UCA

university for the **creative arts**

The Fashion Intern

The Fashion Intern

SECOND EDITION

MICHELE M. GRANGER, EdD

MISSOURI STATE UNIVERSITY

Fairchild Books

NEW YORK

Vice President & General Manager,
    Fairchild Education & Conference Division: Elizabeth Tighe
Executive Editor: Olga T. Kontzias
Assistant Acquisitions Editor: Amanda Breccia
Editorial Development Director: Jennifer Crane
Associate Development Editor: Lisa Vecchione
Associate Art Director: Erin Fitzsimmons
Production Director: Ginger Hillman
Senior Production Editor: Elizabeth Marotta
Copyeditor: Susan Hobbs
Ancillaries Editor: Noah Schwartzberg
Cover Design: Erin Fitzsimmons
Director, Sales & Marketing: Brian Normoyle
Cover Art: Getty Images
Text Design: Tronvig Kuypers

Library of Congress Catalog Card Number: 2009931534

ISBN: 978-1-56367-910-0

GSTR 133004424

Printed in the United States

TP09

Table of Contents

Extended Contents

··❧[EXTENDED CONTENTS]❧··

EXTENDED CONTENTS

Preface

The Fashion Intern, second edition, is written for the postsecondary fashion student preparing to locate, secure, and analyze an internship experience in the fashion industry. The text is developed primarily for use in three types of courses: (1) pre-internship seminar; (2) internship experience; and (3) postinternship, or senior, seminar.

An internship can be one of the most overwhelming and exhilarating learning experiences in the student's academic program. Unlike enrolling in a course that is directed by an instructor who has prepared objectives, assignments, and lectures, the student is responsible, in most cases, for finding a location and sponsor for the internship and then collaborating with the internship sponsor on the goals, projects, and experiences that will facilitate the student's career objectives, fulfill the college or university's academic requirements, and assure that the intern contributes to the day-to-day operations of the internship firm. The internship places the student in the role of a self-directed learner, one who must find the information source for answers; objectively evaluate his or her own performance; and successfully meet the needs of the internship work environment and the academic institution as well as his or her own needs. The intern is often in the position of not being asked the question by the instructor; instead, the intern must generate both the question and the answer. Getting the great job and doing a great job on the job are two very different yet equally paramount aspirations for the student intern.

Organization of the Text

The text is divided into two major parts: (1) pre-internship planning and (2) on-the-job analysis of the internship company. Chapters 1 through 4 offer the tools needed to find internship opportunities and to secure an internship position that will serve as stepping-stones to the student's postgraduate career path. Chapters 5 through 12 provide background information and questions that place the student in the role of business analyst, one whose task it is to assess the business as a whole by reviewing the company's goals, functions, and various departments in their entirety.

Chapter 1, "Getting Started," guides the student through the processes and resources needed to define and plan for the successful internship search. Chapter 2, "Writing a Résumé and Letter of Application," provides step-by-step information on constructing a résumé and letter of application for prospective internship employers. The scannable résumé is examined in this chapter for internship firms that require electronic applications. A résumé critique form is provided for a final analysis. Samples of résumés and letters of applications are models that apply directly to the fashion industry for the student to consider. Chapter 3, "Applying and Interviewing for the Internship," leads the student through the job application and interview process. Interview guidelines, commonly asked questions, portfolio presentation, and post-interview activities are explored. Chapter 4, "Before Settling In," takes a look at standards of professional conduct on the job; the definition and importance of corporate culture; and practical considerations, such as budgeting for housing and transportation.

In the second half of the text, the student is guided through an analysis of the internship organization, beginning with Chapter 5, "The Company Mission, Image, and Location." In this chapter the intern reviews the company's goals and objectives, its image and position in the marketplace, its location(s), and its facility. Chapter 6, "The Nature of the Organization," provides the intern with the opportunity to examine the firm's form of ownership, organizational type, products and services, and extent of departmentalization. In Chapter 7, "The Customer," the internship organization's customer and customer relations are explored. Channels of distribution used to move the product to the customer are also investigated in this chapter. Competition, the economy, social trends, consumer demographics, political and legal issues, nature, and technology have significant influence over a company's performance in the marketplace. These influencers, referred to as the external environment, are reviewed in Chapter 8, which features an emphasis on e-commerce activities. In Chapter 9, "The Product and Pricing," the intern is asked to recognize and classify the products offered by the internship organization. The product life cycle, merchandise assortments, seasonality of goods, brands and trademarks, and packaging and labeling are discussed, in addition to product pricing variables, strategies, and guidelines.

Next, Chapter 10 focuses on product development and design from the perspectives of both the manufacturer and the retailer. Decisions in branding, line planning, and researching trends are made in the product development and design division of a company. The designer's job is also examined in this chapter, as are steps to developing a product and designing a product line. As manufacturing the products follows the development and design process, Chapter 11 takes a look at production. The manufacturing process, including sourcing manufacturers and costing goods, is reviewed for those firms that have a production division. Internships in promotion and publishing have become much more prevalent and sought after by fashion students. Consumer and trade magazines, fashion show production companies, special event planners, and public relations firms are major sponsors of fashion internships and potential employers of fashion graduates. In Chapter 12, "Promotion and Publishing," constructing a message for the customer, establishing the budget, and determining the promotional mix are examined. In addition, visual merchandising as a key form of promotion is discussed, as are various editorial positions in the world of fashion publishing.

Features of the Text

The Fashion Intern, second edition, provides a variety of pedagogical features to be used by a classroom group or by the student individually, as a self-directed learner. Case studies are presented at the end of each chapter to illustrate chapter topics in real-world business scenarios. Models of résumés, information and contact requests, letters of application, and thank-you letters are provided, allowing the student to see samples of these job search tools as they relate to the fashion industry. Boxes feature key points in the chapters, international internship programs and other internship opportunities, profiles of major employers, and interviews with industry professionals. A glossary of key terms is included at the end of the text. The appendices contain a wealth of information and tools, including a learning agreement form, online and print resources for finding and researching prospective internship employers, daily and weekly activity report forms, and evaluation forms for the intern and the internship employer. An instructor's guide is also available to assist with course organization, class discussion, and teaching ideas.

Acknowledgments

To my parents, Sally and John Granger; my sister, Patricia; my brother, Joseph; and my sister-in-law, Wendy, for their support and encouragement. To my beautiful daughter, Annie, I wish a life of success and love. From Annie, I learn that it is never too late to pursue new dreams. To Melody and John, my selected family, for their devotion and love. To Molly, Romeo, Jack, and Myko for the humor and comfort. To Jenn McKelvie for her friendship and her work on all of the visuals in this text. Grateful acknowledgment to Career Services of Missouri State University for its handouts and exceptional student support; to Professor Kirsteen Buchanan, gifted teacher and product developer, for the insightful chapter on product development; and to Carey Kaltenbach for his original material on letters of application, upon which that segment was based. To all my students, past and present, thank you for sharing a passion for fashion and for always teaching the teacher. Finally, thank you to Olga Kontzias, my favorite executive editor and fellow Francophile; Jennifer Crane, editorial development director; Lisa Vecchione, associate development editor; Liz Marotta, senior production editor; Noah Schwartzberg, ancillaries editor; and Erin Fitzsimmons, former associate art director, at Fairchild Books.

Best wishes as you begin your internship experience!

Introduction

To the Student

Congratulations, you are about to set out on an exciting adventure in the fashion industry—the internship. For some, this will be your first work experience. Others have been employed for years, perhaps as a sales associate in a specialty store, a cashier in a department store, or a receptionist for an apparel manufacturer. Regardless of your prior level of experience (or inexperience), this internship journey will provide you with several new opportunities and challenges. As an intern, you will:

- receive exposure to the business organization as a whole;

- construct a written analysis of the internship organization through the completion of this guide and the Daily Activity Journal or Weekly Activity Report (or both);

- fulfill an academic requirement through hands-on experience; and

- receive evaluations from both the internship supervisor and the academic internship sponsor.

These challenges will require you to develop a new perspective—that of a business analyst who studies the organization in its entirety. The purpose of *The Fashion Intern* is to provide a structure for an analysis of your organization as a whole, to help you gain as much from the internship experience as possible. This guide is intended for those employed in any segment of the apparel, accessories, soft goods, and fashion service industries. It can be applied to any organization anywhere along the channel of distribution and serving any market segment. This guide is based on a marketing model, focusing on an organization's decisions about the products, promotion, pricing, and distribution, all with the intent of better serving and growing the target market while managing costs and maintaining profit.

The following assumptions have been made in the preparation of this guide:

- You have a basic understanding of business principles, particularly marketing.

- You are an upper-level student who understands business concepts and practices.

- You will adjust questions to relate directly to your specific internship organization.

- You will review this guide with the academic sponsor and internship supervisor prior to beginning the internship experience.

In each section of *The Fashion Intern,* the main topic will be introduced through a brief outline. Examples are given as to how the topic might be applied to a variety of organizations. Read the introduction and the examples, look critically at your organization, and redefine the question in an appropriate way if necessary. You cannot always depend on the guide to generate the specific question that must be asked. You will be asked to evaluate, analyze, criticize, speculate, and make connections between concepts and practice. Students familiar with the case study method will have an advantage. The intent is to encourage you to think critically. The guide is designed to assist you with the formation of questions that make you think about the organization in its entirety.

Conceptually, *The Fashion Intern* asks you to look critically at the organization (e.g., retail store, museum, factory, design workroom, and so on) as one with its own unique way of relating to:

- its customers;

- the environment to which it must respond;

- formal and informal power structures;

- individual resources and personnel limitations;

- what the internship organization offers (product);

- how it informs potential customers (promotion);

- how it determines what to charge or how to pay (pricing); and

- how it will get that product to its customers (sales and distribution).

In responding to the sections of this guide, descriptions may not be adequate. After the description is formulated, you should take the perspective of a business consultant to this organization and ask, "In what new ways should this organization look at the issue?" If, for example, the issue of social responsibility is one that has apparently never been raised, ask: (1) Why has it not been raised? (2) What are the social responsibility implications for this organization?

(3) What specific issues of social responsibility might the internship organization respond to, and how?

Not only examine the internship organization but also think about competition of the internship operation and about competition as it affects organizations in general. You cannot assume that all retailers, for example, buy only from manufacturers' representatives who visit them in their stores because that is how it is done in the internship organization. Nor can you assume that all apparel manufacturers do pattern drafting by computer just because your organization is fortunate enough to have state-of-the-art computerized equipment.

The Fashion Intern has been designed to (1) respond to a variety of internship experiences available in the fashion industry, (2) allow for any time length required by the academic institution or the internship supervisor, and (3) ask for minimum written requirements from the internship supervisor. The internship may be completed, for example, during a 4-week intersession or a 14-week semester, as required by the academic institution and internship supervisor. Before starting the internship experience, establish a time frame for completing the chapters in the guide. The academic internship sponsor will determine whether the Daily Activity Journal or Weekly Activity Report, or both, will be submitted to the academic internship sponsor following the end of the internship experience or each week. The internship supervisor is requested to complete student evaluation forms at the conclusion of the internship (Appendices F1 and F2). *The Fashion Intern* is designed to help you create a polished and professional product for your portfolio. You can use the text as a place to make notes, to summarize interviews, and to identify those questions that you need to research. The accompanying CD-ROM allows you to input complete answers to the questions and then print a document that provides a total analysis of the internship organization.

CHAPTER ONE

Getting Started

Objectives

- To understand what an internship is and why it is important
- To recognize the significance of planning, organization, and research in the internship search
- To clarify personal and professional goals as they pertain to the internship experience
- To locate prospective internship positions through networking and research
- To construct networking and prospecting letters for locating internship opportunities

What Is an Internship?

An internship is a supervised on-the-job experience that combines work, an analysis of the organization, employer and academic sponsor feedback, and, frequently, special assignments. An internship provides students with an excellent opportunity to apply their education to the work environment; it also allows the employer to assess and train future employees while gaining new perspectives. An internship may be paid or unpaid, and enrolled in for college credit or no credit, depending on the requirements of the academic institution, the students, and the internship organization.

An internship can truly be a win-win situation for all three partners. The student can benefit from hands-on experience, the opportunity to apply academic theory to the real world, and, possibly, procure the additional benefit of post-graduation employment. The internship supervisor can gain a new and enthusiastic perspective from the student as well as a candidate for future employment. The academic internship sponsor is exposed to various fashion industry businesses and given the chance to assess not only student performance on the job but also the relationship between academic course content and current and future industry needs and trends.

There are two categories of internships: formal and informal. A **formal internship program** is most often offered by a large company. For example, a group of student interns may go through preplanned classes and activities in a formal internship program. In an **informal internship,** the internship supervisor and student develop an individual program that will meet the employer's needs, the student's goals, and the academic institution's internship requirements. In an informal internship, developing a specific work plan that meets the needs of the intern, the employer, and the academic sponsor is extremely important.

Why an Internship?

An internship is one of the best ways to get your foot in the door of a fashion business. Interning is a route to meeting and working with successful industry professionals who will model success and may later help you land a position after graduation; it is a path to learning firsthand about the multitude of career options in the industry. This path may not be available to others—those not pursuing a college degree or not enrolled in an academic program that provides the necessary prerequisite training and support. An internship is the part of your education that introduces you to the professional world. Why complete an internship? The following are a few of the many reasons for working diligently to secure and successfully complete the best internship for you.

- **Gain essential on-the-job experience in the industry.** The classroom is the fundamental part of your education and will afford you opportunities to learn about theory, best practices, and techniques; however, one of the most difficult lessons to teach in a classroom is how to work within the industry, with clients, coworkers, teams, and supervisors. An internship provides real-world work experience, such as meeting an immediate and unexpected deadline, pleasing a difficult customer, working with a challenging supervisor, or motivating an uncertain employee.

- **Build an industry network.** Because you will be interning in a showroom, buying office, design studio, retail store, costume collection, or any one of the multitude of places of business in the industry, nearly every person you meet will be someone to add to your career network. Many students say, "It's who you know . . . and I don't know anybody when it comes to finding a job." You know your faculty, alumni, and peers. During the internship, you can expand this network by taking the time to get to know professionals you meet on the job and recording their contact information.

- **Expand your portfolio.** Nothing enhances a portfolio like actual professional work. Your college projects and writing assignments are significant to employers; they show the diversity of your skills and provide outside assessment. Work completed on the job, such as newsletters, memos, trend boards, and other projects, help establish you as a professional.

- **Learn what is out there.** While working as an intern, you will be exposed to many professionals in positions and careers tracks that you may not have studied in college or read about in your research. A former student who interned with a fiber trade organization, Cotton Incorporated, learned that there was an employee who organized sample garments and accessories, catalogued fabric samples, and assisted with the development of trend boards. It was the ideal position for this ultra-organized, color-coded, and fashion-forward young woman. She completed the internship with flying colors and applied for this job when a new graduate. The company knew she was a talented and tireless employee; she got the job.

- **Land a job.** Can you imagine that your job search may be over before it is ever started? Can you envision having a position in the industry before you graduate from college? Many employers prefer to offer an entry-level position to one of their successful, hardworking interns, rather than pay to advertise the position, spend valuable time interviewing candidates, and take a risk in hiring someone with whom they have no experience. Companies offer internships for two main reasons. First, interns provide extra help in the workplace, often offering a fresh look at how business is conducted. Second, an internship provides a company with a test drive of a potential employee. If you are interning for a firm that does not have a job opening now, it may have one tomorrow. In addition, if your internship company does not have a position, the executives may know of another person or business that is hiring. It all comes back to building both a network and a top professional reputation.

Common Internship Questions and Answers

When should I start to plan for my internship?

Begin to plan at least two semesters prior to when you expect to complete the internship. For example, start planning during a current fall semester at the very latest for a prospective internship for the following summer.

What should I do first?

Before contacting prospective employers, it is important to clarify personal goals and expectations for the internship experience. What do you want to do in the internship? Assist in production planning? Learn how to buy? Help plan and coordinate fashion promotion activities? Assist a designer? Work in finance or in control? Learn about visual merchandising or, perhaps, the functions of personnel? Assist in merchandising? Construct patterns? Work in product development?

Now I'm ready to contact employers, right?

Not quite. The next step involves investigation: researching employers and employment opportunities. The Internet is an excellent source of information. Additional resources are presented in this chapter. If you are interested in returning home, or perhaps working in your college town during the school year or summer, you may find it advisable to identify the specific employers you are interested in and to apply directly to those organizations. Knowing something about the company before you begin will help you know how better to present yourself and possibly prevent an embarrassing moment or comment. In addition, the company representative may be impressed by your wealth of knowledge.

So, what next?

Now you are faced with important choices. Do you want to apply for an existing internship program, or should you create your own? For example, Liz Claiborne, Inc., and Saks Fifth Avenue offer structured, or formal, internship programs. Can you complete the internship during the summer or during a semester of the traditional academic year? Can you work full-time or part-time? Applying for internship programs requires careful, long-range planning, perhaps including arranging for a lighter academic load during the appointed internship semester. An internship is a real job that requires time and effort.

After I have decided between creating my own internship and applying for an existing one, how do I present myself?

It is necessary to develop an appropriate résumé and letter of application describing yourself, your experiences, the position sought, and what you bring to this position.

To how many companies should I apply for an internship?

Although there is no right answer, as it depends entirely upon your personal goals and objectives, one should consider a minimum of five to ten applications. If possible, do not limit yourself to one location.

Will I get paid for my internship?

Yes and no. Some companies pay interns the minimum hourly wage; others pay a stipend. Some organizations may not pay at all for the internship experience. It is up to you and your academic institution to decide whether or not you can accept an unpaid internship.

What if I receive more than one offer?

Lucky you! Choosing among offers is never easy. If, however, you have clarified your goals and objectives in applying for the internship early in your search, you will be in a better position to evaluate offers as they are presented.

Recommended Timeline for the Internship

The following schedule has been developed by internship students, alumni, and industry employers. If you prefer to complete the internship during fall or spring semester or during a semester intersession, adjust the plan as needed to accommodate course requirements for your degree program. You may reduce months to weeks if your academic program requires this.

- **Nine to ten months in advance**—Attend student internship presentations, and network with peers, faculty, friends, family, and graduates about internship opportunities. Begin the internship planning process.

- **Eight to nine months in advance**—Research potential employers (e.g., the Internet, Fairchild's Textile and Apparel Financial Directory, Sheldon's Retail, *Standard and Poor's, Women's Wear Daily,* and your college's graduate file). Read *The Fashion Intern* thoroughly.

- **Seven to eight months in advance**—Attend résumé workshops and practice interview sessions. Draft résumés and letters of application. Continue researching potential employers.

- **Six to seven months in advance**—After the résumé and letters of application have been proofread several times, have them printed.

- **Five to six months in advance**—Mail letters of application and résumés to prospective employers.

- **Four to five months in advance**—Follow up on inquiry letters, and schedule both phone and personal interviews. Continue searching and developing new letters of application.

- **Three to four months in advance**—Interview; continue contacting potential employers.

- **Two to three months in advance**—Continue interviewing. If required by the academic institution, register for the internship before leaving campus.

- **One to two months in advance**—Turn in the internship application. Finalize your internship objectives with the academic sponsor and internship supervisor.

- **Showtime**—Complete the actual internship on-the-job work hours.

The Unpaid Internship

Some academic institutions require that students complete unpaid internships. The premise is that this puts all interns on a level playing field and allows for a broader range of internship employers. In addition, because some colleges do not permit the student to receive credit for paid employment, the unpaid internship may be necessary. Some employers also do not permit both college credit and payment. Other employers and universities offer the student the choice of a paid or unpaid internship for college credit. If you have this choice, what should you do?

Do not simply pass up an unpaid internship. Often the experience will bring about more rewards than any paid position. For example, some major design firms in New York City have so many internship applicants from the United States and abroad that they do not pay interns so that they can offer several openings. You may need to ask yourself a few questions: How much can I learn? Who will I meet? Will this position look good on my résumé and help me stand out in the post-graduation job search? Can I afford to do this? There are a number of things you can do to make it without the paycheck from the internship's firm.

- Seek out both scholarships and grants from your college or university to fund the internship experience, or, at the very least, cover the cost of tuition. It never hurts to ask. Sometimes there is money out there that never gets claimed.

- Hit the books. Search for published resources on individual grants, scholarships, and fellowships offered outside of your college or university.

- Ask your parents or relatives for a loan. Promise to do something big for them when you make it big. Meanwhile, set up a repayment plan or contract.

- Apply for financial aid or a student loan.

- Secure a part-time job during the evenings and weekends while you are working on the internship. Some internships are scheduled for only 15 or 20 hours each week, allowing you another 20 hours or more to work in retailing, food service, or another area that will help pay the bills.

Effective Career Planning

To be an effective career planner, use the following checklist to write journal entries as you explore your personal and professional path.

- Understand yourself and your goals, interests, values, aptitudes, and abilities.

- Have a general understanding of the world of work. This requires exposure to different work environments through paid or unpaid jobs, talking to people working in various positions and fields, and reading independently to investigate job and career options.

- Identify your values in terms of career payoffs. In other words, clarify what is important to you. Is it money, status, influence, or the opportunity to make a difference? How will various careers affect your total lifestyle? You will want to select an internship that provides the right environment for personal and professional growth.

- Recognize that getting a job is a job in itself. Plan to spend time and effort in your job search; it is an investment in your future.

A mind map provides an opportunity to assess one's attributes, skills, experiences, and goals from both personal and professional perspectives. Figure 1.1 presents a mind map that encourages the development of short-term and long-term goals in order to evaluate personal and professional strengths and to clarify job contacts. Use this diagram to determine how your personal qualities and experiences fit with your short- and long-term goals. Fill in each bubble with brief descriptions. Once you complete this, evaluate the form to identify the type of internship that is the best match for you. See also Box 1.1, A Case for Mind Mapping.

Following is a list of types of fashion intern employers:

- Retail buying division
- Resident buying office
- Stylist for a media or design firm
- Manufacturer's representative
- Special event producer
- Designer public relations representative
- Fashion trade journals and consumer publications
- Web retailer
- Theatrical costume company
- Modeling agency

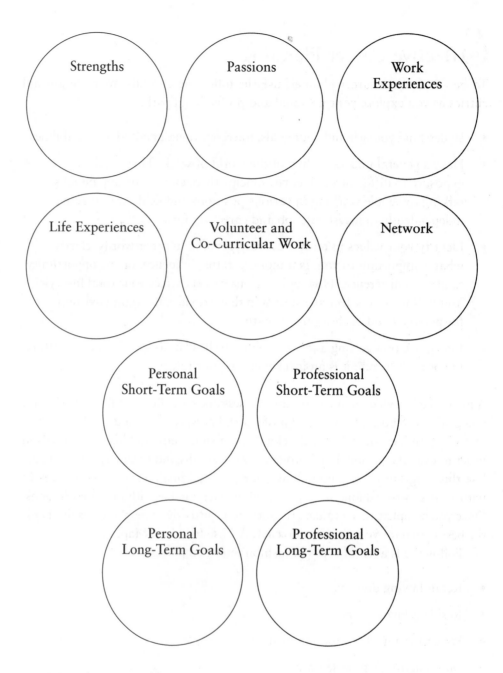

Figure 1.1 Mind-mapping bubbles.

- Mart director's office
- Wardrobe stylist department (for example, theater, film, or television)
- Design studio—interiors, apparel, or accessories
- Visual merchandising department
- Patternmaking department
- Manufacturer's showroom
- Museum gift store or historical costume collection

(continued on page 10)

Figure 1.1 *(continued)*

Looking Further Ahead

Your Ultimate Career Picture (Long-Range)

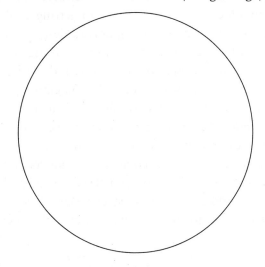

·❊[B O X 1 . 1]❊·

A Case for Mind Mapping

"Would you tell me, please, which way I ought to go from here?"

"That depends a good deal on where you want to go," said the cat.

"I don't much care where," said Alice.

"Then it doesn't matter which way you go," said the cat.

—Lewis Carroll, *Alice In Wonderland*

"If you don't know where you're going, any road will take you there."

—Saint-Onge

- Trend or color forecasting firm

- Retail management

- Production facility

Organizing the Job Search

A job search schedule is presented as Table 1.1 to provide structure to the process. You may decide to set up an Excel spreadsheet to monitor and organize your job search progress. Some students also maintain job search "appointments" with themselves on their computers, iPhones, or BlackBerries (Figure 1.2). Planning the job search and allocating time to the job of getting a job will maximize the quality and number of your internship opportunities.

Organization calls for a systematic way of recording and filing the information that you gather on prospective employers. Index cards are ideal for this purpose, as is a computerized spreadsheet. As you gather pertinent information on job prospects, record it immediately, one company or job prospect to a card or computer file. Enter the name, street address, Web site, e-mail address, and phone number of the company. Add any other information that you feel would be useful, such as the nature of the company's products or services, names and titles of company officers, the person you should contact, locations of branch offices, and so on. Additional notes on correspondence, phone calls, interviews, and needed follow-up work should be included. When gathering contact

Table 1.1 JOB SEARCH WORK SCHEDULE							
Week of _____							
	Estimated Hours To Be Spent						
	M	T	W	Th	F	S	Su
Activity							
Self-Research							
Job Market Research							
Telephone Calls							
Letter Writing							
Job Interviews							
Other							
Daily Totals							
					Weekly Total ____ hours		

Figure 1.2 Schedule job search "appointments" in your week in order to maximize the quality and quantity of your internship opportunities.

information, be certain to spell names correctly and note correct titles. Figure 1.3 illustrates a job search worksheet.

Locating Internship Positions

Where can information about internship positions be found? Internship positions can be located through the following resources:

- **Library**—*Standard and Poor's, Women's Wear Daily, Daily News-Record, Children's Business, Earnshaw's,* and the *Wall Street Journal* are a few of the resources that may be available in the library to provide information on fashion retailers, manufacturers, trend forecasting services, and resident buying offices, among others. Additional resources include *O'Dwyer's Public Relations, The Fashion Resource Directory,* and *Stores* magazine. For internships that are not in fashion retailing, there are directories of textile, apparel, and accessories manufacturers, such as *The Fashion Guide: International Designer Directory.* The Fashion Group International, Inc., and the International Textile and Apparel Association produce membership directories that can be used as resources for locating fashion internships. The Fashion Group International, Inc., has a Web site, www.fgi.org, that often features prospective employers for internships as well as specific positions.

Job Target:
(Use a separate form or computer file for each job target.)

Telephone Calls or Letters:

Date	Person/ Organization	Phone #/ Address	E-mail Address	Objective	Results

Specific Research Objectives:

Date	Sources to Contact	Objective	Results

Other Objectives:
(People with whom to network, information interviews, professional association meetings, etc.)

Related Expenses:
Airfare and lodging, if needed to interview outside of home region; ground transportation; tuition

Figure 1.3 Job search worksheet.

- **Faculty**—Faculty members often have industry contacts or suggestions about resources for the type of internship position you may be seeking. Be sure to ask for their ideas. You will want to provide faculty members with a résumé and a brief description of an internship "wish list." They may hear about the ideal position for you later in the semester.

- **Alumni**—There are many occasions to meet with alumni from the college. Find the right moment to introduce yourself and ask about internship opportunities. If you are unable to visit with the alumni while they are on campus, send a note at a later date.

- **Friends and Family**—Let friends and family know that you are looking for an internship. Tell them about the type of internship you are seeking, the location you would prefer, and the requirements for the internship experience (e.g., number of work hours). Ask them for names, titles, and addresses of industry contacts and refer to the person who helped you in your letter of application.

- **Fellow Students**—Talk to your peers, especially those who have completed internships, about how, what, when, and where they secured their internships. These students may be able to refer you to their former internship employers. Moreover, their parents may have connections with retail operations or design firms.

- **Career Services Department of Your College or University**—Most colleges have counseling centers or career planning and placement offices, or both, that provide information regarding potential employers, on-campus recruiting, and the job search. Attend career fairs held on campus and in the community.

- **Direct Contact with Preferred Employers**—Magazine advertisements and garment hangtags often contain address information for a company's headquarters. Write to the company to request an internship opportunity.

- **Apparel Marts**—Contact the apparel mart directors of several major locations (for example, Kansas City, Atlanta, Dallas, and so on) to ask about positions with the mart director's office or with the manufacturers' representatives. You may want to ask the apparel mart director for a guest pass so that you can distribute résumés to the sales representatives.

- **Industry Organizations**—Some trade and community (e.g., chamber of commerce, mall management, and small business council) organizations solicit members to provide internship opportunities for college students interested in pursuing a career in the fashion industry. Contact this type of professional organization in your area for possible internship opportunities.

- **Guest Speakers at Your College**—Send them thank-you notes for their presentations, and think of contacting them again when seeking an internship.

- **The Internet**—Company Web sites and Internet search engines provide a wealth of information. Many corporate Web sites contain information on the company's internship program. The section that follows further discusses using the Internet as a tool. Also see the Web site links and shaded boxes in Appendix B to investigate a wealth of internship opportunities.

- **Newspapers**—Check the classified sections of newspapers in cities of interest to you for information on job opportunities.

- **Current and Prior Work Associates**—Discuss your internship goals with current and previous employers to seek out new opportunities and specific contact persons.

- **Acquaintances from Volunteer and Professional Organizations**—Community service projects and membership in student organizations provide exposure to people from a variety of backgrounds and industries. Tell them what you are looking for and ask them to share names of who they know.

Be sure to send all network contacts thank-you notes in appreciation of their help and time after they have talked or written to you. Figure 1.4 presents guidelines for constructing a networking letter. Figure 1.5 provides an example of a networking letter.

Researching Employers

Why Research Employers?

Researching a prospective employer is an often missed step when applying for an internship. It is easy to get excited when you believe that you have found a dream career opportunity and the perfect internship position; however, not digging deep into an employer's current situation and past reputation can prove to be a costly mistake. You can be certain that employers are checking your references, online profile, and college credentials before extending an offer. You would be remiss to not do the same with any prospective hiring organization. The more you know about a company, the better able you will be to communicate your value to this employer during your interview. The hard work that you put into your research will almost always pay off by reflecting your interest and enthusiasm to employers and by providing you with the confidence that this is a secure employment opportunity. Taking the time to learn about a company and then to pursue an internship with a firm is a form of flattery to company representatives. Before you complete your letter of application and send out your résumé, we will take a closer look at why you should research employers, what to look for, and how to investigate like a detective.

Your address
Telephone number with area code
E-mail address

Date

Alumnus's or friend's name
Address

Dear (Insert name):

If a recent graduate, it would be acceptable to address the alumnus by his or her first name; however, if the alumnus or friend has been out of college for a length of time and is older than you, address the letter to Ms./Mrs./Mr.

Begin by introducing yourself as a student at _____ (college) in your _____ year, studying in the area of _____.
Tell the person how you obtained his or her name (e.g., your parents, a fellow student, graduate file, and so on) and why you are writing (e.g., for advice or information about a permanent career position after graduation, assistance with relocating to his or her city, help in securing an internship). Be as specific as possible.

In the second paragraph, describe your internship goals and briefly mention a few important things about your background (e.g., courses taken and work experience). It is also helpful to include a résumé. If you have preferences regarding an internship location, be sure to mention this.

In the third paragraph, thank this contact for any assistance given to you. It would be useful to you to try to arrange a time to meet when you are in the area or for you to discuss your internship search further by phone.

Sincerely,

(Your signature)

(Your name printed)

Figure 1.4 Guidelines for constructing a networking letter.

543 Powhatan Avenue
Denver, CO

April 21, 20XX

Ms. Laraine Evans, Dress Buyer
Neiman Marcus
P.O. Box 650589
Dallas, TX 72650

Dear Ms. Evans:

Dr. Smith, professor of fashion merchandising at Ivy League University, suggested that I contact you. She thought that you would be in an excellent position as an alumna to assist me with a career decision.

As a fashion student, I am exploring which career path to pursue. Buying, management, and visual merchandising all sound interesting to me at this point, but I want to go into my campus interviews next semester with a clear sense of direction. I would like to get your advice on the long-term career implications of each path, as well as a better handle on the day-to-day activities and responsibilities of a retail buyer.

I will call you next week to see if we can arrange a brief meeting at your convenience. Thank you for considering my request.

Sincerely,

Marci Winston
(204) 226-1988
mwinston@hotmail.com

Figure 1.5 Sample of a networking letter (modified block format).

Modified and reprinted from *Planning Job Choices: 1999* with permission of the National Association of Colleges and Employers, copyright holder.

The majority of you have held some type of employment, whether as a sales associate, food server, or child caretaker. Some of you had wonderful experiences in these jobs, whereas others may have been wondering what the employer was thinking, how bad it could get, and when it would be over. In the latter case, you learned the hard way to spend dedicated time learning about an employer before applying for a job. Why should you do some investigative work on prospective employers?

- *To determine if the company is a fit for you.* You may find you do not particularly like a specific career path in the industry. You may also dig up unfortunate corporate digital dirt or uncover information on poor employee relations.

- *To decide if you are right for the company.* Some companies or industries may not be the right fit for your skill sets, values, or corporate culture preferences. It is also possible to find that you are not really interested in the company's products or services. Be sure to consider your goals, desires, and ethics to see how they fit given the information you have revealed.

- *To help tailor your résumé and letter of application to the position.* Knowing specifically what makes the company successful can turn your application into the winning ticket.

- *To give you the information required to address effectively the needs of the organization.* Knowing why the company needs to hire an intern is key to addressing how you can help the company.

- *To help you prepare effective interview questions.* Knowing specific industry information or advanced product knowledge can get you closer to an offer as you impress the interviewer with insightful questions and answers.

- *To demonstrate sincere interest in the company.* A common interview question is "Why do you want to work for us?" Having an educated answer puts you ahead of the competition. One of the most important ways to distinguish yourself in an interview is to speak knowledgeably about the organization.

- *To educate yourself about a particular career path in the industry.* Perhaps this internship is in a sector of the industry that is new to you. Get in the know before writing your application and heading to the interview.

When Do I Research Employers?

The best time to research employers is before you prepare your résumé and letter of application to request an interview with a company. By doing some due diligence early, you can quickly rule out firms and internships that do not match your personal needs, academic requirements, or desired career path. It is to your benefit to pull the plug early on a less than reputable internship and turn your focus on positions more worth your effort and time.

Where Do I Start Looking?

Conducting employer research is much like preparing a college assignment or project. The idea is to develop two lists: one of companies for which you are interested in interning and another of resources for researching businesses. Here are a few good places to help you start the second list:

- *Corporate Web Site.* Look for industry information, product or service details, and management information. Most corporate sites indicate company age, size, ownership, locations, and leadership or management details. Check the Web site to see if the company is public or private. A review of annual reports may reveal interesting corporate details, such as the health of the industry and the firm's financial situation, mission statement, and employee numbers.

- *Google.* Search forums, Web sites, blogs, and online articles that will enable you to see what others have to say about the company's products, services, and employee relations. You may be surprised. Take this information for what it is—opinions and comments. Make a decision that is based on facts yet that allows room for majority opinion.

- *Better Business Bureau.* These organizations can alert you to complaints against companies in specific geographical areas or cities. You may want to contact them to see if your prospective employer is on the list.

- *Consumer and Trade Publications.* Research the employer's industry activity through print, in addition to Internet sources. Read magazines, newspapers, trade publications, and journals related to the field and organization.

- *Professional Associations.* Is the company affiliated with an association? Consult association Web sites to see if the prospective employing organization is in good standing and how it contributes to the profession.

- *Chambers of Commerce.* You may want to begin by contacting the chambers of commerce in the communities in which the companies you are interested are located. Often you will find a searchable comprehensive directory online.

- *Employee Handbook.* Ask a representative of the company's human resources department if you can receive a copy of the company's employee handbook to find data on personnel policies, such as vacation time and sick leave. It is amazing how a simple handbook can change your mind or reinforce your desire to intern with a prospective employer.

- *Former Interns and Current Employee References.* Do you know current or former employees or interns? Ask them why they left, who supervised them, and if they would ever work there again. Will the human resources department let you speak candidly to current employees? Getting to know current members of the team is an excellent way to judge if you want to work with this employer in the future.

What Information Should I Uncover?

Begin by locating general information about each company in which you are interested. Keep an accurate record of what you learn. If you are ready to go on the Internet to begin your research, keep the following in mind:

- *Know what you are looking for before you go online.* Keep a list beside you so that you can check off items as you locate them. An electronic spreadsheet is ideal for posting information as you find it. It is easy to get frustrated or disinterested in the research phase without organized records.

- *Bookmark major Web sites as you come across them.* Most browsers will even allow you to create folders or directories to organize the links even further. Print hard copies of important information. If you are concerned about saving trees, you can save a copy of the document to your hard drive instead.

Although the Internet will be an invaluable research resource, your college, university, and local library are still some of the best places to locate information. The reference librarian should be able to point you in the direction of many useful directories and indexes. Examples of resources that you will find in the library are *Dunn and Bradstreet* reports, *Standard and Poor's Corporation Records, World Business Directory*, and *Ward's Business Directory*.

Now that you know *where* to look for general information, you may want to format a spreadsheet of *which* details to uncover. Consider these variables when researching an internship employer:

- Mission, philosophy, and objectives of the company
- Source(s) of funding, including assets, earnings, and losses
- Company ownership (e.g., private or public, sole proprietorship or partnership, foreign or domestic ownership, and so on)
- Company divisions or subsidiaries
- Board of directors or advisory board
- General reputation of the company
- History or background
- Products (to include services) that the company sells or provides
- Target market or clientele list
- Strategies and goals
- Market positioning or repositioning (see Chapter 5)
- Areas of specialization
- New projects and major achievements
- Age of the company
- Size of the company and number of employees
- Patterns of growth or decline

- Forecast of future growth
- Recent issues or events (e.g., layoffs or hiring, closings or expansion, and so on)
- Number of employees
- Location of the company headquarters and length of time it has been established there
- Other company locations
- Office/facility environment
- Personnel policies
- Types of people employed and from where interns are recruited
- Health of the industry
- Compensation and benefits
- Services or products sold or provided
- Career path or other opportunities available

Be sure to consider other details specific to the type of internship in which you are most interested. It is important not to be slow, vague, or inaccurate about this process, as any employer worth your time and effort during the internship is well worth your time and effort now.

The Final Word on Researching before Sending Out Your Résumé

Finding the right internship is work; researching a prospective employer is work, but the results can be very rewarding, especially if your research enables you to find the ideal internship. It just makes sense to do some homework on companies rather than sending out résumés and letters of application to just any firm you hear about or stumble across. You are not simply applying for an internship. This may be the start of your career and the provider of your paycheck in the future. You are your most important investment of time and energy.

Using the Internet as a Tool

There are many ways to locate an internship on the Internet. Many Web sites are created for this purpose. If you do not know where to begin, start by typing in the words *fashion* or *internships,* or both. The following lists several links to introduce you to job openings, résumé postings, and current industry information.

www.fashion.about.com

Here you will find topics on the industry and job openings. Current hiring opportunities are posted under "Fashion Careers & Education." Take a minute to read about a "Day in the Life of a Fashion Professional," with topics changing from fashion stylist to designer to buyer and so on. It is a great tool to help envision the internship experience.

www.fadmashion.net

Information found at this site includes daily fashion news and a networking platform for the fashion industry.

www.monster.com

This is a well-established Web site with a résumé builder, a job locator, and an extensive listing of articles on the retail industry. For example, the "Career Center" page recently had an article titled "Maybe You Can Get Paid for an Unpaid Internship." Articles change weekly and stay current with the industry's fast-paced environment.

www.macysjobs.com

This site provides general career information and details about the paid formal internship programs, located on the East or West Coast with Macy's and Bloomingdale's. Go to www.macyscollege.com/college/internships/ for information about internships in buying, buying/planning, store management, product development, design, and a combined internship in store management/buying.

Companies with Internship Programs

Many companies list internship opportunities and information right on their Web sites. Here are some examples of companies to check out:

Saks Fifth Avenue
www.saksincorporated.com

J.C. Penney
www.jcpenney.com

Women's Wear Daily
www.wwd.com

Glamour
www.glamour.com

Showroom Seven
www.showroomseven.com

Ford Modeling Agency
www.fordmodels.com

Donna Karan
www.donnakaran.com

Liz Claiborne, Inc.
www.lizclaiborne.com

Cotton Inc.
www.cottoninc.com

Internship program information for several of these and other firms are featured in Appendix B.

The International Internship

Some students have successfully completed internships in cities out of the country—London, Paris, and Mexico City, among them. These internships require substantial advance planning and, often, an affiliation with an academic institution. For example, American Intercollegiate University (AIU) and London College of Fashion offer summer programs in London through which the student may elect to complete an internship as part of the course enrollment. Marymount College also offers internship opportunities in London. Paris American Academy provides on-the-job experiences as part of its educational programs in design and merchandising.

Another route to an international internship is to apply through a U.S. company for a position in one of its locations abroad. Barneys, Gap Inc., and Calvin Klein are examples of such global organizations. Alternately, students have had success applying directly to companies overseas. Escada, Zara, and Christian Dior are a few examples. Work permits, language fluency, and cultural awareness are often necessary to obtain an internship position with an overseas firm.

The tragedy and horror of September 11 has severely impacted international internship opportunities. Companies are much more selective when choosing an intern from another country. Documentation, such as work visas, International Student Identification cards, and academic records, is carefully reviewed. In some international locations, such as Paris, liability issues are a great concern now when considering the employment of an American student. For example, if an American student is injured on the job, the legal implications are much more serious than before September 11. However, although it is not as easy as securing an internship in your home country, an international internship can be worth the extra effort. Boxes 1.2 to 1.4 show schools offering international internship programs. Box 1.5 presents an interview with a college graduate who successfully completed one of these internship programs in London.

The Prospecting Letter

Internship candidates may choose to send a prospecting letter on companies they find interesting to an academic institution offering internships abroad. A **prospecting letter** is a brief letter constructed to show interest in the firm and requesting information about any internship opportunities. Figure 1.6 on page 30 provides an example of a prospecting letter.

Internship in Paris through the Paris American Academy

The Paris American Academy is located in the heart of Paris's famous Latin Quarter. Since its founding in 1965, the school has been preparing students for careers in fashion, fine arts, interior design, and creative writing. Paris American Academy offers a three-year bachelor program with specializations in fine arts, interior design, and fashion. University credits may also be earned for transfer to colleges and universities on both the undergraduate and graduate levels. The school provides English language classes for students from all over the world. "We are proud of the bilingual tradition of our school, which almost every year groups together more than twenty nationalities, including Japanese, Finnish, Americans, and Australians," states Monsieur Peter Carman, President of the Paris American Academy.

In describing internship opportunities arranged through the Paris American Academy, Carman says, "We do work with internships for our students. French companies require a three-way written internship agreement, or 'convention de stage,' linking the student, the school, and the company. Most, if not all, internships are unpaid; however, if they last over three months, then some payment is made. Most of the students intern with fashion couture houses, sometimes with trend companies or other design environments."

Web site: www.parisamericanacademy.edu
Mailing address: 275, rue St Jacques
             75005 Paris, France
Telephone: +33 1 44 41 99 20

American InterContinental University: Internships in London

American InterContinental University has been preparing students for the rigors of the real world with practical, career-focused learning for over 35 years. AIU London goes even further by giving students an international education that can set them up for success anywhere in the world—whether in their hometown or farther afield.

AIU London is one of the few universities in the world to be accredited in both the United States and United Kingdom. Students who meet the requisite criteria can earn both U.S. and U.K. bachelor's degrees. AIU London offers bachelor's degrees in business administration, fashion design, fashion marketing, fashion design with marketing, visual communications, interior design, and a master's degree in business administration.

AIU London is located in central London, between Hyde Park and Regents Park, inviting students to experience rich British traditions as they have an opportunity to expand their educational horizons. Whereas numerous American colleges have campuses in London and elsewhere in the European Union, AIU London prides itself on being an international university, not merely an American university that happens to be located overseas. Ninety-five percent of AIU London's student body is international, with students coming from over 100 countries to pursue their degrees. You might not be able to find Nepal or Kazakhstan on a map, but the student sitting in class next to you might call one of these countries home. Overall, AIU London's enrollment is around 1,000 students, about 25 percent of which are study abroad students from affiliated American colleges and universities.

AIU London offers five different start dates throughout the year: October, January, March, June, and July. Each start date coincides with the start of a new ten-week term. Students who want to earn their degrees in as little time as possible usually take classes during all four terms; other students often take the summer term off.

Each term, AIU London professors challenge their students with hands-on classes, career training, and real-life examples. Class size is limited to ensure students get focused attention, and curricula take advantage of AIU's London location by bringing in guest lecturers, staging field trips, and offering internships not usually available elsewhere as part of the degree programs.

Source: www.aiulondon.ac.uk/about_aiu/, accessed June 11, 2009

Details about AIU can be viewed at its Web site, www.aiuniv.edu. Information about AIU's study abroad program can be found at: www.aiustudyabroad.com or by calling 1 (800) 255-6839. The mailing address is American InterContinental University Study Abroad Programs, 2895 Greenspoint Parkway Suite 600, Hoffman Estates, IL 60169.

Congratulations to Christian Siriano for Winning *Project Runway*

March 5, 2008, New York, NY—Christian Siriano, formerly an AIU London student, was selected as the winning fashion designer on Bravo TV's season four finale of *Project Runway*. *Project Runway* provides budding designers with an opportunity to launch their careers in the world of fashion. The hugely successful reality series has become one of television's most-talked-about shows.

Each season, fifteen talented fashion designers are selected from thousands of hopefuls to compete for the opportunity to show their creative work at New York's Fashion Week. Supermodel Heidi Klum heads a panel of industry luminaries, including top womens- and menswear designer Michael Kors and *Elle* magazine fashion director Nina Garcia, who serve as judges and mentors charged with selecting and molding the budding designers. Tim Gunn, chief creative officer at Liz Claiborne, Inc., acts as mentor to the program's contestants. *Project Runway* season four episodes, videos, and collections designed by Christian can be viewed at: http://www.seenon.com/project-runway/.

Christian's winning design abilities were molded while a fashion design student at AIU's London campus from 2004 to 2006. Staff members at AIU London were instrumental in helping Christian land assignments with world-renowned designers Vivienne Westwood and Alexander McQueen.

Source: www.aiuniv.edu/about_aiu/news_events.aspx, accessed December 6, 2008.

AIU's Christian Siriano.

An International Fashion Internship in Italy through Global Experiences

Global Experiences, a company specializing in international fashion internships, provides an 11-week summer internship program for U.S. college students majoring in fashion or interior design to explore the world of Italian fashion, culture, and language. Students have the opportunity to earn credit as interns with Florence's fashion businesses, which are the perfect size for gaining valuable hands-on experience and exploring the business strategies of Italy in the global fashion industry. The program also provides guided excursions and study of Italian fashion history, language, and culture. The program includes:

- custom internship placement and internship orientation;

- four-week intensive Italian language training—20 lesson hours per week in small groups of no more than 12;

- professional seminar and intern shadowing;

- guided fashion-related excursions;

- accommodation in single room;

- 24/7 on-site support, mobile phone, and emergency medical travel insurance;

- pre-departure information and participants' social hours;

- study of the history of fashion in Italy, the rich artisan traditions in Florence, and the fashion-related industries in the region of Tuscany.

The required student attributes include flexibility, self-motivation, maturity, independence, adaptability, willingness to learn, attention to detail, and passion for Italian culture and fashion.
Available placement fields in fashion design are menswear, women's wear, bridal, accessories, and

Global Experiences logo.

Global Experiences intern.

illustration. Fashion business placements are in marketing, merchandising, and showroom sales.

Additional locations for placements in fashion include Spain, London, Australia, and France. Program information is available on the Web site, www.globalexperiences.com/fashion. In all locations, fashion internships are customized to fit the academic requirements and career objectives of each participant. Global Experiences can adjust program structure, length, and assessment procedures as necessary for both the university and the student.

Global Experiences intern.

Interview with International Intern
Jillian Lemaster Nelson

Where did you do your internship?

I did an internship the summer between my junior and senior years of college in London at The Profile Group in its division *Fashion Monitor*. I also did a short internship in New York City when I first moved there at Catherine Malandrino during Fashion Week.

How did you secure this internship?

I applied at American Intercontinental University (AIU). They set you up with an advisor and they help secure the right internship for you based on your education and likes/dislikes.

What school did you go through and how did you work this out with your university?

I went to AIU, and I worked with my university's International Affairs office to make sure all the correct paperwork was filled out and to confirm I would receive credit for the classes I took at AIU and for my internship.

Where did you live?

AIU sets up your housing. I lived in East London in a flat with five other girls from the United States.

Did you need a work permit or visa?
No.

Were you paid?

No, I did an unpaid internship. Most of the internships offered were unpaid, although the company I interned with did give me money for food and transportation on the days I worked.

Jillian Lemaster Nelson, international intern.

What skills did you come up with from the internship that you used to land a great fashion position after graduation?

My internship was based on fashion public relations, learning about London's fashion industry and how important public relations is to fashion companies, brands, and designers. The overall experience I gained helped me land a job in the New York fashion industry.

What did you learn?

At both internships, I learned the professionalism of the fashion industry, the intensity of fashion weeks, and the logistics of fashion public relations and design.

Did prospective employers seem to value your overseas internship?

Yes, it was usually a star point of conversation during interviews, and I feel it encouraged them to have a higher level of consideration for me regarding the possible career opportunity.

Why is an internship important?

An internship is important to get you out there and circulating in the industry. Whatever experience you gain during this time is valuable in so many ways. Learning as many facets as possible within the company you are interning for is important, as it will help you narrow down what you are looking for in a long-term career.

What advice do you have for future interns?

Be enthusiastic, confident, eager to learn, and positive in all that you face during your internship. There is something important you can take away from any task you are asked to do. Your attitude and the relationships you build are extremely important as you make your foundation in this industry in which you are intending to make a lifetime career.

Jillian Nelson graduated with a bachelor of science degree in fashion merchandising and is employed as product design manager at Capelli New York.

849 Baldwin Avenue
Virginia Beach, VA 23467

September 5, 20XX

Ms. Sarah Riley
Director of College Recruiting
Midwest Mercantile Company
4500 Randolf Drive
Chicago, IL 60601

Dear Ms. Riley:

I read your company's description in the *CPC Annual* and would like to inquire about employment opportunities in your management internship program. I want to work in retail management and would like to relocate to the Chicago area after graduation.

I will receive a Bachelor of Science degree in Retail Merchandising and Management this May. My interest in business started in Junior Achievement while in high school and developed further through a variety of sales and retail positions during college. My employment with a large department store convinced me to pursue a career in retail. When I researched the top retailers in Chicago, Midwest Mercantile emerged as having a strong market position, an excellent training program, and a reputation for excellent customer service. In short, you provide the kind of professional retailing environment I seek.

My résumé is enclosed for your consideration. My education and experience match the qualifications you seek in your management trainees, but they do not tell the whole story. I know from customer and supervisor feedback that I have the interpersonal skills and motivation needed to build a successful career in retail management. My relatively extensive experience gives me confidence in my career direction and in my abilities to perform competently.

I know how busy you must be during this time of year, but I would appreciate a few minutes of your time. I will call you during the week of September 22 to discuss internship possibilities. In the meantime, if you need to contact me, my telephone number is (804) 683-8843; my e-mail address is camille@hotmail.com.

Thank you very much for considering my request. I look forward to talking with you.

Sincerely,

Camille Gonzales

Figure 1.6 Sample of a prospecting letter (block format).
Reprinted from *Planning Job Choices: 1999* with permission of the National Association of Colleges and Employers, copyright holder.

CHAPTER TWO

Writing a Résumé and Letter of Application

Objectives

- To develop an eye-catching and effective résumé
- To understand the purposes and potential of tailoring your résumé for specific employers
- To construct a letter of application

How Do I Write a Résumé?

What is a résumé? A **résumé** is a one- or two-page summary of a person's goals, education, experience, and skills. Because it is the primary tool in a job search, a résumé requires many hours of work and several drafts to format it most effectively. When completed, it is continually revised to perfect it and to add new educational and employment activities. Employers who receive a résumé with its accompanying letter of application will assess both its form and content to determine whether to contact an applicant, so every effort must be made to ensure that it is effectively written and well presented. It is important to remember, however, that a résumé does not "get the job." It only opens the door to secure an interview.

A résumé is not a biographical description, but rather a summary that highlights your qualifications for employment in a particular position or career field. In preparing a résumé for one type of internship experience, certain information may be left out yet included in a résumé for another type of internship. The résumé should focus attention on qualifications, achievements, and contributions that you can make to a specific employer. Evaluate your personal characteristics for their job significance. A prospective employer is interested in all your qualifications. Your résumé should be up-to-date and, as a result, rewritten and reprinted often—possibly each time it is sent.

Many career consultants recommend constructing a specific résumé for each prospective employer or for each type of position sought. For example, you may be interested in interning in product development, trend forecasting, and public relations in fashion design. Accordingly, you should develop résumés with three

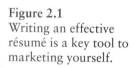

Figure 2.1
Writing an effective résumé is a key tool to marketing yourself.

different objectives that highlight the education and experiences most closely associated with each objective. It is a good idea to tailor each résumé to the position and the company.

There are two primary formats for résumés: chronological and functional. The **chronological résumé** lists a person's education and experience sequentially, with the most recent dates indicated first. The **functional résumé** is one in which a person's education and experiences are grouped by skills and functions, rather than by dates of employment. The majority of executive recruiters, human resource directors, and similar professionals hiring interns in the fashion industry prefer a chronological résumé for several reasons. First, it shows consistency in a person's work history. Second, it illustrates transferable skills to a variety of jobs. Third, at the intern's level, there is often not enough managerial experience to allow for grouping employment experiences by function (for example, product development, merchandising, and retail management). For these reasons, the chronological format is presented in this text.

Résumé Headings

There are several résumé headings that may be used as guidelines to follow for résumé writing. These headings include "Personal Data," "Objective," "Education," "Work Experience," "Related Professional Information," and "References." Box 2.1 features résumé tips to review before you start on the first draft.

Personal Data: Always include your name, street address, e-mail address, and phone numbers (permanent and local, to be optimally accessible). It is not necessary to include data on gender, age, race, marital status, number of dependents, height, or weight. If you have questions on whether or not to include such data, ask yourself if it is relevant to performance on the job; if not, omit it. A photograph is unnecessary, and it is illegal for an employer to request one.

Objective: Make a concise, positive statement about the type of work you are seeking, possibly including both immediate internship and long-range career goals. Indicate the position you think yourself best qualified for, keeping the objective specific enough to fit your internship needs. Tailoring it to fit individual employers is often successful. Many career counselors recommend that job seekers construct different objectives for different résumés, each one specific to the type of internship sought and the company to which the résumé will be sent.

Education: List your highest level of formal education first, then the institution, major and minor (if applicable), and date and title of degree to be earned, followed by the reverse chronological listing of your other levels of education. Grade point average and special courses related to the job objective may be included. If they relate to your objective and would be impressive, include them; if not, omit them. You do not need to include high school information if you have a college education.

Tried-and-True Résumé Tips

No matter if your résumé is scanned and e-mailed, sent through the postal system, or hand delivered, its content is most important. Follow these tried-and-true résumé tips as you work toward résumé perfection:

- Always use spell-check.

- Begin with a goal or an objective. It should include key words.

- For "Education," include your major, minor, and month and year of graduation. Include your grade point average only if 3.0 or higher (this is the general rule).

- "Work Experience" should include internships and part-time jobs (within reason).

- If lacking relevant employment experience, include information about class projects that would relate to the position for which you are applying.

- Include extracurricular involvement, keeping in mind these pointers:

  - Identify the skills and experiences you will need in your target field, and look for organizations on campus where you will get these.

  - Hold an officer position within the organization or head up various committees within the organization.

  - Have a variety of extracurricular experiences to demonstrate your ability to work with a range of people.

- Be involved throughout your college career, not just your final year in school.

- Many companies place a high value on service activities, such as volunteer work on campus or in your community.

- List specific skills related to your career goals, such as computer skills, language fluency, international experiences, and so on.

- You may choose not to list your classes. These can be listed on a separate sheet of paper, or in your portfolio, along with a brief description for those the course title does not adequately explain. You may want to have this information on hand in case an interviewer asks for it.

- Keep it to one page. Although you may have a number of great experiences in college, you likely have not had enough yet to warrant more than a one-page résumé.

- For hard copies, use light-colored, standard size (8½ × 11 inch) paper. Use high-quality paper and a good printer. Choose white, eggshell, beige, or light gray paper. Avoid grainy paper.

- Place your name at the top of each page.

- Do not fold the hard copy of your résumé; send it in a flat envelope.

- Avoid using staples.

Work Experience: When describing your work experience, do not simply say, "I was great." Explain why you were great by citing experiences that relate to the job you are seeking. You will want to quantify your accomplishments. Some employers want to know about all your previous work experience, as they believe doing part-time work during college shows initiative. Other employers are only interested in experience related to the job. Decide for yourself which approach is best for you and the prospective employer. List your most recent job first. Describe for each job:

- **Dates**—Dates should include the entire time you were employed by a particular company. If you worked several summers with a firm, indicate this as "Summers, 2010 to 2011." If you held several positions within one company, those dates should be specified in parentheses after each position. Indicating the years is necessary; the months are optional.

- **Job duties**—Summarize tasks performed, emphasizing those that required the highest degree of skill and judgment. Indicate your specialization and any duties beyond your regular assignment.

- **Scope of responsibility**—Did you hold a supervisory position? How many people did you supervise? Describe your position.

- **Accomplishments**—Outline the outstanding results achieved by your efforts. If possible, give concrete facts and figures, rather than generalities. Following are sample accomplishment statements:

  - Hired, trained, and supervised a staff of nine sales associates

  - Exceeded sales goals annually by 15 to 25 percent

  - Selected newly hired assistant managers in tristate area to train on computerized financial systems

  - Received Sales Excellence Award for top sales volume in region

- **Work actions**—Utilize words such as *developed, organized, planned,* and *researched* to denote action and responsibility in describing the work performed. Begin each job description with an action verb, and maintain parallel construction throughout. For example, you may use *–ed* endings on all verbs for past jobs (for example, "installed displays" and "assisted customers") and use *–ing* endings for your current job. A listing of power words for résumés follows later in this chapter.

- **Volunteer work, field experiences, and practicums**—These should be included in your work history, especially if they are related to your professional objective.

Related professional information: This category should include:

- Licenses and certificates currently held

- Honors, scholarships, awards, and fellowships earned

- Professional organization memberships and offices held

- Publications in which you are featured or have contributed articles

- Special skills, such as fluency in a foreign language, operation of business machines, computer knowledge, etc.

- Internship, study abroad, or field experiences, if not listed under "Education" or "Work Experience"

- Extracurricular activities, including hobbies and outside interests, if relevant to the position

- Affiliations with civic and community groups, including volunteer work

References: References can be handled in a couple of different ways. The current preferred method is to list references' names, street addresses, e-mail addresses, and phone numbers on a separate sheet of paper with the same résumé heading (name, street address, telephone number[s], and e-mail address). Many employers prefer getting a personal telephone recommendation rather than a more generally written letter. Other résumé experts suggest stating on the résumé, "References available upon request," and providing the list when interested employers ask for it. Still other résumé coaches encourage job candidates to eliminate the "References available upon request" statement, as this is assumed information.

However you decide to handle your reference listing, make sure each reference has agreed in advance to take time to write letters or take phone calls concerning your experiences and skills. Providing the reference with an updated résumé will help assure that the most current information will be disseminated. Employment supervisors (past and present), academic advisers, professors, and organization sponsors provide some of the best references. It is important to choose references who will have positive and specific things to say about your work performance and character. This is the type of information the potential employer wants to know.

If your references are listed on a page included with the résumé, follow Figure 2.2 as a model.

Résumé Guidelines

What are some general guidelines for résumés?

- Résumés are written in an abbreviated style, with incomplete sentences or phrases. "I" is understood.

- The layout should lead the reader to important entries.

Figure 2.2
Model for references.

References

Name _____

Title _____

Street Address _____

_____

_____

E-mail _____

Telephone _____

(List home, mobile, and work telephone numbers, if reference approves; remember to include area codes.)

- Entries should be brief, consisting of no more than four or five lines in each block.

- If mailing, the résumé should be printed clearly on good-quality bond paper, preferably white, gray, beige, or ivory. It should match the letter of application and envelope.

- Your e-mail address should reflect a professional image. For example, Fungirl@aol.com does not convey professionalism.

- The size of the typeface should be no smaller than 10 point; 12 point is the easiest to read. The résumé heading can be a larger font than the rest of the résumé.

- Ensure the résumé is "reader centered" as opposed to "writer centered."

- Always choose black for the color of the type.

- Do not fold your résumé. Send it in an envelope that permits it to lay flat.

- If possible, leave at least a 1-inch border. Readers can use the border for notes.

- Avoid using underlines.

- Use company or industry buzzwords.

- Emphasize results and significant responsibilities. Ensure that your qualifications or attributes summary reflects your work style.

- Create a résumé that can be sent by mail, e-mail, or facsimile.

- Include a section about your skills. Speak in terms of proficiency, not familiarity.

- List certificates, licenses, publications, and professional affiliations.

- Include hobbies only if they are relevant to a specific job.

- Begin and end a category on the same page.

- Place the most important information in the top one-third of the page and left half of the page.

- Use the rule "10 years of experience per page" when settling on the length and format of the résumé. Many career coaches recommend that résumé writers with 10 years or less of work experience limit the résumé to one page. Those résumé writers with 11 to 20 years of work experience often work to restrict the length of their résumés to two to five pages.

- Work experience is a mandatory section. It is important to list your most recent experience first, then work backward. All relevant summer employment, part-time employment during the school year, volunteer work, internships, and so on should be identified.

- Military service can be included as a section, if applicable. If you served or are serving in the active military, the reserves, or the National Guard, identify the branch and time spent in the service, and include a statement of the nature of your duties, using easily understood civilian terminology. State the level of security clearance you hold or held.

- Extracurricular activities should be included as a section in the résumé. A prospective employer wants to hire a well-rounded individual who is interested in activities outside of the classroom. Identify the organizations to which you belong and the roles you play in each one, such as serving on committees or holding offices. Highlight any activities that are closely related to career goals or the needs of the employer. If you decide to include outside activities, identify affiliations that will help sell you to an employer or that may help connect you to the person reading the résumé. Conversely, you may want to avoid political, religious, or social affiliations and activities that may alienate the reader.

- An interests section is optional. You should identify personal interests only if they are pertinent to your career goals or the needs of the employer. Do not include this information if it takes up space needed for more relevant information.

- A personal data section is rarely, if ever, used. Whether to include information such as age, height, weight, marital status, health, and so forth should be determined by you. Decide if the inclusion of this information enhances or detracts from your résumé. Employers usually do not request this information because of possible legal complications. If you elect to include this information, place it near the end of the résumé.

The Scannable Résumé

What is a scannable résumé, and how is it different from a traditional résumé? A **scannable résumé** is one that is formatted to be transmitted by e-mail. It is also referred to as an electronic résumé. Computers process data differently from humans and some résumés need to be "computer friendly." Employers will let you know if this is the kind of résumé they desire. Box 2.2 is a summary of recommendations from Lands' End for a scannable résumé. Of particular interest is the company's recommendation to use key words from the internship position posting in your résumé. See also Box 2.3, The Top Ten Pitfalls of Résumé Writing.

Here are additional guidelines to follow when writing a scannable résumé:

- Use standard fonts, such as Arial, Courier, Helvetica, and Times New Roman. Avoid a decorative font.

- Do not use a font size larger than 14 point (10 to 12 is preferred).

- Avoid slang, and always spell out acronyms. Minimize or eliminate abbreviations.

- Avoid italics, underlined passages, and shading or shadows.

- Omit parentheses and brackets. Format phone numbers as 000-000-0000.

- Send your résumé as an attachment (.doc.file) or .rtf.file to maintain its format. Microsoft Word® is the standard program used in most offices.

- Put your name at the top of the page, followed by your address, phone number, and e-mail address, each on its own line. Also put your name on the top of page 2, if applicable.

- Be certain to set tabs for indentations.

- Set margins and tabs to fit 8½ × 11 inch paper. This allows the résumé to be printed or faxed as you intended it to look.

- Center the résumé lengthwise on the page, typed and spaced properly.

- Be brief, precise, and to the point, using phrases rather than complete sentences or paragraphs.

- Only use bullets if you have two or more items.

- Your résumé should contain relevant information about your education, work experience, abilities, and the position you hope to secure.

- Make the most of your experience; this is essentially a sales document.

- Use terminology that stresses managerial and leadership abilities.

- The résumé should be flawless and professional looking; avoid gimmicks, such as floral stationery, or clip art.

- Review it each time it is sent out, updating it as needed.

The Scannable Résumé, Courtesy of Lands' End

Many résumés are scanned and entered by prospective internship employers into a database, where they are reviewed. To ensure that your résumé is scannable, keep the following information in mind.

To maximize the computer's ability to read your résumé, submit the cleanest possible original, and use a standard résumé format. This is not the time to get creative or fancy with your résumé. "But," you may say, "I want my résumé to stand out," or, "I'm in a creative field and I don't want to appear bland." In these cases, send in a standard resume for scanning purposes, and then create another résumé with a more creative layout to be given out at a career fair (along with the scannable one) or interview.

- Use standard, easy-to-read fonts, such as Helvetica, Arial, and Times.

- Use a font size between 10 and 12 points.

- Avoid script, italic, and underlined text. Bold is usually okay.

- Avoid graphics or shading.

- Spell out ampersands (&) and percentage signs (%) because scanners have difficulty interpreting them.

- Horizontal and vertical lines should be used sparingly or not used at all.

- Be sure your name is placed at the top of each page in case the pages become separated.

- Save your résumé in a rich text file (RTF) format. This is readable by nearly all word processors. It could also be sent as an attachment (.doc file).

- Use common résumé headings, such as "Goal" or "Objective," "Work Experience" or "Employment," "Skills," "Accomplishments," "Education," "Professional Affiliations," and so on.

- Use nouns versus verbs if possible. Résumé tracking systems look for nouns (key words) as opposed to action verbs.

- The computer will search for key words in your résumé, so you will want to be sure to include those, as it increases your opportunities for a match. How do you know what key words to include? Here are a few suggestions:

  - Look at the job posting, and notice the words used to describe the duties and requirements of the position. Use these terms.

  - Talk to people in the field. What are some of the industry buzzwords?

  - Meet with someone in human resources to find out what he or she looks for in a résumé.

- Go to the Career Services office of your college, and ask what employers are looking for in interns.

The Top Ten Pitfalls in Résumé Writing

1. **Obviously generic:** An employer should feel you are interested in his or her company, not just any organization. Be sure the objective is specific enough so that the employer can visualize the type of internship you are seeking.

2. **Too long:** Keep it to one page, if possible. Do not exaggerate your work experiences.

3. **Typographical, grammatical, or spelling errors:** Have others proofread your résumé.

4. **Hard to read:** Use a plain typeface, no smaller than 10 point. Use asterisks, bullets, and bold highlighting sparingly. Do not compress spaces between letters.

5. **Too verbose (wordy):** Say as much as possible in as few words as possible. Avoid jargon and slang.

6. **Too sparse:** Give more than the bare essentials. Describe your skills, accomplishments, activities, and so on. Do not downplay your work experiences.

7. **Irrelevant information:** Leave out personal or dated information, such as high school activities, age, weight, and race.

8. **Too snazzy:** Do not use exotic paper, unusual fonts, binders, photos, and graphics. Make it neat, clean, and easy to read.

9. **Boring:** Incorporate action and skill words that make your résumé dynamic and interesting.

10. **Too modest:** This is your chance to sell yourself. Put your best foot forward.

Using Power Words in the Résumé

The following action words will give your résumé the look of achievement:

accomplished	assumed	computed	developed
achieved	attained	conceived	devised
acquired	audited	condensed	devoted
acted	augmented	conducted	directed
adapted	authored	conserved	discovered
addressed	awarded	consolidated	dispatched
administered	began	constructed	dispensed
advanced to*	broadened	consulted	displayed
advertised	brought	contracted	dissected
advised	budgeted	contributed	distributed
advocated	built	controlled	documented
aided	calculated	converted	doubled
allocated	catalogued	cooperated	drafted
amplified	chaired	coordinated	drove
analyzed	charged	copied	earned**
answered	checked	correlated	edited
anticipated	clarified	created	effected
applied	classified	critiqued	eliminated
appointed	coached	dealt	employed
appraised	collaborated	decided	enabled
approved	collected	defined	enforced
arbitrated	commended	delegated	enhanced
arranged	communicated	delivered	ensured
ascertained	compared	demonstrated	established
assembled	compiled	designed	evaluated
assessed	completed	detailed	examined
assisted	composed	determined	exceeded

Note: *"Advanced to" rather than "promoted to"

**"Earned" rather than "was given" indicates a person who does things rather than receives them.

excelled	helped	made	performed
executed	identified	maintained	persuaded
exhibited	illustrated	managed	pioneered
expanded	implemented	manipulated	planned
expedited	improved	mapped	predicted
experienced	improvised	mastered	prepared
experimented	increased	maximized	presented
explained	indicated	meditated	preserved
explored	influenced	mentored	presided
expressed	initiated	met	prioritized
extended	inspected	minimized	processed
extracted	installed	modeled	produced
fabricated	instituted	moderated	programmed
facilitated	instructed	modified	proposed
fashioned	integrated	monitored	protected
financed	interpreted	motivated	proved
fixed	interviewed	narrated	provided
focused	introduced	negotiated	publicized
followed	invented	nominated	published
formed	inventoried	observed	purchased
formulated	investigated	obtained	queried
fostered	judged	offered	questioned
founded	justified	operated	raised
gained	launched	ordered	ran
gathered	learned	organized	ranked
gave	lectured	oriented	received
generated	led	originated	recommended
governed	licensed	overhauled	reconciled
graduated	listed	oversaw	recorded
guided	listened	participated	recruited
handled	located	perceived	rectified
headed	logged	perfected	reduced

reestablished	scanned	stressed	transferred
referred	scheduled	studied	translated
rehearsed	screened	substantiated	tutored
reinforced	selected	succeeded	unified
related	served	suggested	updated
relied	set goals	summarized	upgraded
remodeled	set up	supervised	used
reorganized	shaped	supported	utilized
reported	simplified	surveyed	validated
represented	sketched	sustained	verified
researched	sold	symbolized	volunteered
reshaped	solicited	synthesized	widened
responded	solved	tabulated	won
responsible for	specialized	talked	worked
restored	stimulated	taught	wrote
revamped	strategized	tested and revised	
reviewed	streamlined	theorized	
revised	strengthened	trained	

Using a Résumé Organizational Worksheet

Use an organizational worksheet to help collect and organize information you may want to use on your résumé (Figure 2.3). This format is not for the final résumé. Use it only as a worksheet. Include all details needed, such as dates of employment, employers' titles, addresses, zip codes, area codes, and so on. You may need to add additional sheets of paper for your experience, education, and activities sections.

Reviewing the First-Draft Résumé

After constructing a résumé draft, it is important to take the time to review it carefully before it is printed and mailed. It is also a good idea to have several people review it for you. A résumé critique form is presented as Table 2.1. Suggested persons to review your résumé include faculty, family, employers, members of your college's Career Services office, and friends who are great at proofreading. Following are key questions reviewers may ask about your first-draft résumé.

• Name—Is it most visible? Is it noted on each page, including references?

• Current and permanent street address, phone numbers with area codes, and e-mail address—Are these complete and accurate?

Résumé Hints

General

- Select the best words for your résumé.

- Always use the same tense or ending on words. Use *–ing* verbs for current activities and *–ed* for those in the past.

- Avoid using the same verb more than once.

Personal Data

- Is everything current?

- Have you made yourself easily accessible? (Local and home street address; e-mail address; phone numbers with area codes)

- Is the message on your telephone answering machine or voice mail professional? Is your e-mail address appropriate?

Job Objective

- Are your short-term and long-term goals included?

- Have you kept your qualifications specific, yet not too confining?

Education

- Does the list of your education section start with your most recent schooling?

- Have you included education and training that is not directly related to your internship interests?

- Should you list course highlights?

Work Experience

- Is your experience related to the internship you are seeking?

- Have you listed your most recent job first?

- Internship Goal or Position Objective—Are goals and objectives clear and comprehensive?

- Education—Is it listed from most to least recent?

- Work Experience—Is work experience listed from most to least recent? Are responsibilities defined and articulated with action verbs?

- Honors/Awards (optional)—Are these significant?

- Special Interests (optional)—How do the special interests relate to the desired position?

- References—Are references willing to help? Is all contact information complete and accurate?

A sample résumé for the prospective internship employer is presented in Figure 2.4.

Personal Data (information):

Name _____

Current Address: Permanent Address:

Street _____   Street _____

City _____ State __ Zip _____   City _____ State __ Zip _____

Home Phone (area code) _____

Mobile Phone (area code) _____

Work Phone (area code) _____

E-mail Address _____

Internship Objectives (tailored to types of position or job):

Education:

Course Highlights or Related Courses:

Work Experience (include full-time, part-time, and summer jobs; practicums; and internships):

Competencies and Skills (computer/software knowledge, language fluency, technical skills):

Activities and Honors:

Related Professional Information (certification, publications, professional/honorary organizational memberships, offices held, volunteer work):

References:

Figure 2.3 Résumé organizational worksheet.

Table 2.1
RÉSUMÉ CRITIQUE FORM

Résumé of [name]

Rate the résumé on the points shown below, scoring from a low of 1 to a high of 3 in each of the categories listed. Then compare your rating point total against the highest possible total score of 30. Write comments for each category receiving a score of less than 3.

Item	Score			How It Could Be Improved
	1	2	3	
1. Overall Appearance: Do you want to read it? Is the typeface easily readable?				
2. Layout: Does the résumé look professional, well typed and printed, with adequate margins, and so on? Do key sales points stand out? Is it chronological?				
3. Length: Could the résumé tell the same story if it were shortened?				
4. Relevance: Has extraneous material been eliminated?				
5. Writing Style: Is it easy to get a picture of the applicant's qualifications?				
6. Action Orientation: Do sentences and paragraphs begin with action verbs?				
7. Specificity: Does the résumé avoid generalities and focus on specific information about experiences, projects, products, and so on?				
8. Accomplishments: Has the applicant quantified accomplishments and problem-solving skills?				
9. Completeness: Is all important information included?				
10. Bottom Line: How well does the résumé accomplish its ultimate purpose of getting the employer to invite the applicant in for an interview?				

Rating Point Total _____ (out of a maximum of 30)

What are some other ways that you would suggest to improve this résumé?

_____

_____

_____

_____

_____

MELODY PLACE
melody@gmail.com

Campus Address
Tower Hall, Box 3922
Ivy League University
Tucson, Arizona 85755
(520) 555-1215

Permanent Address
300 West 14th Avenue
Apartment 1-C
St. Louis, Missouri 63021
(314) 855-4213

Objective: To obtain a design internship in the fashion industry that will allow me to use and expand upon my present skills in patternmaking, draping, and illustration, while preparing me for future career employment.

Education: Bachelor of Science in Fashion Design/Product Development
Ivy League University, Tucson, Arizona
Anticipated graduation date: May 2012
Cumulative grade point average: 3.7/4.0 scale

Related Course Highlights

Flat Patternmaking	Retailing
Draping	Accounting I and II
Illustration	Finance
Clothing Construction I and II	Textiles
Product Development	History of Costume

Work Experience: **Alterations Associate,** Custom Fit, Tucson, Arizona, 2010 to present. Serve as night manager of company and supervise team of 5 seamstresses.

Sales Associate, Express, St. Louis, MO, Summers, 2009 and 2010. Assisted customers; checked in merchandise; stocked floor; created interior displays; cashiered.

Desk Hostess, Ivy League University, Tucson, Arizona 2008–2010. Responsible for opening and closing residence hall; assisted visitors and students; handled telephone calls and messages.

Honors/Activities: Fashion Honorary Organization, 2009–present.
Vice President, Tower Hall, 2009–2010.

Additional Skills: Proficient in CAD, Excel, Microsoft Word, Illustrator, and Photoshop
Fluent in French

Figure 2.4 Sample internship résumé.

Constructing a Letter of Application

The internship hunt is not finished yet. A letter of application should accompany the résumé. Some refer to the letter of application as a **cover letter.** Others refer to it as a **letter of interest.** Although these terms are often used simultaneously, a cover letter is used to introduce all types of business correspondence or enclosures, from billing statements to letters of reference. A letter of application, on the other hand, is a document intended to seek out a particular job opportunity. It is a brief explanation about the job you are interested in, how you heard about it, and why your qualifications fit the job. The letter of application includes only the relevant facts and mentions that additional information is contained in the accompanying résumé. It provides an opportunity to specify the reason you are applying to the company, such as a particular internship goal. The letter of application enables you to mention that you are available for an interview at the convenience of the addressee, or indicates when you will be available (for instance, as employment or classes allow).

A letter of application creates a powerful first impression. It ought, then, to observe the conventions governing business letters. No employers want to hire an applicant to whom they will have to teach such skills; they cannot afford the time or the trouble. Your expertise in letter writing is itself a job skill. The form of a letter of application tells as much about the writer as the content on the page. Through your letter, you will compete with other applicants, sell yourself and your ideas, and seek favors (for example, information and contacts). Obviously, no professional can be indifferent to the skills involved in this kind of communication.

It is important to remember that employers expect you to be an asset and to provide more to them than just eight hours of labor each day. As professionals, they expect intangible dividends from you, such as cooperation, genuine interest in the well-being of the company, contribution of ideas, problem solving, good judgment, continued competency in your specialty, and potential skills that can someday serve you in leadership positions. You should do whatever you can in your letter of application to show competency, professionalism, and potential. You must also rely on taste, reason, and a political frame of mind as guides in selling yourself to an employer.

The Structure of a Letter of Application

A letter of application has three parts or sections: an opening, a body, and a closing (Figures 2.5 and 2.6). In the introductory paragraph, indicate specifically the job or internship position for which you are applying.

Opening:

1. Explain who you are.

   Summary beginning: graduation date, degree, and institution

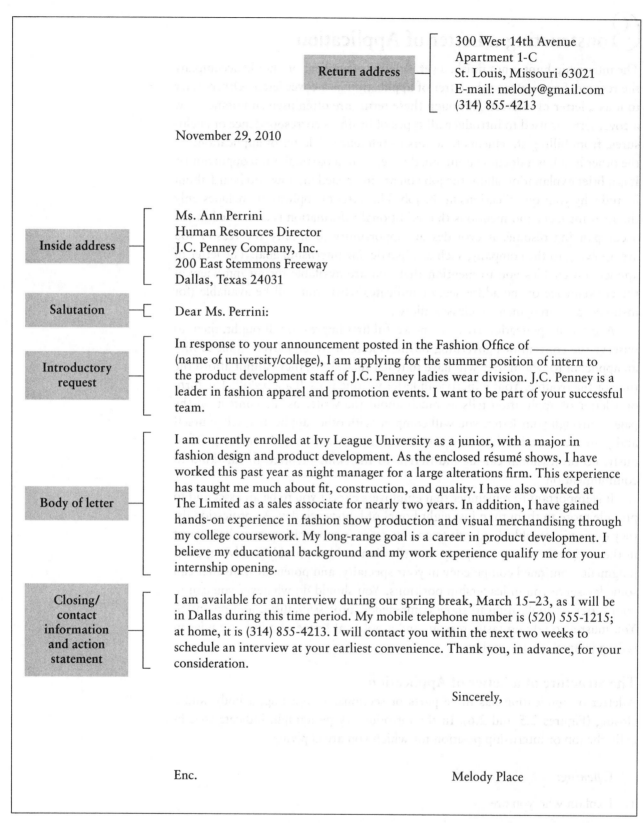

Return address
300 West 14th Avenue
Apartment 1-C
St. Louis, Missouri 63021
E-mail: melody@gmail.com
(314) 855-4213

November 29, 2010

Inside address
Ms. Ann Perrini
Human Resources Director
J.C. Penney Company, Inc.
200 East Stemmons Freeway
Dallas, Texas 24031

Salutation
Dear Ms. Perrini:

Introductory request
In response to your announcement posted in the Fashion Office of _____ (name of university/college), I am applying for the summer position of intern to the product development staff of J.C. Penney ladies wear division. J.C. Penney is a leader in fashion apparel and promotion events. I want to be part of your successful team.

Body of letter
I am currently enrolled at Ivy League University as a junior, with a major in fashion design and product development. As the enclosed résumé shows, I have worked this past year as night manager for a large alterations firm. This experience has taught me much about fit, construction, and quality. I have also worked at The Limited as a sales associate for nearly two years. In addition, I have gained hands-on experience in fashion show production and visual merchandising through my college coursework. My long-range goal is a career in product development. I believe my educational background and my work experience qualify me for your internship opening.

Closing/ contact information and action statement
I am available for an interview during our spring break, March 15–23, as I will be in Dallas during this time period. My mobile telephone number is (520) 555-1215; at home, it is (314) 855-4213. I will contact you within the next two weeks to schedule an interview at your earliest convenience. Thank you, in advance, for your consideration.

Sincerely,

Enc.   Melody Place

Figure 2.5 Sample letter of application.

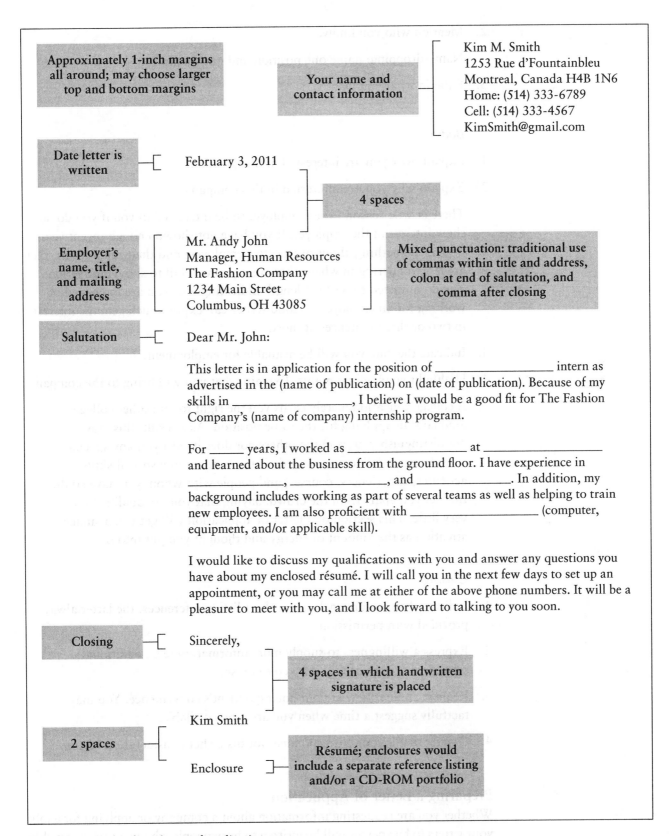

Approximately 1-inch margins all around; may choose larger top and bottom margins

Your name and contact information

Kim M. Smith
1253 Rue d'Fountainbleu
Montreal, Canada H4B 1N6
Home: (514) 333-6789
Cell: (514) 333-4567
KimSmith@gmail.com

Date letter is written

February 3, 2011

4 spaces

Employer's name, title, and mailing address

Mr. Andy John
Manager, Human Resources
The Fashion Company
1234 Main Street
Columbus, OH 43085

Mixed punctuation: traditional use of commas within title and address, colon at end of salutation, and comma after closing

Salutation

Dear Mr. John:

This letter is in application for the position of _____ intern as advertised in the (name of publication) on (date of publication). Because of my skills in _____, I believe I would be a good fit for The Fashion Company's (name of company) internship program.

For _____ years, I worked as _____ at _____ and learned about the business from the ground floor. I have experience in _____, _____, and _____. In addition, my background includes working as part of several teams as well as helping to train new employees. I am also proficient with _____ (computer, equipment, and/or applicable skill).

I would like to discuss my qualifications with you and answer any questions you have about my enclosed résumé. I will call you in the next few days to set up an appointment, or you may call me at either of the above phone numbers. It will be a pleasure to meet with you, and I look forward to talking to you soon.

Closing

Sincerely,

4 spaces in which handwritten signature is placed

Kim Smith

2 spaces

Enclosure

Résumé; enclosures would include a separate reference listing and/or a CD-ROM portfolio

Figure 2.6 Format for a letter of application.

2. Mention who you know.

Name-dropping: name one position and one institution

3. Explain what you want.

Body:

1. Explain why you are interested in this position.

2. Explain why you are interested in this company.

There is little reason for an employer to be interested in you if you do not show interest in the employer. If you have not shown enough incentive to find out something about prospective employers and their reputations, they are left wondering in what other areas you will fail to show motivation. You do not need to write at length indicating why you are interested in working for an employer. A good writer can express such genuine interest in two or three sentences at most.

3. Indicate the date you will be available for employment.

4. Highlight your selling points. Explain what you will bring to the company.

A college education merely earns you the right to join other college graduates in applying for the same position. As a result, this may not distinguish you from the others nor does it earn you any special consideration. What you must do is to point out any special skills, activities, experiences, courses, and people with whom you have studied that set you apart from the crowd. Saying that you are qualified means very little. This section of a letter of application will get you as much attention as the amount of energy and thought you put into it.

Closing:

1. Indicate that you are enclosing a sheet listing references, the latter always provided with permission.

2. Express a willingness to supply more information (e.g., additional references or a portfolio) if asked to do so.

3. Request an interview at your correspondent's convenience. You may tactfully suggest a time when you are most available.

4. Quietly thank your correspondent for his or her consideration of you.

Preparing a Letter of Application

Whether you are requesting information about a company or applying for a job, your letters to businesses will be written to busy people who want to see quickly why you are writing and what they can do for you. Be straightforward, clear, objective, and courteous. Observe conventions of grammar and usage, because these not only make your writing clear but also impress a reader with your care and intelligence.

Business correspondence customarily adheres to one of several acceptable forms. Use either unlined, quality paper measuring at least 8½ × 11 inches or what is called letterhead stationery with your address printed on top of the sheet. The letter should be printed on only one side of the sheet.

The return address heading of the letter gives your address, but not your name, and the date. (If you are using letterhead stationery, only the date must be added.) Align the lines of the heading on the left, and place the whole heading to the right of the page, allowing enough space above it so that the entire letter will be centered vertically on the page.

The inside address should show the name, title, and complete address of the person to whom you are writing, just as this information will appear on the envelope. Begin the address two lines below the heading, at the left side of the page.

The salutation greets the addressee. Place it two lines below the address and two lines above the body of the letter. Always follow the salutation with a colon, not a comma or a dash. If you are not addressing a particular person, use a general salutation such as "Dear Sir" or "Dear Madam" or "Dear Country Classics" (the company name). Use Ms. as the title for a woman when she has no other title, when you do not know how she prefers to be addressed, or when you know that she prefers to be addressed as Ms. If you know a woman prefers to be addressed as Mrs. or Miss, use the appropriate title.

If you do not know the name of the human resources director (or the person to whom your letter is directed), you may want to take a moment to contact the company by phone or e-mail and ask for that person's name (and its correct spelling) and his or her title and exact address. It may take a couple of minutes and a couple of dollars for a long-distance telephone call to get this information, yet it will move you miles ahead in the interview selection process.

The body of the letter begins at the left margin. Rather than indenting paragraphs, place an extra line of space between them so they are easily visible. The letter's close, beginning two lines below the last line of the body, should align at the left with the heading at the top of the page. Typical closes include "Yours truly" and "Sincerely." Only the first letter is capitalized, and the close is followed by a comma.

The signature of a business letter has two parts—a typed one, four lines below the close, and a handwritten one, filling in the space above. The signature should consist only of your name, the same one you use to sign your checks and legal documents.

Below the signature, at the left margin, you may want to include additional information such as "Enc." (something is enclosed with the letter). The envelope of the letter should have your name and address in the upper left corner and the addressee's name, title, and address to the right of the center. Use an envelope that fits and that matches the résumé and letter of application.

Two examples of letters of application are presented in Figures 2.7 and 2.8. Figures 2.9 through 2.12 illustrate letters of application with their corresponding résumés.

1225 Hampton Boulevard
Norfolk, VA 23517

March 15, 20XX

Ms. LeAnn Hinojosa
Manager of Human Resources
Hampton Industries, Inc.
2900 Virginia Beach Boulevard
Virginia Beach, VA 23464

Dear Ms. Hinojosa:

I am applying for the position of intern in the color division, as advertised on March 12 with the placement service at Ivy League University. The position seems to fit very well with my education, experience, and career interests.

Your position requires experience in color, design, and computer systems. With a major in housing and interior design, I have training in CAD, Adobe, and Photoshop. In addition, I worked as a cooperative education student in the design studio of a small home accessories operation, where I gained knowledge in product development. My enclosed résumé provides more details on my qualifications.

My background and career goals seem to match your job requirements well. I am confident that I can perform the job effectively. Furthermore, I am genuinely interested in the position and in working for Hampton Industries. Your firm has an excellent reputation and comes highly recommended to me.

Would you please consider my request for a personal interview to discuss further my qualifications and to learn more about this opportunity? I will call you next week to see when a meeting can be arranged. Should you need to reach me, please feel free to contact me at (303) 683-4388 or by e-mail at randees@hotmail.com.

Thank you for your consideration. I look forward to talking with you.

Sincerely yours,

Randee Stemmons

Figure 2.7 Sample letter of application (full block format).

Modified and reprinted from *Planning Job Choices: 1999,* with permission of the National Association of Colleges and Employers, copyright holder.

Elizabeth Wilson
1008 Montana Avenue
Los Angeles, CA 90403
(310) 394-7000
(310) 394-8090
Wilson3@gmail.com

February 26, 2011

Mr. Alexander Dust
Manager, Human Resources
Divine Design Firm
1234 Corporate Boulevard
Dallas, TX 95655

Dear Mr. Dust:

This letter is in application for the position of design intern as advertised in the *Dallas New Leader* on February 14, 2011. Because of my skills in design, management, leadership, and computer programs, I believe I would be a good fit for Divine Design Firm's internship program.

For one year, I worked as a fashion intern at Abercrombie and Fitch and learned about the business from the ground floor. I gained experience in customer relations, office management, and visual merchandising. In addition, my background includes working in the university's theater department as a costume designer and seamstress as well as helping train new employees. I am proficient in Illustrator and Microsoft Office.

I would like to discuss my qualifications with you and answer any questions you have about my enclosed résumé and CD portfolio. I will call you in the next few days to set up an appointment, or you may call me at either of the above phone numbers. It will be a pleasure to meet with you, and I look forward to talking to you soon.

Sincerely,

Elizabeth Wilson

Enclosures: Résumé and CD portfolio

Figure 2.8 Sample letter of application.

Modified and reprinted from *Planning Job Choices: 1999,* with permission of the National Association of Colleges and Employers, copyright holder.

DAYNA C. POLLARD
1117 E. Delmar Street
New York, New York 10001
(212) 555-4343
dpollard@hotmail.com

Ms. Wendy Cox
Internship Coordinator
Nordstrom Human Resources
47 West County Center
Des Peres, MO 64133

December 15, 2011

Dear Ms. Cox:

My name is Dayna Pollard. I am a junior majoring in fashion merchandising with an art minor, attending Liberal Arts College in New York City. My graduation date is May 2012, and an internship is an upper-level degree requirement. I am interested in securing a managerial internship with Nordstrom's this coming summer.

"Our goal is to make as many friends as possible in St. Louis County and introduce them to what Nordstrom's has to offer," stated Jason Price, store manager and guest speaker in one of my fashion classes. I, too, want to help Nordstrom's show customers why it is one of the leading fashion retailers, through an internship. This internship would be an opportunity for me to work with all levels of management and receive an understanding of fashion retailing at its best. During my time as a student, I have always worked in customer service jobs. This has increased my understanding of the customer's needs and wants. I have learned time management through balancing college and a full-time job. In addition, my fashion merchandising courses have helped me to gain a better understanding of management, marketing, and product development as it relates to fashion retailing. These are just a few qualifications that would make me an asset to Nordstrom's.

As I am originally from St. Louis, arranging an interview will be uncomplicated. My phone number is (212) 555-4343. I will contact you in the next two weeks to schedule an interview at your convenience.
Thank you for your time and consideration.

Sincerely,

Dayna Pollard

Enclosures: Résumé and references

Figure 2.9 Sample letter of application.

DAYNA C. POLLARD

1117 E. Delmar Street
New York, New York 10001
(212) 555-4343
dpollard@hotmail.com

OBJECTIVE
To secure managerial or marketing internship in the retail sector of the fashion industry.

EDUCATION
Liberal Arts College, New York, NY
Bachelor of Science in Fashion Merchandising; minor in Art
Planned graduation date: May 2012

SKILLS
- Computer skills in Excel, PowerPoint, and Access
- Oil, watercolor, and acrylic painting
- Time management skills developed from working 40 hours per week and attending school full-time
- Customer service abilities enhanced by service-oriented jobs
- Creativity strengthened by design and art classes

CURRICULAR EXPERIENCE
- Selected to design logo for spring 2010 fashion show "Jet Setting"
- Student designer, spring 2009, "Inspired by Decades of Fashion," juried fashion show
- Member of Association of Fashion Majors, October 2009–present
- Attendance at annual Fashion Group International, Inc., Career Seminars

JOB EXPERIENCE
Server, September 2010–present
Fox and Hound English Pub and Grille, New York, NY
- Operate cash register and handle customer payments in cash and credit card, totaling in excess of $3,000 weekly; gratuity exceeding others by 23 percent.
- Train servers on serving alcoholic beverages and dining protocols.
- Advise customers on choosing the menu items and provide suggestive selling.

Finance Intern, May–August 2010
Stifel Nicolaus and Co., Inc., St. Louis, MO
- Called prospective clients in St. Louis and its vicinity to provide free financial plans.
- Recorded customer postal addresses and mailed promotional materials.

Chef's Assistant, May–August 2009
Holiday Inn, Wentzville, MO
- Assisted chef in preparation of regular meals and desserts.
- Designed presentation of food during the absence of chef.
- Provided hospitality services when needed.

AWARDS
Third place in "Design Your Future" trend board, Fashion Group International, Inc., competition, September 2010
Dean's List, Spring 2010
Employee of the Month Award, Holiday Inn, July 2009

Figure 2.10 Résumé to accompany letter of application (Figure 2.9).

Carlee Evans
Evans228@gmail.com
911 China Circle
Paris, Texas 74059
(555) 728-4160 (mobile)

January 26, 2011

Dear Mr. Kim:

It is with your organization that I desire a position in the marketing division. I am certain that my skills and experiences, when combined with the vision of your company, will serve to create productive results. I have learned of the position after researching job openings on your Web site and in *Women's Wear Daily.*

I will be completing my Bachelor of Science in Fashion Merchandising at Texas State University in May 2012 and will be available for employment at that time. This past summer I completed an internship in New York City, at *Shape* magazine. I worked alongside very knowledgeable and prestigious people who gave me great opportunities and experiences. I was given progressively significant daily tasks and individual projects. I also accompanied my bosses on assignments.

As a senior at Texas State University, my education in the Department of Fashion and Interior Design has been highly beneficial and rewarding. My work background and coursework have supplied me with many skills and an understanding of the fashion industry. For example, I have acquired a solid reputation from my professors and peers as a responsible leader and strong networker in the industry. In addition to my academic endeavors, I have put my knowledge and creativity toward the involvement of fashion in the community. I have participated in planning and judging fashion shows for the university and local boutiques. I have also assisted a professor in a weekly television segment titled "Dr. Fashion." Along with fashion, I have a passion for photography and have been asked to photograph merchandise from boutiques and stores for publication in local magazines. I am consistently energized by opportunities to enhance my knowledge of and experience in the fashion industry. I have had the opportunity to travel and experience China, London, and Paris, where I was able to observe diverse global fashion markets contributing to this enormous and fast-paced industry.

I have enclosed a copy of my résumé with additional information about my qualifications. I look forward to the opportunity to speak with you and discuss the job position. I believe I can contribute to the creative needs and further advance the visibility of your organization. Thank you for your time while looking over my résumé. The best time to reach me is Monday through Friday, between 9:00 a.m. and 6:00 p.m. I will call you in two weeks to inquire about the best time for an interview. Thank you for your consideration.

Sincerely,

Carlee Evans

Enclosure: Résumé

Figure 2.11 Sample letter of application.

Carlee Evans

Evans228@gmail.com
911 China Circle
Paris, Texas 74059
(555) 728-4160 (mobile)

Objective: To obtain a job in the magazine industry in which I can apply my skills and experience in public relations, visual merchandising, and marketing

Education

Texas State University	**May 2012**
Candidate for a Bachelor of Science in Fashion Merchandising with a minor in Marketing	

Internships

Shape Magazine, New York, NY   **June 2011–August 2011**
Assistant to the Director of Public Relations
- Produced segments for online video clips featuring style director.
- Accompanied director of public relations to weekly national broadcasted segments.
- Pitched ideas relevant to latest issue of *Shape* and breaking world news.

Jeffrey Sweet Photography, Springfield, MO   **January 2011–June 2011**
Photographer's Assistant/Intern
- Assisted company owner/photographer with studio shoots (portrait, commercial, fashion).
- Helped arrange layouts for ads and magazines.
- Took photos of clothing and other items for advertisements in local magazines.

417 Magazine, Springfield, MO   **August 2010–December 2010**
Style Coordinating Assistant
- Accompanied style coordinator on variety of photo shoots.
- Selected merchandise and themes for different features.
- Operated Photoshop and other software programs for magazine layout.

Work Experience

BCBG MaxAzria Springfield, MO   **Fall 2010–present**
Sales Specialist
- Calculate daily/weekly/monthly sales plans and goals.
- Assist in reorganizing floor sets and inventory of merchandise.

Activities

- China and Paris fashion study tours (2009, 2010)
- Attended Fashion Group International seminars in Kansas City, Chicago, and Dallas (2008–2010)
- Fashion show production public relations leader, Association of Fashion and Design (2009)
- Fashion show production public relations leader (2009)
- Vice president, *Rho Lambda*, national women's sorority leadership recognition society (2009–present)
- Executive public relations officer, Business and Professional Women's Foundation (2009–present)
- Vice president, Order of Omega Greek honor society (2010–present)

Volunteer Services

- Help Give Hope
- Hurricane Katrina Relief efforts
- Donated series of original photographs that were auctioned to raise money for student scholarships

Figure 2.12 Résumé to accompany letter of application (Figure 2.11).

What Recruiters Look for in a Nutshell (and Other Tips on Conducting an Internship Search)

Your résumé:

- Keep it simple and to the point; a résumé is like a prospectus, an offering to a prospective buyer.

- Tell the truth and nothing but the truth. Do not find yourself in the position of having to explain a point that is not factual.

- The résumé should help you get through the door but does not tell the whole story.

- You need to be ready to jump in and to fill in the gaps.

Supporting the résumé:

- Write a good letter of application (cover letter).

- Your letter should be short and to the point. Make sure the recipient knows what you want (e.g., a permanent job, an internship, an informational interview, a contact, and so on).

- Provide your contacts.

- Ask alumni; they want to help if they can. Use family and hometown contacts. This is how you develop your network, one that you will build throughout your career.

- Make use of the informational interview.

- Identify key decision makers, and schedule a meeting to learn more about the business or the career path. Contact people both in human resources and in other areas. The more people in support of you, the better.

The interview (see also Chapter 3):

- Be prepared. Research the company and the industry before the interview.

- Come prepared with good questions (even better if you know the answers).

- Be polite and courteous. You are building your professional reputation.

A well-written follow-up letter is very important, especially if this is an off-campus interview. Points to keep in mind:

- **Be strategic and focused**—Even if you do not know exactly what you want, sound like you at least have an idea.

- **Understand the reality of the workplace**

  - Service businesses in the fashion industry are good places to look. Be creative.

  - New industries and businesses have fewer old rules to inhibit your growth.

  - Think about what environments you would like to work in (e.g., a large company, a big city location, a formal structure, and so on)

  - Find a good training program. Down the road you will benefit greatly from a good foundation. Sales and retail management often have the best.

- **Consider the merits of graduate school**

  - More and more young professionals have advanced degrees. They are likely the ones you will compete with further on up the career ladder.

  - Consider working first. You may want to gain some experience in the workplace so that you can add value to further education. Sometimes, employers will pay for graduate coursework.

- **Enjoy yourself—Have fun!**

- **Be realistic**—You are looking for an internship; hopefully, a career will result from this experience.

- **Consider yourself fortunate to have a general education**—Your college or university has provided you with a solid foundation and diverse exposure. Recruiters like that.

- **Remember to sell yourself**—Many doors can be opened for you, but it is up to you to sell yourself in order to walk through.

Wrapping It Up

Finding the right internship is a full-time job in itself. The amount of effort expended is proportionate to the type of internship secured. The letter of application and the résumé are the keys to securing an interview; however, no matter how effective these are, research on prospective employers will provide the door that these keys may open. Remember not to limit yourself: "They'll never hire me; I don't have enough experience," "I can't afford to live in New York City." These types of thoughts will block any opportunities that may arise. Where there is a will, there is a way. In the next chapter, skills for applying and interviewing for internship positions are presented.

CHAPTER THREE

Applying and Interviewing for the Internship

Objectives

- To learn how to complete the job application form

- To prepare for the interview

- To succeed in the actual interview

- To actively follow up on the interview

- To evaluate and negotiate position offers

- To withdraw, refuse, or accept an internship position professionally

How Do I Apply for an Internship?

After you have developed a résumé and letter of application, you are ready to begin the first active step toward securing an internship: applying and interviewing for the position. Now you will be presenting yourself in person, rather than through the written picture given by the résumé. It will be time to think on your feet. Following is a discussion of pre-interview considerations, then an explanation of what to do during and after the actual interview.

The Job Application Form

Some employers ask for a completed job application form even if a résumé is provided and often before an interview is scheduled. The information requested is basically the same on all applications: personal data, education, past work experience, and references. Each application will ask for the information in varying detail. Because many applications cannot be taken home, it is a good idea to carry an information sheet with you so that names, dates, and addresses of past employers and job references are handy. Accuracy and neatness are critical. Forms that are scratched out or left blank, or that contain misspelled words and illegible writing, do not make positive impressions.

Be sure to read the directions on the job application form carefully. The directions usually state exactly how to fill in the application and can save you much time and error. Avoid abbreviations unless they are commonly known, such as state abbreviations (e.g., PA, CA, NY). Any questions that do not apply to you should be marked "Not Applicable" or "N/A" or crossed out by drawing a line through the blank space. For questions concerning salary, indicate an expected rate in hourly or monthly terms as a salary range, or simply write "open" or "negotiable." If you are applying for an unpaid internship, simply note this in the salary or wage section. An example of employment application form for a retail operation is shown in Figure 3.1. Figure 3.2 illustrates an employment application form for an apparel manufacturing and design firm, and Box 3.1 includes tips on completing a job application. After the job application is complete, the interview is often the next step. Preparation is the key to a low-stress, successful interview. Next, tips to prepare for the interview are presented.

EMPLOYMENT APPLICATION

As an equal opportunity employer, Garland, Inc., does not discriminate in hiring or terms and conditions of employment because of an individual's race, creed, color, sex, age, handicap, or national origin.

_____/_____/_____
Date of Application

| Position Desired: _____ |
| Schedule Desired: [ ] Full time [ ] Temporary or or [ ] Part time [ ] Permanent |
| Salary Expected: $ _____ per _____ |
| Date Available: _____/_____/_____ |

PERSONAL INFORMATION

Last Name	First Name	Middle Name	Are you a Citizen of the United States? [ ] Yes [ ] No
Present Street Address	City	State Zip	How long have you lived there? ____ Yrs. ____ Mo.
Previous Street Address	City	State Zip	How long did you live there? ____ Yrs. ____ Mo.
Home Phone Number	E-mail Address	Social Security Number	Are you under 18 years of age? Yes ☐ No ☐

EDUCATION

Type of School	Name and Location of School	Degree/Area of Study	Number of Years Attended	Graduated [Check One]
HIGH SCHOOL	Name City State			Yes ☐ No ☐
JUNIOR COLLEGE	Name City State			Yes ☐ No ☐
COLLEGE	Name City State			Yes ☐ No ☐
GRADUATE SCHOOL	Name City State			Yes ☐ No ☐
OTHER	Name City State			Yes ☐ No ☐

ACADEMIC AND PROFESSIONAL ACTIVITIES AND ACHIEVEMENTS

Academic and Professional Activities and Achievements, Awards, Publications, or Technical-Professional Societies. Indicate type or name. Exclude organizations that indicate race, creed, color, sex, age, handicap, or national origin of its members.	Date Awarded

SPECIAL SKILLS

Computer Programs Used (e.g., Excel, Microsoft, Photoshop)	Other Equipment Operated

Other skills applicable to position applied for

MILITARY SERVICE

Branch of Service	Technical Specialization	Rank Attained	Date Entered	Date Discharged
			___/___ mo. yr.	___/___ mo. yr.

Figure 3.1 Employment application for a retail firm.

EMPLOYMENT HISTORY

List employment starting with your most recent position. Account for any time during this period that you were unemployed by stating the nature of your activities. If you have less than four places of employment, include personal references to be contacted. May we contact your present employer? [ ] Yes [ ] No

DATES	NAME AND ADDRESS OF EMPLOYER	POSITION HELD AND SUPERVISOR	LIST MAJOR DUTIES	WAGES	REASON FOR LEAVING
From: __/____ mo. yr.	Name	Your Job Title		Starting	
To: __/____ mo. yr.	Address Phone	Supervisor		Final	
From: __/____ mo. yr.	Name	Your Job Title		Starting	
To: __/____ mo. yr.	Address Phone	Supervisor		Final	
From: __/____ mo. yr.	Name	Your Job Title		Starting	
To: __/____ mo. yr.	Address Phone	Supervisor		Final	
From: __/____ mo. yr.	Name	Your Job Title		Starting	
To: __/____ mo. yr.	Address Phone	Supervisor		Final	

MISCELLANEOUS

Is there any additional information involving a change of your name that will permit us to check your work record? If yes, please explain.

Have you ever been employed by a division of Garland, Inc. before? [ ] Yes [ ] No	When:	Where:	Position:

List names of friends or relatives now employed by Garland, Inc.:

List any hobbies or special interests you have:

Have you ever been convicted of a felony? [ ] Yes [ ] No	If yes, please explain:

Do you have any impairment that would prevent you from performing the activities involved in the job(s) for which you applied? Please explain.	If there are any jobs for which you do not wish to be considered or duties you cannot perform because of physical, mental or medical disabilities, please explain.

PERSON TO CONTACT IN CASE OF EMERGENCY

This information is to facilitate contact in the event of an emergency and is not used in the selection process.

Full Name	Address	Phone	Relationship to you?
Place of Employment	Address	Phone	

PLEASE READ THIS STATEMENT CAREFULLY

I hereby affirm that the information given me on this application for employment is complete and accurate. I understand that any falsification will be immediate grounds for dismissal. I authorize a thorough investigation to be made in connection with this application concerning my character, general reputation, personal characteristics, and mode of living, whichever may be applicable. I understand that this investigation may include personal interviews with third parties. I further understand that I have the right to make a written request within a reasonable period of time for a complete and accurate disclosure of the nature and scope of the investigation.

It is understood that as a prerequisite to consideration for employment, I agree to submit to such future examinations, physical or other, as may be required by the company. The company will pay the reasonable cost of any such examination that may be required.

If I am hired, I agree that my employment and compensation can be terminated with or without cause and without notice at any time at the option of Garland or myself. I understand that no store manager or other representative of Garland, Inc. other than a Vice-President has authority to enter into any agreement for employment for any specified period of time or to make any agreement contrary to the foregoing.

I have read and affirm as my own the above statements.

_____   _____
Signature   Date

APPLICANTS IN THE STATE OF MARYLAND ONLY

Under Maryland law an employer may not require or demand any applicant for employment or prospective employment or any employee to submit to or take a polygraph, lie detector or similar test or examination as a condition of employment or continued employment. Any employer who violates this provision is guilty of a misdemeanor and subject to a fine not to exceed $100.

_____   _____
Signature   Date

Figure 3.1 *(continued)*

Application For Employment

We consider applicants for all positions without regard to race, religion, creed, gender, national origin, age, disability, handicap, marital or veteran status, sexual orientation, or any other legally protected status.

If you need assistance in completing this application for employment or require a reasonable accommodation to the testing process, please notify the Human Resources Department.

Position(s) Applied For	Location	Date of Application

How Did You Learn About Us?
❏ Advertisement   ❏ Friend   ❏ Walk-in
❏ Employment Agency   ❏ Relative   ❏ Other _____

Last Name	First Name	Middle Name

Address	Number	Street	City	State	Zip Code

Telephone Number(s)	E-mail Address	Social Security Number

If you are under 18 years of age, can you provide required proof of your eligibility to work?   ❏ Yes   ❏ No

Have you ever filed an application with us before?   ❏ Yes   ❏ No

If Yes, provide date _____

Have you ever been employed with us before?   ❏ Yes   ❏ No

If Yes, provide date _____

Are you currently employed?   ❏ Yes   ❏ No

May we contact your present employer?   ❏ Yes   ❏ No

Are you **prevented from lawfully becoming employed in this country because of visa or immigration status?**
Proof of citizenship or immigration status will be required upon employment.   ❏ Yes   ❏ No

On what date would you be available for work? _____

Are you available to work: ❏ Full Time   ❏ Part Time   ❏ Shift Work   ❏ Temporary

Are you currently on "lay-off" status and subject to recall?   ❏ Yes   ❏ No

Can you travel if the job requires it?   ❏ Yes   ❏ No

Have you been convicted of any felony, misdemeanor, or other offense that a reasonable person would view as substantially relating to the requirements and circumstances of the job for which you are applying?   ❏ Yes   ❏ No

If yes, please explain _____

WE ARE AN EQUAL OPPORTUNITY EMPLOYER

Figure 3.2 Employment application from an apparel manufacturing and design firm.

Educational Background

	Name and Address of School	Course of Study	Years Completed	Diploma Degree
High School				
Undergraduate College				
Graduate Professional				
Other (Specify)				

Indicate any foreign languages you can speak, read, and/or write.		
	BELOW AVERAGE	AVERAGE	ABOVE AVERAGE
SPEAK			
READ			
WRITE			

Describe any specialized apprenticeship, skills, licenses, and extracurricular activities.

_____
_____
_____
_____

Describe any specialized job-related computer skills.

_____
_____
_____
_____

Figure 3.2 *(continued)*

Employment Experience

Start with your present or last job. Include any job-related military service assignments and volunteer activities. You may exclude organizations that indicate race, color, religion, gender, national origin, handicap, or other protected status.

1. Employer	Dates Employed	Work Performed
Address		
Telephone Number(s)	E-mail	Hourly Rate/Salary
Job Title	Supervisor	
Reason for Leaving		

2. Employer	Dates Employed	Work Performed
Address		
Telephone Number(s)	E-mail	Hourly Rate/Salary
Job Title	Supervisor	
Reason for Leaving		

3. Employer	Dates Employed	Work Performed
Address		
Telephone Number(s)	E-mail	Hourly Rate/Salary
Job Title	Supervisor	
Reason for Leaving		

4. Employer	Dates Employed	Work Performed
Address		
Telephone Number(s)	E-mail	Hourly Rate/Salary
Job Title	Supervisor	
Reason for Leaving		

If you need additional space, please continue on a separate sheet of paper.

List professional, trade, business, and civic activities and offices held.
You may exclude membership that would reveal gender, race, religion, national origin, age, ancestry, disability, or other protected status.

_____

_____

_____

_____

Additional Information

Other Qualifications

Summarize special job-related skills and qualifications acquired from employment or other experience relating to the position for which you are applying.

Specialized Skills

Mark skills/equipment operated with VP (very proficient), P (proficient), or N (none)

Production/Mobile
Machinery (list):

Other (list):

___ CRT/Terminal   ___ Photoshop

___ PC   ___ Adobe

___ EXCEL   ___ Microsoft Word

___ U4ia   ___ Illustrator

___ Gerber   ___ Kaledo

State any additional information you feel may be helpful to us in considering your application.

References

1. (Name)   (Title)   Phone #

   (Address)   E-mail

2. (Name)   (Title)   Phone #

   (Address)   E-mail

3. (Name)   (Title)   Phone #

   (Address)   E-mail

Applicant's Statement

I certify that answers given herein are true and complete to the best of my knowledge.

I authorize investigation of all statements contained in this application for employment as may be necessary in arriving at an employment decision.

(This application for employment shall be considered active for a period of time not to exceed 45 days. Any applicant wishing to be reconsidered for employment beyond this time period should inquire as to whether or not applications are being accepted at that time.)

I hereby understand and acknowledge that, unless otherwise defined by applicable law, any employment relationship with this organization is of an "at will" nature, which means that the Employee may resign at any time and the Employer may discharge Employee at any time. It is further understood that this "at will" employment relationship may not be changed by any written document or by conduct unless such change is specifically acknowledged in writing by an authorized executive of this organization.

In the event of employment, I understand that false or misleading information given in my application or interview(s) may result in discharge. I understand, also, that I am required to abide by all rules and regulations of the employer.

I affirm that everything is true and correct, and I acknowledge that I can be terminated at any time if it turns out that any information I supply is false. I affirm that I have a genuine intent and no other purpose in applying for a job with the company.

I further understand that my employment may be conditioned on satisfactory results of a physical examination, including substance abuse screening. Refusal to participate following receipt of a conditional offer will result in the rejection of my application.

Signature of Applicant   Date

FOR HUMAN RESOURCES DEPARTMENT USE ONLY

Arrange Interview   Yes   No

Remarks _____

INTERVIEWER   DATE

Employed   Yes   No   Date of Employment _____

Job Title _____   Hourly Rate/Salary _____   Department _____

By _____

NAME AND TITLE   DATE

Figure 3.2 *(continued)*

Job Application Tips

- Learn about the target employer.

- Do not miss any deadlines.

- Complete company application forms neatly, accurately, and thoroughly.

- Type whenever possible.

- Fill in all the blanks.

- Include details such as area code, zip code, and apartment number.

Interview Guidelines

Preparing for an interview is often just as important as the interview itself. Here are some guidelines for interviewing successfully:

Before the Interview

Practice

- Questions you may be asked

- Questions you want to ask about the position and the organization

- Role-play the interview; videotape and critique it to observe your behavior, using the assistance of your university's career services office when available

Self-Assessment

- Goals

- Skills, abilities, accomplishments

- Work values (important factors you look for in a job)

- Experiences

- Personality

Research

- Obtain company literature

- Write to or visit the organization

- Talk to people familiar with the organization

- Obtain references

Figure 3.3 Arriving for your interview a little early will assure that you do not feel rushed and worried about being on time.

Figure 3.4 No small surprise: plan your interview outfit in advance, ensuring that it fits and is pressed. Make sure that your shoes are also professional. Do not wear sneakers on the interview.

Plan ahead

- Directions to the interview site

- Time of arrival (get there with at least 10 to 15 minutes to spare)

- Attire to be worn to the interview: pressed and altered to fit

- Makeup (if applicable) and hairstyle

Summary of Pre-Interview Considerations

Keep the following in mind when preparing for your interview:

- Find out the exact place and time of the interview.

- Be certain you know the interviewer's name and how to pronounce it if it looks difficult.

- Research the company with which you are interviewing. Talk to people about it, and read the company literature and review its Web site to know what its products or services are, where its offices are located, what its growth has been, and how its prospects look for the future.

- Be up to the minute on current events. Read the newspaper; check out the news online or on television. An interviewer will often break the ice with an opening conversation about general world events.

- Think of two or three good questions you would like to ask during your interview.

- Plan to arrive at the designated place for your interview a little early so that you do not feel rushed and worried about being on time.

- Plan to dress in a manner appropriate to the company with which you are interviewing.

Practice to Interview Successfully

Practice, practice, practice—the best advice for a top-notch interview. Practice the questions you will have to answer. Practice the questions you will ask. Think about what you will wear and what messages your body language will give. Practice how you will conclude the interview session. Following is information on practicing for interviews: pre-interview preparation, body language, questions to ask and answer, and how to dress for interview success.

Interview Preparation Tips

- Prepare with practice questions that illustrate an interest in the particular company.

- Plan to go alone to the interview. This is not the time or place to bring a friend.

- Dress professionally and appropriately for the business of the prospective employer. (Further discussion on dressing for the interview is provided later in this chapter.)

- Plan to arrive early. Arriving late to an interview may be enough to lose the position before you are even interviewed.

- Speak in a conversational tone at a comfortable pace. When nervous, some people speak too loudly or rapidly. Are you prone to either interview faux pas?

- Answer the questions completely. Include a brief example when appropriate.

- When asked if you have any questions, ask approximately three. This guideline allows you to ask what you need to know without dominating the interview.

- Do not talk too much. This can turn off an interviewer.

- Plan to close the interview session with an appropriate statement or question. This is very important, as it leaves a final impression. Then thank the interviewer; express your interest in the company and the internship; and, if possible, inquire about when the decision will be made and how you should follow up.

Body Language during the Interview

- Make eye contact. Avoid shifting your eyes and glancing downward, but do not stare.

- A slow nodding of the head shows that you are listening and not in a hurry.

- Be careful not to tap your fingers or feet, swing your legs, or show other nervous behaviors.

- A firm handshake is important.

- Be yourself.

- Smile genuinely to show your interest.

Assessment Questions Asked by Professional Interviewers

Most employers will ask many questions during the interview. Every question has a specific purpose. The manner in which you respond, and the thought you put into the response, will affect the decision either to invite you back for a follow-up interview, to offer you the position, or to send you a rejection letter.

Many questions professional interviewers ask today reflect a significant movement away from standard direct interview questions toward more open-ended ones. Common topics involve the application of your analytical, problem-solving, and decision-making skills; leadership development; creativity; teamwork; and ability to assess and implement confidentiality. It is important to note that, during the interview, an employer may want to evaluate how responsible and discreet you will be about the plans, data, and interpersonal relationships within the organization. (Further discussion of confidentiality is presented in Chapter 4.) The top three questions the interview candidate should prepare to answer are:

1. What do you know about this organization?

2. Why are you interested in this organization? What internship position would you like to have? Why?

3. What can you contribute to this company?

The following questions and statements are examples of other types of questions interviewers may ask:

- What can you tell me about yourself?

- What school activities have you participated in? If you have not been active on campus, why not?

- Describe a leadership position you have held; give two key principles you learned.

- In looking at your academic program, which classes did you enjoy the most? The least? Why?

- Describe a mistake you have made; relate the lessons you learned and the impact they had on you.

- Give me an instance when you felt most pressured and stressed in your work or school. How did you cope?

- Describe a time when you were assigned to teach others a new skill or a new way of doing something.

- Do you feel you have done the best scholastic work you are capable of doing? Why or why not?

- What are your greatest strengths? weaknesses? (Identify several specific strengths and one weakness.)

- What do you think determines an individual's success in a work situation?

- What personal characteristics do you think are necessary for success in your chosen field?

- What qualifications do you have that make you feel you will be successful in your chosen field?

- Are you a leader or a follower? Why?

- Do you prefer working with others or by yourself? Why?

- Provide your definition of cooperation.

- How do you define success?

- What jobs have you held? How were they obtained? What did you like or dislike about the jobs? Why?

- What are your short-term goals? long-range?

- What are two or three things that are most important to you in a job? Why?

- Tell me about the most difficult or frustrating person with whom you have worked. Did you manage to develop a good working relationship with him or her? How?

- Describe a time you took an idea and turned it into a program or project.

- Tell me about a time when you contributed to the success of a team/committee/project.

- Describe a time when you presented your ideas to others for new programs, procedures, or processes.

- How do you go about organizing your work and scheduling your time?

- Describe a major problem you faced and how you dealt with it.

- Are you willing to relocate? If so, do you have a geographical preference? Would you consider traveling?

- What do you expect from an employer?

- Describe the relationship that should exist between a supervisor and subordinates.

- What kind of work environment do you prefer?

- If you were hiring a graduate for the position for which you are applying, what qualities would you seek in the candidate?

- Why should we hire you? (Address this answer to meet the company's needs or job requirements.)

- What is your problem-solving process?

- What do you consider to be your most significant accomplishment? Why?

- What goals have you set for yourself? How are you planning to achieve them?

- Who or what has had the greatest influence on the development of your career interests?

- What factors did you consider in choosing your major?

- Where do you see yourself in your career 10 years from now?

- What two or three things are most important to you in a position?

- What kind of work do you want to do?

- What can you tell me about a project you initiated?

- What are your expectations of your future employer?

- What is your grade point average? How do you feel about it? Does it reflect your ability?

- How do you resolve differences with others?

- How would you evaluate yourself in regard to your strengths and weaknesses?

- What work experience has been the most valuable to you, and why?

- What was the most useful criticism you ever received, and who was it from?

- Can you give an example of a problem you have solved and the process you used to solve it?

- Describe a project or situation that best demonstrates your analytical skills.

- What has been your greatest challenge?

- Describe a situation in which you had a conflict with another individual, and explain how you dealt with it.

- What were the biggest problems you encountered in college? How did you handle them? What did you learn from them?

- What are your team player qualities? Give examples.

- Describe your leadership style, and provide an example of your leadership success.

- What interests you about the position or the company? What concerns you?

- What was your greatest challenge in a particular leadership role you had?

- What idea have you developed and implemented that was particularly creative or innovative?

- What characteristics do you think are important for this position?

- How have your educational and work experiences prepared you for this position?

- How do you think you have changed personally since you started college?

- Tell me about a team project of which you are particularly proud, and discuss your contribution.

- How do you motivate people?

- Why did you choose the extracurricular activities you did? What did you gain? What did you contribute?

- What types of situations put you under the most pressure, and how do you deal with that pressure?

- Can you tell me about a difficult decision you have made?

- Give an example of a situation in which you failed, and explain how you handled it.

- Can you tell me about a situation in which you had to persuade another person to take your point of view?

- What frustrates you the most?

- Knowing what you know now about your college experience, would you make the same decisions?

- How would you react to having your credibility questioned?

- What characteristics are important in a good manager? How have you displayed one of these characteristics?

- What challenges are you looking for in an internship position?

- What two or three accomplishments have given you the most satisfaction?

- Describe a volunteer role you held, and discuss why you committed your time to it.

- How are you conducting your internship search, and how will you make your decision?

- What is the most important lesson you have learned in or out of school?

- We are looking at a great number of excellent candidates. Why are you the best person for this internship position?

- How would your friends describe you? your professors? your previous employers?

- What else should I know about you?

- Is there anything else you want to tell me about yourself?

Questions Candidates Ask Employers

Sometime during the interview, you may find a lull in the conversation. This may be an excellent moment to ask some of the questions on your mind. As the interview draws to a close, the interviewer will likely ask if you have any other questions. Having well-thought-out questions demonstrates your interest in and knowledge of the employer's organization.

Your questions should show a sincere interest in this particular employer, an awareness of the employer's needs, and how you can fulfill those needs. What is a good question? In general, good questions are those that are basic but not so general that the interviewer assumes you have not researched the company. Ask the most important questions first. Recognize that the employer may be on a tight time schedule. You may be able to ask less important questions during a follow-up interview.

Too many employment applicants spend all their time worrying about what questions employers will ask them. Too often, they fail to ask the vital questions that would help them learn if a job is right for them. Although some applicants do have the opportunity for a second contact through a follow-up interview, many do not have this option. After the job offer has been received and accepted, it may be too late to ask significant questions.

The following are examples of questions internship applicants have asked. Modify the wording of the questions to reflect your own speaking style.

- What is the employer's management philosophy?

- What is the nature of the training program and supervision given in the internship?

- Has your organization hired interns from this school in the past? If so, what is their success record?

- What will be expected of me as a new intern?

- How much training and support are offered interns?

- Is there any time scheduled for an internship review? When will it be conducted?

- Is this a new internship position or a vacated position?

- What new plans or projects are being developed to maintain or increase the company's market share?

- Have any new product lines been added recently? Is the sales growth in the new product line sustainable?

- Who are the people with whom I will be working? Will I meet with some of them?

- May I have a copy of the internship position description?

- What might be a typical first assignment?

- What is the potential for promotion in the organization? In promotions, are employees ever transferred between functional fields?

- What is the average time to get to the next level in this career path?

- Is it your policy to promote from within, or are many senior jobs filled by experienced people from the outside? Do you have a job posting system?

- What type of training will I receive? When does the training program begin?

- About how many individuals work in your internship program?

- What is the normal routine of an intern like? Can I progress at my own pace, or is the internship structured?

- How much travel is normally expected? Is a car provided to traveling personnel?

- How much freedom is given to and how much self-direction is required from interns? How much input does the intern have in decision making?

- What is the short-term housing market for interns in _____ (city)? Is public transportation adequate?

- How much contact and exposure to management is there?

- If I am selected for the internship, how soon would I be expected to report to work?

- When do you expect to make your decision on the internship position?

Failing to ask important questions during the interview often leads to no job or a job that offers neither interest nor challenge. Too often, uninformed applicants accept positions, hoping that these will develop into something more meaningful and rewarding later.

Inappropriate Questions for the Interview Candidate and Interviewer

Questions that do not directly pertain to the employing company, or that are extremely general, should be avoided by the interview candidate, such as "How do you feel the economy will affect fashion retailing?" Also, questions that scream "It's all about me" are inappropriate, such as vacation time, daytime-only hours, and so on. A poor question for the interview candidate to ask early in the process is one that deals with salary and benefits. Remember, the preliminary part of the interview process is a screening interview. Both you and the interviewer are trying to determine if there is any interest. If there is, there will be ample time to discuss salary and benefits.

Inappropriate (and often illegal) questions for interviewers to ask include those that pertain to race, religion, sexual preference, national origin, age, marital status, veteran status, and disabilities or handicaps that do not impact job performance. For example, if you are applying as an intern in a manufacturing plant, it is appropriate to be asked if you can lift ten pounds, assuming that is part of the job. Plan ahead to answer this type of question, if asked. Most interviewers are aware of the types of personal questions that should be avoided due to law; however, preparing to deflect or deal with such queries is highly recommended.

Common Reasons for Rejection

Employers reject applicants for many reasons. A good number of these can be easily avoided by the job searcher. Review the following list of reasons for passing on a job applicant before each interview to prevent you from losing a potentially great job because of an avoidable error.

- An overbearing, overaggressive, conceited, superior, or know-it-all attitude

- An inability to express oneself clearly; poor voice, diction, grammar

- Lack of planning for the interview or, more important, for one's career; purpose and goals are unclear

- Lack of interest and enthusiasm

- Failure to participate in part-time work, student activities, or volunteer activities

- Overemphasis on money; interested only in the best dollar offer

- Poor scholastic record; just "got by"

- Uses profanity or inappropriate language during interview

- Asks no questions about the position

- Lack of knowledge about the employer

- Late for the interview

- Sloppy data sheet, résumé, or application form

- Poor eye contact during interview

- Extreme nervousness

- Indefinite responses to questions; talks too much or not enough

- Lack of confidence and poise

- Indecisive; lacking initiative

- Condemnation of previous employers or professors

- Unwilling to start at the bottom; expects too much too soon

- Makes excuses, is evasive, hedges on unfavorable factors in record

- Lacking in courtesy; ill-mannered

- Lack of leadership qualities

- Timid; lacking sufficient degree of assertiveness

- Questionable long-term potential for advancement

- Poor personal grooming

- Inappropriately dressed

Dressing for the Interview

Make a good first impression at the interview by dressing for success. In the past, it was simple to describe the executive interview uniform: a business suit; sensible, well-polished shoes; and a pressed shirt. Today, many employers are seeking young professionals who reflect the company image by being a reflection of the brand. The conservative interview uniform may cost the internship candidate the position, for example, in an informal Internet firm retailing activewear. However, there are some guidelines that are applicable to most companies:

- For men and women, a clean, pressed, two-piece suit is usually appropriate for most types of business. For some companies a more casual look will provide a better image fit. For all companies, avoid athletic-type sportswear or club wear. For women, low necklines and high-slit skirts are not appropriate for an interview.

- Clean, polished shoes (for women, closed-toe shoes, with low or medium heels).

- A neat hairstyle (if your hair is going to get in your face, wear it back).

- Piercings and tattoos may put off some employers. Use common sense in determining whether these "accessories" fit the employer image or not.

- Clean, trimmed fingernails. Go light on the jewelry, perfume, and makeup. Project a healthy appearance.

- Avoid smoking or chewing gum. Smokers should not smoke on the way to an interview.

Figure 3.5 Think twice about making a statement with your personal accessories. Determine whether your look fits the employer's image or distracts from what you are saying.

Figure 3.6 Dressing for success with style: traditional, with a fashion twist.

- Carry a light briefcase or portfolio. Women should choose a small briefcase rather than a purse. If you carry a purse *and* a briefcase, it becomes a juggling act, and you are likely to leave one behind.

- Avoid bulky items, such as a winter coat, if possible. Leave heavy outerwear in the reception area closet when available.

Collaborating on Your Internship

As a former internship employer in the industry who is now working with college interns and their fashion industry employers, I would like to include some observations that may be helpful in your approach to the interview process. From these experiences, and through conversations with a wide variety of other intern employers, the following general observations are worth noting.

Formal internship programs in retailing and fashion merchandising may be offered only during the academic semester, rather than in the summer. Saks Fifth Avenue, Dillard's, and Macy's are a few of the retail operations that offer structured, formal internship programs, with a limited number of openings, during the fall and spring semesters. These are difficult positions to secure and may require a semester away from school. The advantages of these selective programs are many. They are most often paid positions offering a highly competitive salary. They are carefully planned and structured to expose interns to a wide variety of departments, personnel, and executives in the company. Firms with formal internship programs often hire graduates of their programs for entry-level executive positions. Figure 3.7 illustrates a description of a formal internship program offered by Land's End.

If you do not have the opportunity to be part of a formal internship program, you have another viable option: the informal internship. The informal internship may be paid or unpaid. It may take place in a single-store entrepreneurial firm or in the branch store of a specialty chain, for example. The informal internship plan is often created by the intern and supervisor to meet the needs of the student, the academic institution, and the industry employer. Informal internship programs may offer more time flexibility and may be more readily available, if you take the time to investigate them. The term *internship* often frightens the employer with no formal internship program. *Always* be honest and upfront with a prospective employer. Ask the employer if you can work, for

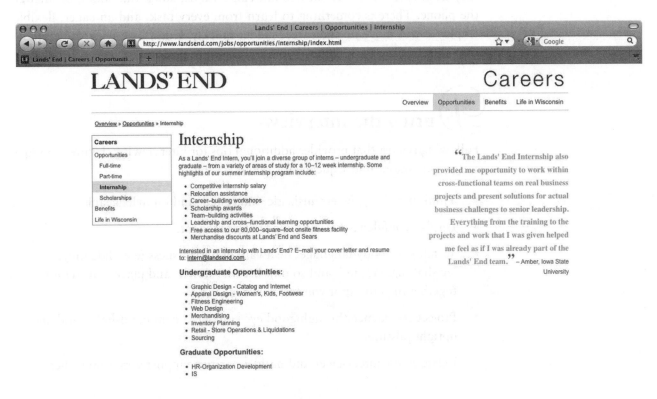

Figure 3.7 Formal internship program offered by Lands' End.

example, a minimum of 200 hours; if you will receive exposure to all or most aspects of the business; and if your direct supervisor would be willing to complete an evaluation form on your work performance at the conclusion of your employment. You may want to clarify that you expect to work primarily as a sales associate or receptionist or design assistant (or whatever position for which you are applying) but would like the opportunity to observe other departments. You may even offer to observe the other departments on your own personal time when not "on the clock." If all this is agreeable to the prospective employer, then an informal internship program may be an option with this company. Now is the ideal time to show the prospective employer your textbook and to let him or her know you will be responsible for completing this guide as part of your internship work experience.

Ask for an informal internship. Let the employer know that your college program, academic sponsor, and textbook help structure the program for the employer and place the responsibility for it on the student. The student does 95 percent of the internship's written work; the employer is asked to expose the intern to the organization as a whole and to fill out an evaluation form. This way you may not need to find a formal internship program to fulfill your academic requirements, depending on the requirements of your academic institution.

Let your prospective employer know what assets you will bring to the internship organization, including your enthusiasm, education, and work experience. Let the employer know you are willing to start at the bottom, as a "gofer." You may need to vacuum the showroom, run errands, stock the floors, or answer the phone. There is something to learn from every task, and an eager, flexible employee will move up the career ladder quickly. Good luck with your internship search. Keep looking until you find the right position for you.

During the Interview

Following is a list that provides additional tips for interviewing. Figure 3.8 illustrates a common time sequence for the interview.

- Think positively. Be enthusiastic, interested, and knowledgeable.

- Display confidence without appearing arrogant.

- Watch your body language. Be aware of nervousness (e.g., fidgeting, leg shaking, tapping, and so on). Breathe slowly, and place your hands together in your lap if you feel nervous.

- Project confidence through good eye contact, a firm handshake, and an upright posture.

- Relate to the interviewer and build a positive rapport with him or her.

Figure 3.8 The interview process and sequence.

Minutes	
0–5	**Size it up.** Be impressive. You and the interviewer are both evaluating each other. First impressions count.
5–20	**Sell yourself.** This is the time for you to explain your résumé. Know which parts of your background to stress. You will be judged on how well you organize your thoughts. Don't be shy about your accomplishments. Describe yourself, but remember the time. If interviewers ask you a yes or no question, answer it that way. If they want you to elaborate, they will ask.
20–25	**Let them sell themselves to you.** Ask questions about the organization. Why is it such a great place to work? Remember, this is an important decision for you.
25–30	**Wrap it up.** Determine what will happen next. Will they call you or should you contact them? A follow-up letter is always needed, as an opportunity to highlight your compatibility and to say thank you.

- Listen and observe; react and respond to the interviewer. Be aware of the questions the interviewer asks. Understand what is really being asked (e.g., are you dependable?) and answer the underlying concern. Answer with information relevant to the question and position. Provide a direct and brief answer with an example, if appropriate.

- Think about the questions you will ask. These questions should indicate that you know something about the job. Avoid questions that could easily be answered elsewhere (e.g., through research).

- Obtain information you will need to know to be satisfied with the job. Keep in mind that interviewing is a two-way process.

- Salary and benefit questions should be asked after a job offer appears highly probable or after an offer is presented. Use your judgment with these types of inquiries.

- Achieve an effective closure. Restate your interest and ability to perform the job. Emphasize your key skills and show confidence and enthusiasm. Smile and end with a firm handshake. If you want the job, say so. Employers want to hire people who are enthusiastic about working for their companies.

- Arrange to call back. Ask when the employer expects to make a decision. Establish a specific time and date to contact the employer to ask further questions or learn more about your status. Obtain the employer's business card, if possible. It will be useful when writing a follow-up letter.

The Professional Portfolio

For years, some professions have encouraged candidates to demonstrate their skills by showing samples of their work. A portfolio is a compilation of products or samples that show a person's work skills and values. Candidates interviewing for design, graphic, and public relations positions are expected to present an art portfolio. All job seekers, including those in merchandising, management, and production, can benefit from preparing their own professional employment portfolios and using them in an interview.

Why Should You Develop a Portfolio?

- A portfolio shows you how far you have come and how much you have grown.

- It makes you stand apart from other candidates and demonstrates your unique talents and abilities to the employer.

- The items in your portfolio illustrate your style, abilities, and creative potential. They support what you tell the employer.

- A portfolio is your marketing tool, your billboard. It provides an easy way for you to show and discuss who you are and what you've done.

Organizing the Portfolio

Begin to craft your portfolio through serious self-assessment. Take inventory of your knowledge, skills, and abilities. Decide what skills and experiences you have that relate to the needs of the employer. Your goal is to make sure that during an interview you will be able to demonstrate your strengths and most marketable skills through the contents of your portfolio.

Begin by asking yourself, "What will I be asked during an interview?" After you develop a list of potential questions, choose items for the portfolio to help answer them. The following items can be included in a professional portfolio:

- A program, DVD or CD-ROM, or press release (or a combination of these) from an event you helped plan and execute. A brief description of the project or event, a responsibility list, and a calendar of the project's deadlines will clearly show your contributions to the activity.

- Awards, honors, certificates for special training or seminars (e.g., Fashion Group International, Inc., career days), or recognition on the job and in school

- Items you have created (e.g., trend boards, art projects, original designs, market research, and other special reports)

- Documentation, such as presentations and spreadsheets, of technical or computer skills that could benefit the employer

- Letters of commendation or thanks from people with whom you have worked

- Newspaper or magazine articles that demonstrate your achievements

- Reports of career-related work experiences (e.g., your internship summary)

- Writing samples

- An official copy of your transcript

- An extra copy of your résumé

These items are just a few possibilities. Brainstorm—think of every possible item that might assist you during an interview. Then, for each interview, carefully choose the ones that will help you tell your story to win that job. As you progress through your academic program, you may want to remove some items and add new ones of a higher quality. Remember to make corrections on items that need them, as suggested by your instructors, before including them in your portfolio. Make color copies of finished original design pieces for a professional appearance and to save the original images. You may want to photograph items that demonstrate special skills you have and then include them in your portfolio. For example, you may not want to carry garments or oversized trend boards to an interview. You also may decide to create an e-portfolio that will require digital imagery. A discussion of the print and electronic portfolio options follows.

Presenting the Portfolio—Print or Digital
For either a print or electronic portfolio, organize the employment portfolio so that it tells your story. You may want to begin with a résumé, followed by a table of contents, and then add index dividers with tabs for easy review. Make it "reader friendly" so that the interviewers can easily observe the skills you are trying to communicate. Keep in mind that your portfolio displays your abilities to an employer, therefore, it must present you in a professional manner. For a print portfolio, buy a professional-looking binder and a supply of plastic page covers for the items you have selected.

What Is an E-Portfolio?
A portfolio is defined as a case for carrying papers, such as writings, photographs, and drawings, or the materials collected in such a case, usually for presenting a person's work. With this definition, the portfolio is primarily a grouping of printed hard copies intended to tell a story—your professional story. In contrast, the **e-portfolio** is a computer-generated resource that allows a person document academic, work, and extracurricular achievements, reflect on past experiences, and display this work on the Web. The e-portfolio is also referred to as a **digital portfolio**. The easiest way to develop an e-portfolio is to make a CD-ROM of your print portfolio pages. Often, the majority of these files are readily accessible on your computer, as your résumé, assignments, and

letters are usually saved electronically. You can scan projects that are done by hand, such as product development sketches, and save them as they are or enhance them through appropriate software programs, such as Illustrator and Photoshop. Digital files are easily and inexpensively reproduced, allowing you to give a copy of your portfolio, in the form of a CD-ROM, to each prospective employer you want to impress.

E-portfolio components may be identical to those in a print portfolio. They may, however, include the addition of personal information in the form of a narrative describing career short-term and long-term goals. Some e-portfolio developers also add an introductory section called the **e-portfolio abstract**, a summary of the sequence of the portfolio, much like a table of contents. A listing of possible e-portfolio sections follows.

- Résumé/personal information

- Portfolio abstract

- Integration statement (e.g., goals; how education, work experience, travel, and volunteer activities combine to support the writer in meeting the résumé objectives)

- Education

- Learning experiences—artistic, cross-cultural, leadership, research, and volunteer experiences

The most important part of designing an e-portfolio is to create it so that the reader is guided from section to section, and from page to page, seamlessly.

Just as you would add or remove pages in your print portfolio to tailor it to a particular prospective employer's needs or to one of your specific internship goals, you can add or remove electronic files in the e-portfolio. Remember to burn the portfolio onto a CD-RW so that it can be rewritten and added to easily. Because CD-ROM discs are inexpensive, you can create multiple copies that can be generously distributed and that may even include voice, music, or animation.

E-portfolios sent by e-mail with related documents (e.g., your résumé) can be very effective in securing an interview, or even an internship position, in the fashion industry. You may be located far from the location of your dream internship and not have the funds to travel to and from this location for an interview or two. This gives you the chance to get your résumé in the door, show your work, and demonstrate your technological abilities. The e-mailed portfolio is usually sent as an attachment to an online letter of application, in addition to a resume. There are two warnings to sending this important "personal billboard" via e-mail. The first caveat is to be certain to use a common software that is located on most computers or to send the pages as a PDF file that can be interpreted by Adobe Acrobat or Acrobat Reader. Second, it is critical to send this information to the right person in the company, whether owner, manager, designer, human resources director, or another. Researching industry journals, newspapers, and Web sites, as well as telephoning the company, are efficient ways to investigate who is the right person and what is his or her correct e-mail address.

Web-Based Portfolios

You can show your e-portfolio to the world with another step forward. A Web-based portfolio is formatted digitally so that it can be viewed on the Internet. Web pages can be developed for placement on a wide number of Web sites geared for employment, including internships. Many Career Services Offices of colleges and universities now offer this service for students and graduates of their institutions. Check with this office at your school to learn if there is a career placement Web site at which prospective employers can view students' portfolios.

E-Portfolios for Fashion Merchandising Students

An excellent book for fashion merchandising students preparing a portfolio is *Developing and Branding the Fashion Merchandising Portfolio* by Janace Bobonia-Clarke and Phyllis Borcherding (2007). This title is also a great tool for fashion design, product development, and interior design student portfolios, particularly in its discussion of "branding yourself." Bobonia-Clarke and Borcherding describe this strategy as follows:

> A digital portfolio offers a unique way for you to brand yourself. If accompanying a printed portfolio, the images need to be compatible and have one to three elements in common, such as a logo, a signature, or an image. The digital portfolio offers more options to show presentation and technology skills that may set you apart from the competition. (p. 83)

Bobonia-Clarke and Borcherding also declare the external packaging of the CD-ROM featuring your digital portfolio a "branding opportunity that introduces you and your work to a potential employer" (p. 88). This is a great idea for an e-portfolio on a CD-ROM that is mailed via the post office, with a letter of application and résumé, or hand delivered during an interview. A CD-ROM cover contains front and back visual spaces that are ideal places—in essence minibillboards—to entice the viewer to take a look at what is inside (see Figure 3.9). The same branding imagery that is used on the letter of application and résumé and within the portfolio pages should be repeated on the CD-ROM cover, in addition to your name and contact information.

Inform the employer in your letter of application or on your job application that you can either mail (e-folio) or bring to the interview an employment portfolio that demonstrates your skills. When the employer begins to ask questions, you can use your portfolio to support your responses. You may need to find an opening in the interview to present your portfolio. Think of it as your marketing tool, and plan to introduce it early in the interview session. This is the time to be assertive in seeking a job.

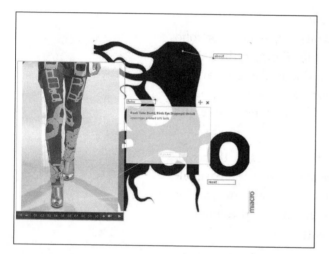

Figure 3.9 Screenshots from www.miacrodesign.com, a small start-up company's digital portfolio Web site. (See also these images in the color insert.)

$\mathcal{E}$valuating Job-Seeking Assertiveness

How assertive are you (or will you be) as you interview for the internship position? Listed below are questions that will help you evaluate your assertiveness.

Yes	No	
____	____	Do you make an effort to research a company before an interview?
____	____	Do you prepare several questions that you want to ask?
____	____	If an interviewer asks an inappropriate personal question unrelated to the job, can you tactfully deflect it?
____	____	If an interviewer gives you a hypothetical job-related problem, do you have confidence in your ability to respond in a timely and succinct manner?

_____ _____ If the interviewer seems distracted or uninterested during your interview, can you steer the interview back on track and regain his or her attention?

_____ _____ When you meet the interviewer, would you be the first to introduce yourself and begin the conversation?

_____ _____ If the interviewer continually interrupts when you are responding to his or her questions or when you are giving information about yourself, can you politely handle this?

_____ _____ If the interviewer never gives you the opportunity to talk about yourself and you only have 5 minutes remaining in the interview, have you thought about phrases or ways to redirect the interview?

_____ _____ Have you planned a way to introduce your portfolio into the interview process?

_____ _____ When the interviewer begins to close the interview, can you ask questions concerning where you stand, what the determining factors are for candidate selection, and by which date you will have an answer?

After the Interview

Following the interview, you should do the following three things:

1. Record the interview date, the interviewer's name, the company name, and the expected notification response date for future reference.

2. Write a follow-up letter, thanking the interviewer for his or her time and highlighting your fit to the position.

3. About a week or two after the expected decision date, call if there has been no response from the employer.

Writing a Follow-Up Letter

Writing a follow-up letter after an interview is often overlooked, yet many employers believe that this is the deciding factor between several equally quali-fied job candidates. The follow-up letter should be typewritten, approximately one page in length, and consist of three to four paragraphs. If you are interested in a position for which you had an interview, you should *immediately* follow up that interview with a letter.

The letter should be directed to the person who interviewed you. Its purposes are, first, to thank the interviewer for his or her time and interest, and, second, to reemphasize the qualities you would bring to the position if hired. In addition to a sincerely stated thank-you for the interviewer's time and interest, you may want to restate your qualifications for the position in a brief, straightforward manner. Next, describe how your qualifications fit well with those being sought out by the interviewer. Show a match, indicate your high level of interest, and make yourself available. Let the interviewer know that you are interested in another meeting if he or she would like. In some cases, you may decide to make a follow-up phone call or e-mail as well. As in all aspects of a job search, follow-ups must be approached with balance in mind. The point is to remind the employer about your skills and enthusiasm without making a pest of yourself. Be attentive to the reaction your letter or phone call elicits and take your cue from there. It is a challenge, this balancing act. Some employers wait to see if the internship candidate is eager for the job, enthusiastic, and assertive by waiting for him or her to call. Other employers have such busy schedules that it takes many attempts to reach them.

In writing the follow-up letter, use the guidelines given in Figure 3.10 and the sample shown in Figure 3.11. Many internship graduates recommend that candidates also send brief follow-up letters containing a sincere thank-you to the person they were introduced to and spoke with during the interview. If you ask for the business card of each person you meet, you will know how to correctly spell the individual's name and you will know each person's job title when you write your letters.

Evaluating an Internship Offer

There are three key areas that can help you evaluate an internship offer:

1. Your personal and professional goals
2. The company culture
3. The employer as an educator

The personal and professional goals that you articulated in the mind map prior to researching prospective employers should guide your internship decision. If, for example, you established that living in New York City is a personal goal, and the position is located there, you now have an opportunity to accomplish that goal. In addition, you will want to compare the job objectives of the position with your professional goals. Ask yourself if you have the skills and attributes to do the job well, if you believe you will like it, and if you feel good about the prospect of working with this company.

Next, evaluate the firm's corporate culture. If it is comfortable, supportive, and student friendly, then this may be the place for you. Assess the growth potential of the company and your potential for advancement and career opportunities with this firm. Finally, compare your skills, interests, and values with those of the potential employer.

The ideal employer is one that "grows" employees. To grow, you will need the resources to get the job done, regular and productive performance reviews, clear

Mailing address
E-mail address

Date
Interviewer's name
Job title
Company name
Mailing address

Dear Ms./Mr. _____:

    In the first paragraph, thank the interviewer for her or his time and interest in meeting with you.

    In the second paragraph, mention some of the qualities that you think make you the best candidate for the position. You may have discussed these during the interview, but this is an opportunity to reemphasize why the employer should hire you.

    In the third paragraph, it is a good idea to state why you are particularly interested in the employer's organization. Share some of your knowledge about the positive attributes of the company. Mention information you have gathered about the company's current activities and future plans, and information you were pleased to learn during the interview.

    In the closing paragraph, state that you look forward to hearing from the interviewer in regard to her or his decision. You can also mention that you are willing to provide other materials to support your application (a transcript, letters of recommendation, or samples of work) and to meet with her or him again. Close with an action statement indicating when you will telephone to find out about the employment decision.

Sincerely,

Your name
Area code and phone number

Figure 3.10 Guidelines to writing a thank-you letter.

300 West 14th Avenue
Apartment 1-C
St. Louis, Missouri 63025
E-mail: melody@gmail.com

March 28, 2010

Ms. Ann Perrini
Human Resources Director
J.C. Penney Company
200 East Stemmons Freeway
Dallas, Texas 24031

Dear Ms. Perrini:

Thank you for taking the time to interview me in Dallas on March 22nd. It was a pleasure to meet you and the product development staff members. In addition, it was a wonderful experience to tour the headquarters of the J.C. Penney Company.

I am extremely interested in the summer internship position we discussed. I believe I possess the qualifications and experience you described as prerequisites for the job during our interview. My employment as a manager at an alterations company has provided me with excellent on-the-job training in adjusting patterns, perfecting fit, and satisfying customers who return asking for me. During my sophomore year at Ivy League University, I was able to assist with the production of garments for a major fashion show for an audience of 600 persons.

In a summer internship with J.C. Penney, I could draw upon my background and expand my skills by assisting with the product development activities of the ladies wear division. J.C. Penney Company is on the cutting edge of fashion retailing, as shown through its recent expansion as well as its future growth plans. To be a team member for the private label lines of one of the top retailers in the country would be an exceptional opportunity for me.

I look forward to hearing from you within the next two weeks. I have enclosed an additional copy of my résumé for your convenience. If you would like any other materials to support my application, I would be pleased to forward them to you. My college transcript and a CD-ROM of the fashion show production are available at your request. I will phone you in two weeks, unless I hear from you before then. Thank you for your time and consideration.

Sincerely,

Melody Place
(314) 855-7402

Enclosure: Résumé

Figure 3.11 Sample thank-you letter following an interview.

expectations about your work, and people who can answer your questions and provide guidance. The hierarchy of authority and the company's decision-making process will also affect your on-the-job performance. If you are satisfied that your goals are likely to be achieved, that the corporate culture is a match, and that the employer is willing to educate you, your next step will involve negotiation.

Use the following checklist to compare several internship opportunities:

Yes   No
____   ____   An effective and interested internship supervisor
____   ____   An organized plan of meaningful assignments
____   ____   Effective mentoring
____   ____   Networking opportunities
____   ____   Measurable objectives
____   ____   A formal evaluation process
____   ____   Exposure to the total organization or to contacts in the organization's various areas

electing the Right Internship

When making your internship selection you should consider the following:

- What do you want from an internship? It will cost you time and money.

- Good internships should offer real-world experience, that which is not available at college or as part-time work.

- When the internship concludes, you should have had the opportunity to develop identifiable skills and expertise and have had the accomplishment of completing at least one project.

- Seek internships offering meaningful work, to develop your skills and abilities. Ask yourself, "What will I do in the internship? What will I be expected to get done?"

- Who will select the intern? Who will supervise the intern? Avoid an internship working under a supervisor with little or no authority and little or no part in the selection process.

- Find a job in which you can undertake tasks on your own and have your own projects. Will you have responsibility for an area or task? Will you accomplish something you can cite in future interviews? Will you be viewed as a young professional or as "the intern"? You want quality hands-on experiences.

What do you want to be able to tell future employers you are capable of accomplishing? You must have the work experience to prove it.

Table 3.1 provides an assessment chart to help you evaluate internships. Adjust it to reflect your individual academic needs, as well as personal and professional priorities, values, and goals.

Table 3.1	
INTERNSHIP EVALUATION AND COMPARISON	
	Internship Evaluation Ranking
Company Name:	**Ranking scale: Best (5) Worst (1)**
1) Financial considerations: Paid or unpaid	_____
Number of weeks ___ hours per week	_____
Housing costs	_____
Food expenses	_____
Commuting and parking	_____
Cost of living (higher in cities)	_____
Travel to and from internship site (air and ground)	_____
Clothing (professional dress costs)	_____
2) Intrinsic value: Learning and personal growth	_____
3) Extrinsic value: Money/compensation and industry contacts	_____
4) Geographic location	_____
5) Duration of internship	_____
6) Academic credit and requirements	_____

Negotiating the Offer

Salary, benefits, job-related expenses, and time are typical negotiation areas for an intern. Some internship organizations pay interns an hourly wage or a monthly salary, whereas others provide a stipend, or flat fee, for the internship. For postgraduation jobs, the issue of benefits is involved. Full-time employees often negotiate for such benefits as health insurance, stock options, retirement plans, and vacations. In most cases, the intern's opportunity for benefits is limited to merchandise discounts, travel expenses, and possibly sales commissions. You will want to clarify:

- if you will be paid;

- how much you will be paid;

- how often you will be paid;

- what job-related expenses you will incur and if they will be reimbursed; and

- if the company assists interns with housing arrangements.

There are a number of Web sites that enable you to estimate costs for living expenses in a specific location. You can budget rent, utilities, transportation, and even parking costs through this research.

Some internship employers will assist with finding a short-term place for the intern to live; others will not. Some will reimburse the intern for travel expenses to and from the job; others will not. It is important for the prospective employee to be diplomatic and professional in negotiating travel and housing—to recognize if and when you are being a potential liability, rather than an asset to the company.

Next, it is important to reiterate the academic requirements of the internship. A quick review of your university's expectations, such as number of on-the-job hours, assignments, and the evaluation component, will clarify your needs while reminding the internship supervisor of his or her commitment. It is a good idea to take brief notes during the negotiation in order to include critical points in the follow-up letter.

Finally, time is another variable for possible negotiation. When you will begin and end the internship, how many hours you will work weekly, if overtime is unusual or standard procedure—these are critical questions that you need answered and may want to use as bargaining tools. Remember that negotiation often requires compromise and that both parties should ultimately feel as though they have won.

Writing a Follow-up Letter

A follow-up letter is appropriate in the following situations:

- After sending the interview thank-you letter, following two or three weeks of no reply.
- When you have been refused a job.
  - Express your regret that no job is available.
  - Ask if you might be considered in the future.
- To accept a job, even if you previously did this in person or by phone (Figure 3.12).
  - State your acceptance.
  - Reiterate the agreement (e.g., starting date, salary, job description before beginning work).
  - Avoid asking favors.
- To refuse a job offer (Figure 3.13).
  - Graciously decline the offer.
  - Sincerely state that you appreciate the offer.
- To withdraw a job application (Figure 3.14).
  - State reason for withdrawal.
  - Be courteous, and thank the person for his or her time.

Be certain that your follow-up letter demonstrates the attitude, quality, and skills of a professional.

507 Shore Drive
Hampton, VA 23501
sriley@hotmail.com

April 20, 2012

Mr. John Andrews, Division Manager
Home Design International Corporation
1212 Corporation Lane
Richmond, VA 23312

Dear Mr. Andrews:

I am writing to confirm my acceptance of your employment offer of April 16 and to tell you how delighted I am to be joining Home Design International in Richmond. The summer internship program (12 weeks at 40 hours per week) is exactly what I have prepared for and hoped to do. I feel confident that I can make a significant contribution to the corporation, and I am grateful for the opportunity you have given me. Enclosed you will find copies of the Learning Agreement and university requirements for the internship that we reviewed during my interview.

As we discussed, I will report to work at 8:00 a.m. on May 21. Additionally, I will complete all employment and insurance forms for the new employee orientation on May 22. I look forward to working with you and others on the Home Design team. I appreciate your confidence in me and am very happy to be joining your staff.

Sincerely,

Sarah Riley
(555) 765-4321

Enc: Learning Agreement and Internship Guidelines

Figure 3.12 Sample letter accepting a job offer.

Modified and reprinted from *Planning Job Choices: 1999* with permission of the National Association of Colleges and Employers, copyright holder.

351 Seaside Road
San Diego, CA
mollymay@hotmail.com

March 25, 2012

Ms. Mary Best, Director
Promotion Division
Design International, Inc.
570 7th Avenue
New York, NY 10018

Dear Ms. Best:

Thank you very much for offering me the position of promotional intern with Design International, Inc. I appreciate your discussing the details of the position with me and giving me time to consider your offer.

You have an excellent organization, and there are many aspects of the position that are very appealing to me. However, I believe it is in our mutual best interest that I decline your kind offer. This has been a difficult decision for me, but I believe it is the appropriate one for my career at this time.

I want to thank you for the consideration and courtesy shown me. It was a pleasure meeting you and your staff.

Sincerely,

Molly May
(555) 872-9248

Figure 3.13 Sample letter refusing a job offer (block letter format).

Modified and reprinted from *Planning Job Choices: 1999* with permission of the National Association of Colleges and Employers, copyright holder.

4621 Chester Lane
Virginia Beach, VA 23466
slawson@hotmail.com

April 20, 2012

Ms. Karla Vaughn, Personnel Director
Bridal Boutique
8989 Princess Anne Road
Virginia Beach, VA 23465

Dear Ms. Vaughn:

I am writing to inform you that I am withdrawing my application for the internship position with Bridal Boutique. As I indicated in my interview with you, I have been exploring several employment possibilities. This week I was offered an internship position with a local specialty store and, after careful consideration, I decided to accept it. The position provides a very good match for my interests at this point in my career.

I want to thank you very much for interviewing and considering me for your position. I enjoyed meeting you and learning about the innovative merchandising programs you are planning. You have an excellent organization, and I wish you and your staff well.

Sincerely,

Shannon Lawson
(555) 888-0002

Figure 3.14 Sample letter withdrawing a job application (full block format).

Modified and reprinted from *Planning Job Choices: 1999* with permission of the National Association of Colleges and Employers, copyright holder.

CASE STUDY 3A

A Tough Decision

Angela Lopez is a student majoring in fashion merchandising at a state university in Florida. As part of the university's requirements for graduation, she must complete an internship in her prospective field of employment during the summer between her junior and senior years. The university, in conjunction with the Textile and Apparel Department, has established these guidelines for the internship requirement:

- The student must successfully complete the pre-internship seminar before enrolling in the internship.

- The student must complete a minimum of 200 work hours on the job during the summer of the internship.

- The internship must be directly related to the student's anticipated field of employment.

- The student must fill out the internship workbook approved by the department and participate in an oral presentation on internships for freshman- and sophomore-level students.

- The student, academic internship sponsor, and employer must jointly approve the internship initially and then communicate regularly throughout it.

- The student must receive a passing evaluation from the internship supervisor.

Six months prior to the anticipated start of her internship position, Angela constructs her résumé and drafts a letter of application with assistance from the university's Career Center. She discusses internship possibilities with senior-year students who have completed this requirement. She attends the departmental internship workshops and reviews the bulletin board for available internship openings. Through these announcements, Angela obtains information about several internship opportunities with retail operations that appeal to her and are located near her summer residence.

After completing interviews with six prospective employers, Angela finds that two positions interest her equally. In both cases, the employers have offered her an internship position. She is now at the point in which she will have to make a decision about which opportunity will best meet her goals and objectives.

The first position is with a small, heavily traveled specialty store operation. The store owners are extremely enthusiastic about the prospect of working with a student intern and are particularly impressed with Angela's past experience in retail sales. They have offered her full-time employment for the entire summer at minimum wage plus commission. Although her primary job responsibility would be assisting customers on the sales floor, the owners have offered to teach Angela about their total retail operation by taking her with them to the regional apparel market, allowing her to participate in advertising meetings, encouraging her to work on in-store displays, and permitting her to assist them with accounting and receiving duties. Angela genuinely likes the store owners and the store itself, and she believes that here she would learn how a specialty store operation functions—from the inside out.

The second internship position that Angela is considering is with a major department store. The store has a formal internship program in

(continued on next page)

APPLYING AND INTERVIEWING FOR THE INTERNSHIP   101

which ten student interns participate. The interns are paid two dollars per hour above minimum wage for the program's duration. There is also the possibility of employment after the conclusion of the internship program if an opening exists at that time. During the six-week program, the group of interns receives one week of in-class training and five weeks of working in all of the major divisions of the store, from the advertising department to the human resources division. Actual on-the-floor selling is a minimal part of the job description. The department store is well known and has branch stores located throughout the Southeast. As approximately one hundred students have applied for the company's internship program, Angela is thrilled to be one of the top ten invited to participate. She believes that she would receive in-depth exposure to a department store operation.

Both internship opportunities meet the requirements of the university and department. As Angela evaluates the pros and cons of each position, she becomes more and more confused about which job she should accept.

Because Angela is at an impasse in regard to her internship decision, she consults with one of her favorite college instructors, Dr. Jean Hamilton. Dr. Hamilton is the academic sponsor for the department's internship program. Angela tells her that she does not know which position would be best for her in terms of her long-range career plans. Dr. Hamilton suggests that Angela carefully evaluate three areas: her goals and objectives for an internship, her goals and objectives for a career, and her prior work experience. She recognizes that her career objectives may change but that right now her ultimate goal is to own a successful retail store. As to her prior work experience, Angela was employed as a waitress during her high school summers, and during college she worked as a student assistant in the Textile and Apparel Department. She was also a resident advisor in the university dormitory where she lived. Angela is looking forward to her summer internship, as it will be actual retail store work experience.

1. If you were in Angela's position, what would you do?

2. Which factors do you believe are the most critical in making this decision? Create a list of pros and cons needed to make a selection.

Finalizing Internship Plans

Even though you may receive an initial offer, you may decide to pursue other opportunities if it is not your dream internship. A prospective employer will not expect an immediate decision. Ask for a reasonable amount of time to carefully assess the offer, and then provide a response as negotiated. After you have verbally accepted the position, it is often good to confirm it in writing. Some universities will require a letter from the employer summarizing the internship arrangement (starting date, salary, position description, and so on) for your records and for the academic sponsor.

Next, notify any prospective employers you have scheduled interviews with that you have accepted a position elsewhere. Write letters to all reference and network contacts who assisted you in the internship search to thank them for their help and to advise them of your decision. Finally, update your planning calendar to reflect the dates relating to your new accomplishment: the internship.

A Mixed Message

The Zipper is an apparel chain of more than 100 store units that caters to a target market of males and females between the ages of 12 and 30 years. The merchandise is fun and fashionable, and the sales staff is young and energetic. Twenty-year-old Elizabeth Wilson has been with the company for more than two years as a part-time sales associate. She is presently working in one of the branch stores, located in a Los Angeles suburb; however, she is leaving this area in a few months to attend college in San Diego. Elizabeth hopes to secure an internship position in The Zipper's San Diego branch store in order to fulfill her internship requirement while attending classes at the university.

Elizabeth is informed by her present store manager, Lila Chase, that there will be an internship position for her with The Zipper team in San Diego. Lila says that all Elizabeth needs to do is to contact Mary Jean Zachary, the San Diego store manager, upon her arrival at the university. She encourages Elizabeth to schedule an appointment to go into the store for a brief, informal meeting with Mary Jean. "You will have no problem getting an internship there," she concludes. "It will be a simple transfer that will not even require another interview." Elizabeth is relieved that she will be able to build upon her part-time sales employment with The Zipper because she enjoys working in the company and knows the merchandise, store policies, and procedures well. "It will be great to have a position that I am familiar with," she thinks, "because I will need to really concentrate on my classes and complete this internship."

When Elizabeth arrives in San Diego, she contacts Mary Jean and goes to the store to meet her a few days later, on Saturday. When she finally arrives, Mary Jean asks her to come back at the beginning of the week, when the store is not so busy. As Elizabeth's schedule is hectic, several days pass before she is able to return to the store. Mary Jean hands Elizabeth an employment application to complete before they begin their discussion. Although Elizabeth is a little surprised that she is required to fill out the form, she assumes that it is necessary for her employment file at this branch store. Mary Jean then briefly interviews Elizabeth. She asks about the requirements of the internship and mentions that she is too busy to spend a lot of time explaining everything she does. She does not appear interested in hearing about Elizabeth's college course work. Mary Jean concludes the interview with the question "What do you believe that you can do for our team here?" Elizabeth replies, "I think that I have a good deal of knowledge that I can share with your employees and that I could become a leader as an intern."

Mary Jean wraps up the interview by thanking Elizabeth for her time and interest in an internship with The Zipper. "It was a pleasure to meet you, Elizabeth," she says. "If you do not receive a telephone call from me by the end of the week, then good luck with your internship search."

"Good luck with my internship search?" Elizabeth thinks as she leaves the store, "I am not supposed to be hunting for an internship position. This is my position—it was supposed to be a simple transfer between stores!" Elizabeth hopes she is wrong, but she does not receive a phone call from Mary Jean by the end of the week.

1. If you were in Elizabeth's position, what would you do?

2. What would you recommend to Elizabeth to avoid this type of situation in the first place?

CHAPTER FOUR

Before Settling In

Objectives

- To maximize the opportunities provided by the internship experience

- To recognize professional on-the-job conduct, including office, online, and phone etiquette

- To examine and prepare for possible internship obstacles

- To understand the implications of changing the internship plan

- To plan for expenses and develop an internship budget

How Do I Prepare for the Internship Experience?

After securing the internship position, you can look forward to joining the real-world workforce. On-the-job requirements and expectations are often very different from those of the academic environment. For example, submitting an assignment late in an academic course usually carries the penalty of a lower grade; however, in business, it can mean losing a job or forfeiting a positive reference from an employer. As a student, you may be able to sit through a lecture course without participating and still pass the course with a satisfactory grade. In the industry, success depends on positive contributions to the day-to-day activities of the company. A lack of participation in business usually means a lack of continued employment. Tips for success in the fast-paced world of the fashion industry are presented next.

On-the-Job Tips

The internship experience is intended to help develop professional work skills. Such experience and skills will increase your opportunities for obtaining a good job after graduation. Success in your career also requires developing excellent personal qualities and work habits. The following attributes will help an intern get the most out of the internship experience and give the most to the internship organization.

A Positive Attitude

Approach every job with a positive attitude. It is damaging to your image and unproductive to dwell on negative factors or complain about a previous job, supervisor, or the company to fellow workers. Not all the tasks you are given will be exciting or challenging (which is true of most jobs), and yet, you will find you can learn something new from whatever you do. Show enthusiasm and a willingness to pitch in. Employers appreciate cooperation and collaboration.

Initiative

Take an active role in the job. After completing assigned work, do not sit around and wait for another assignment. Instead, do the following:

- Ask the supervisor for another project.

- Offer to assist someone else in the office.

- Learn as much as possible about the company and its policies and procedures by reading company literature.

- Read professional literature in the field. This will identify you as an interested and serious professional.

- Using good judgment: choose an appropriate time to ask your fellow workers and your supervisor questions about the company.

- After becoming familiar with the procedures required to perform your job responsibilities, you should be able to anticipate the next step. Take the initiative and do it. Your efforts will save your employer time and will increase your value as an employee.

Assertiveness

Achieving goals in a direct, honest, and open manner, instead of being either meek or pushy, is being assertive. The objectives stated in the learning agreement are the goals you as an intern will be working toward. It is up to you, with guidance and assistance from your supervisor, to attain these goals. Being responsible, being flexible, speaking up, and having a positive attitude are all aspects of assertive behavior. Knowing when to speak up and how to express yourself calmly and clearly are keys to successfully projecting assertiveness.

Confidentiality

The issue of confidentiality is one that should be understood before beginning the internship experience. Internship employers have varying degrees of comfort about the type and amount of information they provide. Some internship employers will completely open their books to an intern, whereas others prefer total privacy when asked to give information about inventory shortages, payroll, sales volume, and so on. If the internship employer is not forthcoming in providing the specific information necessary to complete this guide successfully, do some independent research to determine industry norms. For example, the National Retail Federation annually publishes *Retail Industry Indicators*, a directory that contains industry averages (low, middle, and high) for most merchandising statistics (for example, maintained markup, stock turn, shortages, sales per square foot, and so on) for all types of retail operations. Some internship supervisors may feel more comfortable with providing a range for such statistics, rather than specific data.

Regardless of the amount of information the internship supervisor will supply, the responsible intern owes it to the employer to be discreet about any information received. A worker respects the employer's right to privacy. This means that, as a professional, it is inappropriate for you to discuss with others (including fellow employees) information such as hourly wages, sales performance, interpersonal relationships, and similar topics related to the internship organization. Discretion is key.

Student's Top Ten Tips for Interns

by Bradley Richardson

1. **Do not be afraid to talk to people.** Do not be intimidated because you are a student. People are sometimes too busy to roll out the red carpet, so you may have to make the first move to talk with coworkers and supervisors.

2. **Find the right things to do.** Do not wait to be told what to do. Solving problems and taking initiative are the best ways to stand out in a crowd.

3. **Learn all you can about the industry.** Talk with people in different departments as well as clients and vendors, if appropriate. It is important to recognize that internship supervisor guidance is essential before approaching and speaking with customers and vendors in many organizations.

4. **Read everything you are authorized to.** You will not find everything you need to know in the training manual. Reading reports, letters, memos, press releases, and trade publications will help you become informed about all elements of the business—as long as you are permitted to view these materials. Remember that you do not have the right to access or duplicate anything without the authorization of your internship supervisor. Use discretion at all times.

5. **Do not gripe about the grunt work.** There is always something more to learn. How long you do grunt work depends on what you make of it. Everything has a purpose, so learn how the small tasks fit into the big picture.

6. **Milk the fact that you are a student.** As a student, you are not threatening to most business associates and often have more access to opportunities than a full-time employee. Most people want to help a student learn.

7. **Hitch your wagon to a star.** Learn from the people who are the superstar performers and most respected individuals in the office. Learn from the best.

8. **Get in the information loop.** Decisions are not always made in a conference room.

9. **Ask to attend meetings and events.** You will learn how things really get done. When invited to attend, be sure to arrive early. In fact, be sure to do everything on time.

10. **Do not burn any bridges.** You never know when you will encounter someone later in your career.

The Reality Check

Next is a list of helpful hints to remember when planning for and working at an internship.

- **It is OK to call back . . . several times.** The individual you are speaking to about an internship position is undoubtedly extremely busy, and chances are that the contact person does not even know you called twice last week to speak to him or her, even if you left messages.

- **Get it in writing.** If at all possible, get the terms of your internship in writing. This is especially important if your internship is a paid position and your only means of income. Several weeks before you are to begin, you may want to write a follow-up letter to your internship supervisor, letting him or her know how excited you are about the position and verifying your understanding of details of the internship. Such details may include your start date and time, salary (if applicable), hours and days to be worked, duration of internship, and so on.

Figure 4.1 Do not hesitate to call back; fashion professionals are extremely busy and may not even be aware that you have attempted to contact them before. Use common sense, but be assertive.

- **Keep a daily journal.** This journal should include a recap of the day's events, new things learned, things you need to do, and questions for the internship supervisor or your academic sponsor. This journal is essential when you sit down to complete your final internship assignment to be submitted to your academic sponsor. The CD-ROM included in this book allows you to create an electronic journal detailing your internship experiences.

- **Keep a running list of contacts.** Now is the perfect time to start compiling your list of contacts in the industry. No matter how unimportant the person you meet may seem, write down his or her name and contact information (you never know!).

- **Never say no.** Gladly accept any responsibility you are given. Once again, you never know who you may meet or what you may learn.

- **Keep a camera accessible at all times.** Many times, the only way to keep a record of the work you do, or the projects you create, is to snap a picture of them. Remember that it is only appropriate to take a photograph after receiving permission from your internship supervisor.

- **Maintain a project list.** Write down tasks and assignments, deadlines, project coordinators, and colleagues' names.

Corporate Culture

Corporate culture refers to the way things are done in a company. A company's culture is defined by its management and embodied by the employees. It is a system of shared characteristics and values held by the organization's employees and management. It also has to do with how employees work together within the business and how they dress.

For example, Gap employees casually dress in khakis, jeans, tank tops, and T-shirts. Talbots, however, prefers the suit-and-blouse approach. Many companies nurture a culture in which everyone's opinion is valued regardless of rank. In other companies, the culture dictates a more hierarchical approach. To be successful in creating an organizational culture that supports the goals of the company, businesses must establish beliefs and core values that are upheld on a day-to-day basis.

As an employee, it is in your best interest to understand the nuances of your company's culture. Part of a company's culture is its view of office Internet, e-mail, and telephone etiquette. Next, this part of the company culture is explored.

Office Etiquette

As an intern, you should understand the nuances of **office etiquette**, the protocol of professional conduct in most business settings. It is important that you make a good impression at work. If you make a good impression on your boss, he or she is more likely to give you more responsibility and visibility. This, in turn, can lead to promotions and raises. According to http://careerplanning.about.com/od/workplacesurvival/tp/good_impression.htm, here are seven ways to make a good impression at work:

1. **Use proper office etiquette.** Using good manners will make a good impression with your boss and your coworkers. Office etiquette includes everything from making proper introductions, thanking associates for assistance, and using e-mail properly to knowing when, where, and how to use your cell phone while at work.

2. **Represent your company well in and out of the office.** When you represent your supervisor at a business meeting or your company at a conference, making a good impression on others will consequently help you make a good impression on your boss. Think of yourself as an ambassador for both the internship organization and your college or university. Dress appropriately, network on your employer's behalf, and bring back information.

3. **Be accountable when you make a mistake at work.** Everyone inevitably makes a mistake at some point. Do not ignore your error or place the blame on others. Take responsibility, and come up with a solution to fix your mistake. Your supervisor may not be thrilled about the mistake but will likely be impressed with your response.

4. **Know when to call in sick to the office.** Do you think coming to work when you are ill instead of staying at home shows your supervisor how dedicated you are? Reasonable employers know that not only is a sick employee unproductive but also he or she may spread an illness around the office, rendering everyone else unproductive as well. Call in sick when it is truly necessary.

5. **Be the solution instead of the problem.** Few things go as planned. When the unexpected happens at work, who will make a better impression on the boss: the employee who worries and does nothing or the one who springs into action? Dealing with a crisis quickly and effectively, while being the calm center of the storm, makes you a valuable team member with potential to be a future leader in the firm.

6. **Know which topics not to discuss and what to do to avoid offending your colleagues.** Avoiding inappropriate or controversial subjects may not help you make a good impression at work, but it will keep you from making a bad one. Subjects that do not make for productive workplace conversation include gossip or rumors, politics, religion, health problems, and other personal concerns. Always show respect for your coworkers. The last thing a supervisor wants to hear about is the uncivil conduct of an employee.

   Having loud telephone conversations, not cleaning up after yourself in the break room, taking credit for another's work, complaining about other employees, exhibiting a condescending attitude, or asking a subordinate to do work unrelated to the job (i.e., running errands) are all examples of disrespectful behavior toward colleagues.

7. **Manage your time efficiently.** Your ability to complete projects of quality in a timely manner will help make you an office star. You can demonstrate that you know how to manage your time effectively by submitting assignments on, or even before, deadlines. A discussion of time in the office should also include a caveat on clock watching. It is not impressive to arrive on the dot at the work start time or to be watching the clock so that you can leap out the door when the workday officially ends.

Netiquette

What is netiquette? Simply stated, **netiquette** is the use of good manners to communicate online. The term is a **portmanteau,** a blending of two words, in this case, *network* and *etiquette.* Netiquette refers to the protocol and decorum prescribed by authority to be necessary in social or business situations; it is the set of social conventions that facilitates personal and professional interaction over the Internet, the guidelines for polite and professional communication via the Internet.

When you enter any new culture (and the Internet has its own culture), you are likely to unknowingly commit a few social errors. You may offend people without meaning to. You may misunderstand what others say and be offended unnecessarily. Most important in this culture, you are typing on a keyboard and transmitting your message in seconds. The written word, and the speed and ease of the Internet, make it easy to forget that we are interacting with real people. Next are twelve general guidelines to Internet communication that will serve to present you and your message in a positive and professional light (adapted from www.albion.com/netiquette/corerules.html):

1. **Remember that you are dealing with people and that people have feelings.** E-mail is a contextual channel of communication. You should not use it if there is any chance that your message will be taken out of context or misunderstood. If your message is complex, personal, or difficult to express, choose a telephone call or personal meeting instead of e-mail. If your message is a reply, remember to include the original message with your response to help keep context intact.

   Before you send a message, take a moment to imagine how you would feel if you were the person receiving and reading it. When communicating by e-mail, the person you are "talking" to sees only a computer screen. The recipient of your message does not have the opportunity to read facial expressions, body language, and tone of voice to understand your meaning. Words are all you and your correspondent have. Ask yourself, "Would I say this to this person's face?" If the answer is no, rewrite and reread until you would feel as comfortable saying these words face-to-face with the person as you do e-mailing him or her.

A good rule is to never use e-mail to deliver bad news, as this form of communication lacks the benefit of body language, facial expression, intonation, and care. Taking the time and having the courage to schedule a one-on-one discussion is a demonstration of respect. The recipient has the opportunity to ask questions and absorb the shock of the news. It is very important to take care that you are not relying on e-mail to the exclusion of personal contact. Although certainly at varying levels, we all appreciate and need human interaction. Especially in the age of technology, relationship skills are at the heart of professional and personal success. Your e-mail communication should supplement regular meetings, informal conversations, and personal attention.

In addition to civility, another reason to be careful about what you send online is that, because your words are written, they are stored where you have no control over them. There is the risk that they can come back to you when you least expect it or be forwarded to someone you did not intend to read them. There is more on this in guideline three.

2. **Recognize the limitations of others' time and bandwidth.** When you e-mail, you are taking up others' time. It is your responsibility to ensure that the time they spend reading your message is not wasted. Bandwidth refers to the information-carrying capacity of the tools that connect us via Internet. There is a limit to the amount of data that can be received at any given moment, even with state-of-the-art technology. Bandwidth is also used to refer to the storage capacity of a host system. When you accidentally send the same note with large attachments or photos to the same recipient several times, both time (yours and the reader's) and bandwidth are wasted. As a result, your future postings may be deemed less important by those recipients.

3. **Think before you send sensitive information.** Avoid using e-mail to discuss either a coworker's or manager's performance with peers or supervisors. You are responsible for conducting yourself with professional courtesy in person and online. E-mail is filled with too many perils for disclosing sensitive or confidential communication; you could strike your group list key accidentally, sending negative comments about an employee's work to everyone in the organization, as in Box 4.2 on page 119. Remember that e-mail messages may be subject to discovery and subpoena in litigation. Unless you are ready to have your words read by an unintended reader, avoid e-mail: it is simply not secure enough.

4. **Know where you are on the Internet.** As many news-reading programs are slow, simply opening a posted article can take a while. It may be better to send the link or Web site address. If you forward an e-mail that was previously forwarded to you (and, perhaps, to many others ahead

of you), the recipient must wade through numerous and often lengthy header information to get to the actual message. Have you ever been the reader who is not pleased when the message turns out not to be worth the trouble?

5. **Think about to whom you are sending messages.** Today, you can copy your entire e-mail address list with the strike of a key. Maybe this is why *mailing list* and *listserv* could become dirty words of the 21st century. Before you copy others on your messages, ask yourself whether they really need to know what you're sending. If the answer is no, value their time. If the answer is maybe, think twice before you click the "Send" button. The best guideline is to copy with care by sending e-mail messages only to readers who have a legitimate need for the information. If you find yourself copying e-mails to others strictly out of habit, rethink that pattern. People have less time than ever today, precisely because they have so much information to absorb. Think twice before you click the "Reply to all" button. The general rule is to address your message to the person you want to motivate to act and to send copies as a courtesy to keep those with a need-to-know in the communication loop. As copy recipients are not required to reply to messages, you should not be concerned if responses are not forthcoming. Moreover, the blind copy (Bcc) may not be as invisible as you believe. On many computer systems, when the recipient clicks "Reply All," the e-mail address or name of the person to whom the e-mail was originally blind-copied, or both, is displayed. Finally, when thinking about e-mails and copies, think green. The computer stores your incoming and outgoing messages for later perusal. You probably do not need e-copies and hard copies of all the messages and other documents that go through your computer. Print when you need to, but think about it first in recognition of your time and the organization and the world's resources.

6. **Look good online.** As you are reading this book, it is safe to assume that you are interested in some sector of the fashion industry. As such, you know how important presentation and appearance are and how significant a first impression is. In e-mail communication, you will be judged by the quality of your writing and the clarity of your thoughts. Spelling, grammar, sentence structure, meaning, and brevity of communication do count. Text messaging and instant messaging have generated shortcuts, abbreviations, and acronyms that have no place in a professional e-mail message. If your job search and, later, your internship position require spending a great deal of time writing (on or off the Internet), and you are not confident in these areas, it is time now to brush up on them. Take a course in business writing or copyediting and proofreading. Read some books on the *how to*'s of writing well, and refer back to them often.

7. **Know what you are talking about, and say it well.** One prospective intern e-mailed her letter of interest and received an online reply from the firm's

design director saying, "What are you talking about? What do you want? Adult, experienced reader here." It is clear: that was not the internship she secured, but it was the one she most wanted. There may be one chance only to make a positive impression; make sure your messages are clear and logical. It is possible to write a paragraph containing no grammar or spelling errors that makes no sense. Make your message flow logically. Keep it simple. Be pleasant and polite. Do not use offensive language or slang. Provide all the necessary information. Proofread it. There you go, a great impression.

8. **Help keep flame wars under control. Flaming** is the term used to describe when a person expresses a strongly held opinion online without holding back any emotion. In certain situations, flaming is acceptable; however, netiquette does forbid the perpetuation of flame wars. **Flame war** describes a series of angry letters, most of them from two or three people directed toward each other, that can dominate the tone of an exchange and destroy the camaraderie of the senders and recipients. **Flame bait** refers to the e-mail that started the fire.

9. **Respect the privacy of others, as you want your privacy to be respected.** You would never go to the company mailbox and open your colleagues' letters. You should not read their e-mail messages either. Failing to respect another's privacy is not just bad netiquette—it could cost you your job as well. Forwarding an e-mail without the permission of the writer is also an invasion of privacy. Ask before you forward. This applies not only to a person's messages but also to e-zines and electronic newsletters, as these may be copyright protected.

10. **Do not abuse Internet power.** Some people involved with technology have more knowledge or access than others, such as system administrators, administrative assistants, technology consultants, and even the resident office "techie." Knowing more than others, or having more power than they do, does not give one the right to access or interfere with e-mail communication.

11. **Be patient with others.** Everyone was a network newbie once. Whether it is a spelling error, unnecessarily lengthy answers or attachments, overuse of e-mail, sending of chain letters, or forwarding of your e-mail to another without permission, be kind. If it is a minor error, you may not need to say anything. If you decide to inform someone of an e-issue, point it out privately and politely.

12. **Learn quickly about your internship organization's personal-use policy.** Some employers address attachments in their written e-mail policies and may go as far as prohibiting the opening of externally delivered e-mail attachments altogether. Other companies have no written e-mail policies at all. Before sending an attachment, ask if the recipient prefers to receive

the information as an attachment (and which software program in which to send it), as part of the message itself, or via fax or postal mail. Some organizations allow employees free and unrestricted personal use of office e-mail, whereas others ban or limit personal time. Recognize that office e-mail is intended primarily as a business tool. Learn your company's computer culture early in the internship, rather than assume that you know what constitutes appropriate online content and conduct in the workplace.

Responsible Use of the Internet

The Responsible Use of the Network (RUN) Working Group of the Internet Engineering Task Force (IETF) has created an excellent online netiquette resource, RFC 1855: Netiquette Guidelines (www.dtcc.edu/cs/rfc1855.html). It provides a minimum set of guidelines for individuals and businesses, both users and administrators. RFC 1855 is referred to by business professionals, directors of executive training programs, Internet business owners, and many others. Although not intended to specify an Internet standard of any kind, the document provides a minimum set of guidelines for network etiquette that many organizations have adapted for their own use. Following are the guidelines for individual users:

- Unless you have your own Internet access through an Internet provider, be sure to check with your employer about ownership of electronic mail. Laws about the ownership of electronic mail vary from place to place.

- Unless you are using an encryption device (hardware or software), you should assume that mail on the Internet is not secure. Never put in a mail message anything you would not put on a postcard.

- Respect the copyright on material that you reproduce. Almost every country has copyright laws.

- If you are forwarding or re-posting a message you have received, do not change the wording. If the message was a personal message to you and you are re-posting to a group, you should ask permission first. You may shorten the message and quote only relevant parts, but be sure you give proper attribution.

- Never send chain letters via electronic mail. Chain letters are forbidden on the Internet. Your network privileges can be revoked. Notify your local system administrator if you ever receive one.

- A good rule of thumb: Be conservative in what you send and liberal in what you receive. You should not send heated messages (as already mentioned, these are called "flames") even if you are provoked. On the other hand, you should not be surprised if you get flamed, and it is prudent not to respond to flames.

- In general, it is a good idea to at least check all your mail subjects before responding to a message. Sometimes a person who asks you for help (or clarification) will send another message that effectively says, "Never mind." Also make sure that any message you respond to was directed to you. You might be cc-ed rather than the primary recipient.

- Make things easy for the recipient. Many mailers strip header information that includes your return address. To ensure that people know who you are, be sure to include a line or two at the end of your message with contact information. You can create this file ahead of time and add it to the end of your messages. (Some mailers do this automatically.) In Internet parlance, this is known as a ".sig" or "signature" file. Your .sig file takes the place of your business card (you can have more than one to apply in different circumstances).

- Be careful when addressing mail. There are addresses that may go to a group but the address looks like it is just one person. Know to whom you are sending.

- Watch cc's when replying. Do not continue to include people if the messages have become a two-way conversation.

- In general, most people who use the Internet do not have time to answer general questions about the Internet and its workings. Do not send unsolicited mail asking for information to people whose names you may have seen in RFCs or on mailing lists.

- Remember that people with whom you communicate are located across the globe. If you send a message to which you want an immediate response, the person receiving it may be at home asleep when it arrives. Give them a chance to wake up, come to work, and log in before assuming the mail did not arrive or that they do not care.

- Verify all addresses before initiating long or personal discourse. It is also a good practice to include "Long" in the subject header so that the recipient knows the message will take time to read and respond to. Over 100 lines is considered "long."

- Know who to contact for help. Usually you will have resources close at hand. Check locally for people who can help you with software and system problems. Also, know who to go to if you receive anything questionable or illegal. Most sites also have "Postmaster" aliased to a knowledgeable user, so you can send mail to this address to get help with mail.

- Remember that the recipient is a human being whose culture, language, and humor have different points of reference from your own. Remember that date formats, measurements, and idioms may not travel well. Be especially careful with sarcasm.

- Use mixed case. UPPER CASE LOOKS AS IF YOU ARE SHOUTING.

- Use symbols for emphasis. That *is* what I meant. Use underscores for underlining (e.g., _War and Peace_ is my favorite book.)

- Smiley faces are sometimes used to indicate tone of voice, but use them sparingly, if at all. Do not assume that the inclusion of a smiley face will make the recipient happy with what you say or wipe out an otherwise insulting comment.

- Wait overnight to send emotional responses to messages. If you have really strong feelings about a subject, indicate it via FLAME ON/OFF enclosures. For example:

FLAME ON:
This type of argument is not worth the bandwidth it takes to send it. It's illogical and poorly reasoned. The rest of the world agrees with me.
FLAME OFF

- Do not include control characters or non-ASCII attachments in messages unless they are MIME attachments or unless your mailer encodes these. If you send encoded messages, make sure the recipient can decode them.

- Be brief without being overly terse. When replying to a message, include enough original material to be understood but no more. It is extremely bad form to simply reply to a message by including all of the previous messages: edit out all the irrelevant material.

- Limit line length to fewer than 65 characters and end a line with a return.

- Mail should have a subject heading that reflects the content of the message.

- If you include a signature, keep it short. Rule of thumb is no longer than four lines.

- Just as postal mail may not be private, e-mail is subject to forgery and spoofing of various degrees. Apply common sense "reality checks" before assuming a message is valid.

- If you think the importance of a message justifies it, immediately reply briefly to an e-mail message to let the sender know you got it, even if you will send a longer reply later.

- "Reasonable" expectations for conduct via e-mail depend on your relationship to a person and the context of the communication. Norms learned in a particular e-mail environment may not apply in general to your e-mail communication with people across the Internet. Be careful with slang or local acronyms.

- The cost of delivering an e-mail message is, on the average, paid about equally by the sender and the recipient (or their organizations). This is unlike other media such as postal mail, telephone, television, or radio. Sending someone mail may also cost them in other specific ways like network bandwidth, disk space, or CPU usage. This is a fundamental

A True E-Disaster

When the CEO of Cerner Corporation elected to use e-mail to express his dissatisfaction with employee performance, he intended to motivate his 400 managers to act quickly. That they did. They posted the CEO's disturbing message on Yahoo! where it was read by an audience of 3,100 Cerner employees as well as financial analysts, investors, and Yahoo! subscribers. In three days, Cerner's stock, valued at $1.5 billion the day of the CEO's e-mail, fell 22 percent, from $44 to $34 per share. An excerpt from the CEO's e-mail follows:

"We are getting less than 40 hours of work from a large number of our K.C.-based EMPLOYEES. The parking lot is sparsely used at 8 A.M.; likewise at 5 P.M. As managers—you either do not know what your EMPLOYEES are doing; or you do not CARE. You have created expectations on the work effort which allowed this to happen inside Cerner, creating a very unhealthy environment. In either case, you have a problem and you will fix it or I will replace you.

"NEVER in my career have I allowed a team that worked for me to think they had a 40 hour job. I have allowed YOU to create a culture which is permitting this.

"NO LONGER . . .

"You have two weeks. Tick, tock.

Source: Flynn, N., & Kahn, R. (2003). *E-mail Rules: A business guide to managing policies, security, and legal issues for e-mail and digital communication.* New York: AMACOM.

economic reason why unsolicited e-mail advertising is unwelcome (and is forbidden in many contexts).

- Know how large a message you are sending. Including large files such as images or programs may make your message so large that it cannot be delivered or at least consumes excessive resources. A good rule of thumb is to not send a file larger than 50 kilobytes (KB). Consider file transfer as an alternative, or cutting the file into smaller chunks and sending each as a separate message.

- Do not send large amounts of unsolicited information to people.

- If your mail system allows you to forward mail, beware the dreaded forwarding loop. Be sure you have not set up forwarding on several hosts so that a message sent to you gets into an endless loop from one computer to the next to the next.

Take some time to go online (www.dtcc.edu/rfc1855.html) and review this document. It contains suggested strategies for group e-mails, administrators, information service, and security considerations, among other topics. Because you

Netiquette in a Box

Netiquette basics:

Help the newbies

Research before asking

Remember emotion

People are not organizations

Netiquette of sending:

Be brief

Use white space

Use descriptive subject lines

Stay on topic

Be careful sending attachments

Copy the minimum number of people

Include your e-mail address

Respect noncommercial spaces

Avoid flaming

Netiquette of replying and forwarding:

Summarize for the group

Check current information before replying

Reference past communications

Acknowledge important communications

Netiquette of confidentiality:

Do not publicize others' e-mail addresses

Never send what you don't read

Remember archiving

Respect copyright

Source: www.livinginternet.com/i/ia_nq.htm

likely use e-mail personally, and will use it professionally during your internship, this is an ideal time to learn more about "megabyte manners."

Cell Phone Protocol in the Office

When it comes to using your cell phone at work, you have to be considerate of your coworkers and your employer. You also need to get your work done. To help you accomplish both, a list of guidelines for cell phone courtesy in the office follows. Keep in mind that some of these guidelines may also be applied to the use of text messaging and personal digital assistants in the workplace.

1. **Turn off your cell phone ringer, and do not bring your cell phone to meetings.** If you have your cell phone at work, it should not ring. The

sounds of different ring tones going off all the time can be very distracting in the office. If you do not want to turn off your cell phone completely, at least set it to "vibrate"—yet, even on this setting, you may be tempted to see who a call is from if you receive one during a meeting. Also, the phone can be heard when on "vibrate." This is impolite and a clear signal to your boss that your mind is not fully on the meeting.

2. **If you choose to have your cell phone at work, use it only for really important calls.** What is an example of an important call? A true family emergency that you must deal with immediately is important; your friend calling to chat or your mom calling to tell you that your cousin is engaged is not. While you are at work, if you are in doubt as to the importance of a call, let voice mail pick it up. It will take much less time to check your messages than it will to answer the call and then tell the caller you cannot talk.

3. **Find a private place to make cell phone calls.** It is acceptable to use your cell phone at work for private calls during breaks. Find somewhere private to talk, even if your conversation is not confidential. You may be on a break, but your coworkers may be trying to work. Find a place where your conversation cannot be overheard. You should never make a phone call in the restroom. You never know who is in there, the person on the other end of the line may hear that is where you are, and it is an invasion of your coworkers' privacy.

Source: http://careerplanning.about.com/od/workplacesurvival/tp/cell_phone.htm

Internship Obstacles

Situations may arise during your internship that require direct communication and professional conduct such as the following:

- Unchallenging, routine work

- Inadequate amount of work

- Unclear assignments

- Ambiguous feedback or lack of performance review

You may find you are spending most of your time on routine clerical work instead of performing tasks that would develop new skills. Ask the internship employer for additional responsibilities after successfully completing assigned tasks. Show initiative, accuracy, and speed—then the internship employer will be eager to give you additional work. It is important to keep in mind, however, that there is something to be learned from every job and that routine clerical work must be done in order for the organization to function. If the situation arises that you do not have enough work to do, choose a good time to approach your internship employer and explain your concerns. Be clear and specific in

Figure 4.2 Do the routine tasks well, and then courteously voice your desire to take on additional responsibilities so that you can develop new skills.

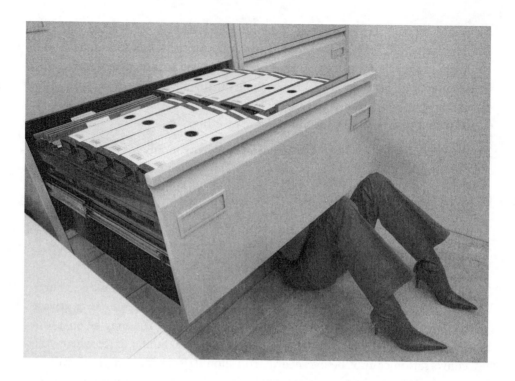

stating your problem, not belligerent or whining. If this is unsuccessful, then speak to your academic internship sponsor. Problems should be handled as soon as possible; you do not want to waste half your internship in an unproductive situation.

You may also be given an assignment that you do not understand. Never hesitate to ask questions for clarification. It is also important to learn how to listen carefully. If you do make a mistake, it is best to admit it rather than attempt to cover it up. You should also communicate with your employer and receive feedback. You may have completed several projects yet not know if the supervisor is satisfied with your performance. As part of your professional growth, you will need to know how you are performing. Schedule a time when it is mutually convenient to discuss your work performance: areas of strength, areas for improvement, and new opportunities. When receiving feedback, listen carefully without responding defensively. Take constructive criticism as an opportunity to grow and learn. It is important to exhibit a professional attitude in the workplace. Keep the tips from Box 4.4 in mind while at your internship.

Changing Internship Plans

The internship is both a job and an academic requirement. It does, however, differ from academic work in many ways. It is a professional relationship and, after you have begun your internship, you may not withdraw from it in the same way as you would from an academic course. If there is an extraordinary circumstance causing you to leave, you will need to discuss the specific situation with

Top Ten Tips for the Workplace

1. **Work a full day, every day.** You are expected to be on the job during working hours. Working late does not make up for arriving late, especially if your boss needs something done at 8 A.M. Missing work time will not only displease your supervisor but also it will make your hardworking coworkers resentful.

2. **Keep absences to a minimum.** Missing a day of work may be more serious than missing a class. Lateness or absence is excusable only if you are physically ill or have a serious personal emergency. If these are the reasons that keep you from work, call your supervisor immediately, and tell him or her about your situation and when you expect to return to work. When planning your schedule, keep in mind that academic holidays are not necessarily work holidays.

3. **Get your work done on time.** In college, you may be able to turn papers in late, but finishing work assignments after the deadline is unacceptable. Excuses do not help. If you are having trouble completing an assignment, tell your supervisor as soon as possible so that she or he may call in more help. Be realistic about your limitations and the number of assignments you can undertake. It is important to stay focused on the task, and to know when to ask questions, in order to avoid missing deadlines. In the workforce, arriving late or submitting late work can cause you to lose the job.

4. **Your boss is your boss.** Be respectful and follow orders. When you feel you have a special insight that would help solve a problem, by all means, speak up. It is important not to argue over the small things. A reputation as a complainer is difficult to reverse.

5. **No job is fun all of the time.** Every job has its share of tedium and frustration. It stands to reason that the newest and least experienced employees will be asked to complete most of the routine tasks. Do not be discouraged. Do your best, as cheerfully as possible, and watch for opportunities. Your chance for a plum assignment will come.

6. **Be honest.** Everybody makes mistakes. Do not be afraid to own up to yours. Blaming someone else can be damaging to your career and conscience.

7. **Observe professional staff members.** Note how employees dress, and use these observations as your guidelines. Some organizations have more rigid standards than others. Regardless of your taste in dress, some degree of conformity is expected.

8. **Keep a notebook.** It is difficult to remember everything that a supervisor and others tell you, so put it all in writing. This will also help you manage your time and set work priorities as well as keep track of your internship experiences.

9. **Always ask for a business card.** Record names and phone numbers of people you meet; some of these contacts may be helpful to you in the future.

10. **Build your portfolio.** If you produce a project, write an article, or the like, ask your supervisor for a copy to include in your portfolio. It may be useful when you are looking for a position in the future.

your academic sponsor in order to receive approval to withdraw from the internship position. Examples of extraordinary circumstances include illness (whether it's yours or your employer's); a drastic change in the internship organization, such as a merger or the elimination of your business; or an employee transfer that relocates your direct employer, possibly leaving you with a new internship supervisor who is unwilling to commit to your internship requirements. Your academic sponsor will confer with you (and possibly the internship supervisor) to assure that every effort has been made to fulfill the original requirements of the learning agreement (Appendix A).

Similarly, changing internships, after you have begun, should only be done if all efforts have been made to resolve any problems. For example, you may have made arrangements to complete your internship in the children's wear division of a department store. It is not permissible for you to change divisions without the approval of your academic sponsor. In some cases, the original learning agreement will specify that you will work in a wide range of departments. If it does not, approval from the academic sponsor to alter the original agreement must be received.

The Internship Evaluation

The internship employer will review you formally at the conclusion of the internship work experience through a written evaluation form available in the appendices. It is a good idea to take the time to review the criteria listed on the evaluation form often during the internship. This will help you to keep in mind the qualities the internship employer will be critiquing as she or he reflects on your performance at the end of your work experience. You will have the opportunity to evaluate the internship organization, your supervisor, and yourself at the conclusion of the internship (see Appendices). The academic internship sponsor will usually review the evaluations, assess the written responses, and calculate a final grade for academic internship credit.

Other Practical Considerations

In addition to the internship itself, other practical considerations must be taken into account. Housing, transportation, and apparel are among the expenses for which the intern must prepare.

Housing

If completing the internship in a location away from home, an intern will need to find a place to stay. It is an intern's responsibility to find housing, not the employer's. Although the employer may have some excellent ideas about housing alternatives, and you should not be afraid to ask for suggestions, responsibility for this is ultimately yours. Students have previously used the following solutions to internship housing:

- **Colleges/Universities**—This is the top-ranked alternative. Find the residential college located nearest your internship location and contact the college's student life office for short-term housing options and prices, meal plans, and furniture needs. Sometimes the college will require a letter of introduction from the academic internship sponsor. Often, the dormitory will require a deposit to reserve housing. New York University (NYU), for example, provides dormitory rooms, apartments, and meal tickets at reasonable fees, but they are reserved quickly. A deposit must be sent early in the year to secure a place at NYU for the summer.

- **Graduates of the institution**—You may decide to write to alumni soliciting housing suggestions. Be certain to include the dates and exact location of your employment situation. Former interns have successfully exchanged child care and house-sitting for free board.

- **Sublets**—The classified section of newspapers, along with craigslist.com and other Internet sites, provides information on short-term leasing. Remember to ask about telephone and utility deposits, monthly utility costs, and furniture needs. In addition, you may elect to search for furnished apartments in the appropriate city. It is a good idea to take someone with you when you look at rental property or goods for sale from an online source. Always think about safety.

- **Others**—These may include friends of your family, church, or club contacts, your student friends and their parents.

Transportation

Remember to check out the buses, taxicabs, subway systems, and car rental options in the internship location. You may be able to walk or ride a bicycle to

Figure 4.3 Research transportation availability and costs to ensure you arrive on time to your internship every day.

work. If not, however, you should include transportation costs as part of the internship expense budget. Travel to and from the internship location may also be a significant expense.

Dressing for Success

Some companies prefer employees to wear clothing produced or sold by them. In return, they often offer substantial discounts on their merchandise to enable employees to dress accordingly. For example, former interns of Express retail outlets and Hollister apparel were encouraged to wear merchandise sold by their respective firms. To assist employees in building a work wardrobe, these retailers offer substantial discounts on purchases. In these cases, you may want to wait to buy a work wardrobe until you get the job. Some businesses have a formal dress code, such as requiring suits; others encourage casual dress, such as jeans and tennis shoes.

You may not be able to make a judgment call on appropriate apparel for the internship position based solely on observations made during the interview. Although the sales personnel and the receptionist in an apparel manufacturer's showroom may be dressed in sophisticated sportswear, the patternmakers and sample hands in the adjacent factory may be wearing slacks and comfortable shoes. Clothing choices often depend on your particular position within the company. Before purchasing clothing or packing that suitcase for the internship work experience, it is entirely appropriate to ask your internship contact person to describe the firm's dress preferences for your job.

Other factors to consider when determining a work wardrobe are weather conditions, "off-duty" clothing needs, and the variety of your job requirements. If the internship is with an apparel manufacturer, for example, you may be required to work in the factory some days, sell in the showroom on other days, and entertain clients with the manufacturer's representative in the evenings. Remember, this is the fashion industry, and your appearance makes a significant impression.

Modeling the Way

It is important to recognize that, as an intern, you are a representative of your academic institution. As an ambassador for your school, you have the opportunity to influence future internship placements for better or for worse. If your work is below par and your attitude is bad, it is likely that internship opportunities for future students from your school will be jeopardized. As you begin the internship, take time to reflect on the positive impact you can have on the reputation of your college and opportunities for future interns. Follow these ten tips to be the model intern.

Top Ten Tips for Success

1. Know how your job fits into the organization. Learn all you can about the industry.

2. Put your effort into the tasks that your supervisor values. You earn an A when you please your boss, not necessarily when you do what you think is important.

3. Do not be afraid to ask questions. Know when to ask questions. Learn where to go for answers.

4. Tactfully let other people know when you have done a good job. Being good is not enough; people have to know you are good.

5. Learn to communicate effectively and to the right people.

6. Always share credit; never share blame.

7. Stay cool and reasonable. Do not let your emotions control your actions.

8. Be sensitive to office politics.

9. Remember the importance of networking.

10. Learn how to manage stress before the need arises.

Is It Worth It?

Emily was a fashion marketing and management major who planned to graduate in May after completing an internship. Emily held a part-time position as a bank teller for two years. She enjoyed it, but she knew that she needed some type of retail employment before she graduated, so she started to look for an internship position to gain experience and fulfill her internship requirement. Emily applied at a large retail chain, Molly's. She interviewed with the manager of the misses' dress department, Heather, and was offered a paid position that met her internship needs and guaranteed Emily 30 work hours a week. This was necessary because Emily was going to have to leave her regular job where she worked 30 to 35 hours a week.

Emily was very excited about starting her new position. Her manager was very nice and seemed interested in helping her meet her internship goals. During the first few weeks of Emily's new job, she noticed she was not scheduled for all of the hours for which she was hired. Emily decided it was because she was new and that management wanted to start her off slowly. After the next couple of work schedules were issued, Emily realized her weekly schedule was only 17 to 20 hours, instead of 30 hours. Emily had worked for Molly's a little over a month when she decided to speak with her manager. Heather apologized to Emily and promised her more hours for the next week. That week, when Emily received her schedule, it still did not show enough hours. This concerned Emily for a number of reasons. First, she needed to work at least 30 hours each week to complete her internship requirements in time for May graduation. Second, Emily based her personal expenses on income from working at least 30 hours per week. Emily spoke with her manager several more times about her hours. Heather continued to promise her that she would have more hours. Finally, Heather told Emily that she did not have any extra hours to give her because sales were down for the entire store, and the payroll had to be reduced. In light of the payroll problem, she stated that she could give Emily only 17 to 20 hours a week. Emily walked away upset and angry. She felt she had been lied to about the job. She was confused about what to do. She needed more hours, but she also needed the experience for her degree and future career.

1. What should Emily have done about her job at Molly's?

2. If you were the university's academic internship sponsor, what would you advise Emily to do?

The "Too-Good-to-Be-True" Intern

Thomas Scott was concluding his first six weeks as an intern to the buyer of the men's sportswear division for a major resident buying office located in New York. In the resident buying office's internship program, the interns are "promoted" through relocation to a new department. The rationale is that if the intern has accomplished the responsibilities of one area, he or she is rewarded with a move to a new department in order to gain more experience and exposure. The most successful interns work in two or three departments during a three-month internship. Thomas was scheduled to receive his first internship evaluation through a personnel review by Michael Johnson, the men's sportswear buyer—a requirement for the internship. Mr. Johnson was a respected executive in the menswear market with nearly 40 years of buying experience. He had worked successfully as a retail store buyer, then as a resident buyer in both ladies' and men's apparel.

Thomas was confident that his first evaluation would be a positive experience. He was anxious to receive the recommendation that would support his move to another department, increasing the exposure and opportunities of his internship. Almost daily, Mr. Johnson commented on Thomas's superior work performance. Over the six weeks of his internship, Thomas had learned quickly and worked diligently. Mr. Johnson had come to count on Thomas in nearly every aspect of the buying job. Mr. Johnson had expended much time and effort to train Thomas, allowing him to handle responsibilities greater than those of the other interns.

After two weeks of exposure to the buying position, Thomas eventually became responsible for communicating with the client stores monthly, following up on shipments due from the manufacturers, placing reorders on hot sellers, maintaining the on-order records, visiting the vendors to preview new items or lines, and summarizing the sales reports. Michael Johnson frequently referred to Thomas as his "right arm." The client store buyers regularly relied on Thomas for assistance with returns to vendors, cooperative advertising requests, and promotional suggestions. He felt appreciated by his internship supervisor and valued by the buying office's retail accounts. Thomas believed that he would soon receive the departmental move he had been working toward. His evaluation meeting the next week would determine whether he had reached this goal.

As they sat down for their evaluation meeting, Mr. Johnson brought out a list summarizing Thomas's strengths and his areas that needed improvement. The number of strengths substantially outweighed the areas that needed improvement. Johnson cited Thomas's strengths as follows: his exceptional oral and written communication skills, quantitative analysis abilities, "people skills," ability to learn quickly, and to retain information. Mr. Johnson did note, however, that Thomas needed to work on his delegation skills when given a major project and on his enthusiasm when presenting merchandise to the client store buyers. Thomas agreed with the evaluation's points and was pleased to receive a fair and helpful review.

Mr. Johnson concluded, "Thomas, I don't believe that you're ready yet to move into the internship position that will be available next week in ladies' accessories. First, you need more time in this department—time to learn more about the men's sportswear business and to work

(continued on next page)

on the areas where you need improvement. You're young and have just started in this business. You will have plenty of opportunities. Second, you don't have any experience in the ladies' apparel division. Finally, I can't imagine how I'd get along without your help. Normally it takes months to train an intern to do what you do." He continued, "I am going to recommend that you remain in this department and continue interning for me, Thomas. Don't let it get you down—your time will come soon enough." Thomas thanked Mr. Johnson for his candid evaluation and quietly left the office.

By the time Thomas arrived home, his head was whirling. He had really wanted that transfer to ladies' accessories. He questioned whether or not he had made himself too valuable in his present internship position. Thomas began to feel resentment toward Mr. Johnson as he wondered if Johnson was intentionally holding him back for his own personal benefit.

Thomas replayed the evaluation session in his mind and attempted to formulate the questions he should have asked. He decided that he would develop a plan that night and deal with his questions and concerns at work the next day.

1. If you were in Thomas's position, what would you do?

2. Develop a brief response that Thomas could give following the evaluation session.

CHAPTER FIVE

The Company Mission, Image, and Location

Objectives

- To analyze or develop a mission statement for the internship organization and the intern

- To articulate the objectives and goals of the internship organization and those of the intern

- To examine market positioning and repositioning efforts of the internship organization

- To examine the components of the organization's image and image perception inside of the company by employees and outside of the company by consumers

- To explore the location decisions of the internship organization—regional, state, city, and site

- To review the layout of the company facility, whether it be a brick-and-mortar retail store, a showroom, a factory, or a Web site, among others

What Is the Foundation of the Internship Company?

The internship company is directed by its vision, one that is often articulated through its mission statement. The company's goals and objectives produce an image, a company personality, and a culture. The places it chooses to locate its products and workforce contribute to this image. All are examined in this chapter.

The Company Mission Statement

The company mission statement is intended to coordinate the individual efforts of members of the organization. The **mission statement** articulates the firm's vision and guides it. An effective mission statement answers the following questions:

- What is the existing business?

- Who is the customer?

- What is the company's value to the customer?

- What potential business opportunities exist for the company?

The purpose of a mission statement is to motivate company employees through a shared sense of direction, opportunity, significance, and achievement. Under the company mission statement, employees can work independently yet collectively toward realizing the organization's potential. The mission statement should define the business domains in which the organization will operate in terms of its products, technologies, customer groups, and external influences. The mission statement can be as long as a paragraph or as short as a single sentence.

Figure 5.1 Nike president and CEO Phil Knight helped start a sports business revolution in the 1970s, changing old-fashioned tennis shoes into highly specialized equipment and promoting them as symbols of athletic prowess and success.

The corporate giant Nike, manufacturer of athletic apparel and footwear, sums up its mission statement in two pithy sentences: "To bring inspiration and innovation to every athlete in the world. If you have a body, you are an athlete." (www.nikebiz.com/company_overview/)

5.1   Indicate the mission statement of the internship organization. If the organization has not developed a formal mission statement, compose one that will guide and inspire the business's constituencies by answering the questions introduced at the start of this chapter.

_____

_____

_____

Some companies develop mission statements to guide the firm in focusing on one particular vision that is foremost in constituencies' minds. Box 5.1 provides Nordstrom's mission statement on diversity.

The Company Objectives and Goals

The mission statement is turned into a detailed set of supporting objectives for each level of management. These objectives are later converted into specific quantitative goals to obtain planning and control, such as "increase market share to 20 percent by the end of the year." Goals are often objectives that have been made specific with respect to numbers and time.

··❦[B O X 5 . 1]❧··

Example of a Mission Statement on Diversity

At Nordstrom, we value the richness that diversity brings to our workforce—it makes our Company better and the communities we serve stronger.

Our Diversity Mission Statement:

To maintain a workforce that represents many backgrounds, while remaining deeply committed to cultivating an environment where the contributions of every employee, customer and vendor are valued and respected.

Nordstrom is an equal opportunity employer, committed to recruiting, hiring and promoting qualified people of all backgrounds, regardless of sex; race; color; creed; national origin; religion; age; marital status; pregnancy; physical, mental or sensory disability; sexual orientation; gender identity or any other basis protected by federal, state or local law.

Source: http://about.nordstrom.com/aboutus/diversity/mission_statement.asp

---

For example, Nike established the following goal for the years 2008 to 2013. At the end of that time, Nike will reevaluate the goal, which may remain as it is or may change, as determined by the board, management, employees, and customers. The goal of Nike is "to carry on the founders' legacy of innovative thinking, whether to develop products that help athletes of every level of ability reach their potential, or to create business opportunities apart from the competition and provide value for (our) shareholders" (www.nikebiz.com).

5.2 Discuss the objectives and goals of the internship organization. If goals and objectives have not been specified for the organization, develop a list of goals and objectives that will help implement the company's mission statement.

_____

_____

_____

Developing a Mission Statement to Chart Your Internship Course

What Is a Personal Mission Statement?

Nearly every major company has a mission statement. A company mission statement is a short, descriptive statement of the common objectives and focus of the organization. It is the company's purpose for existence. A personal mission statement describes your purpose, your individual and work intentions. It provides you with clarity and direction, defining who you are (or want to be), what you value, and how you want to live as an individual and as a professional. A personal mission statement specifies how you intend to meet your personal and professional goals and when and where outcomes to measure your progress will be forthcoming. Writing a personal mission statement offers the opportunity to establish what is important and create a road map before you ever begin your career track.

How Do I Write a Personal Mission Statement?

When writing a personal mission statement, begin with the following activities—the 5Ds:

- Describe your best personal, individual characteristics and how you express them as well as those you want to develop.

- Describe your best professional attributes and how you express them as well as those you intend to develop.

- Define both personal and professional goals and objectives that will result in measurable outcomes.

- Determine deadlines, such as December 31, the midpoint in the internship, or the seventh week of the internship.

- Draft a handwritten or typed page that you will revise and shorten as you review it.

Most people find it easiest to define the values and characteristics they have and want to attain first and then to develop objectives that will result in outcomes in their personal and professional lives, thus implementing the chosen values and characteristics.

Ideas for Your Personal Mission Statement—Individual Values and Qualities

Next, here are examples of values and personal qualities to give you a starting place:

- To remember where I have been and where I will go through maintaining positive relationships with family and friends

- To choose the ethical way by making a personal commitment to honesty and integrity

- To find peacefulness within myself by looking inward, while using my heart to guide my dreams and desires and my mind to pursue knowledge

- To create balance among all my obligations

- To content myself in my surroundings so that I will always know where security lies within my life

- To build a reputation of being dedicated to every goal I choose to pursue

- To commit to having successes in both my personal and professional life

- To enjoy every moment along this journey, finding laughter, love, and happiness with each day that passes

- To find happiness, fulfillment, and value in living, I will seek out and experience all the pleasures and joys that life has to offer

Ideas for Your Personal Mission Statement— Professional Values and Qualities

Nearly all major companies have corporate mission statements that are designed to provide direction and drive to those within the organization. The company mission statement acts as an invisible hand that guides the people in the organization toward the same goals and values. Although a personal mission statement is a bit different from a company mission statement, the fundamental principles are the same. A personal mission statement helps job seekers identify their core values and beliefs. In his time management book *First Things First* (1994), Stephen Covey states that a personal mission statement is "an articulation of what you're all about and what success looks like to you." Covey refers to crafting a mission statement as "connecting with your own unique purpose and the profound satisfaction that comes in fulfilling it" (p. 113). He goes on to explain that one way to develop a personal mission statement is to visualize your 80th birthday or 50th wedding anniversary and imagine how your family, friends, colleagues, and employer will describe you.

Developing your personal career focus will help you clarify your vision of who you are and where you want to go in your career. Begin your summary statement with the words "My personal career mission is . . ." and finish with qualifying words and phrases to describe your mission. Following are some examples of personal career mission statements: "my personal career mission is to become a world-class trend forecaster in the global fashion industry"; "my personal career mission is to continually learn and apply the leading Web development tools and become a first-in-class Web developer in the fashion industry"; "my personal career mission is to become an editor for one of the U.S. fashion magazines."

Your personal mission statement should be tightly focused on the first three to five years of your career (short-term) and more loosely describe the next five years (long-term). You can give specifics about the job type and industry, as appropriate. This personal career mission statement will form the foundation of your career focus and will guide you toward successful completion of your internship experience. The career portion of the personal mission statement allows you, the intern, to identify the shared values and beliefs of the internship organization, to better assess benefits and opportunities to be had during your internship. The biggest problem most interns face is not in wanting to have a personal mission statement but in actually developing and writing it. To help you get started on a personal mission statement that includes your internship, there is a five-step mission-building process. Take as much time on each step as you need, and remember to think carefully in order to develop a mission statement that is both authentic and honest. To assist you in moving through the process, an example of one job seeker's process in developing her mission statement will be presented.

Steps toward Building a Personal Mission Statement with Career Goals

Step 1: Identify Past Successes. Spend some time identifying four or five examples that illustrate your personal success in business in recent years. These successes could take place on the job, volunteering on campus or in your community, or working with family and friends. Identify the common themes among these examples, and write them down.

Step 2: Apply Core Values. Use the list of attributes that you identified earlier—who you are (or want to become) and what your priorities are.

When your list is complete, see if you can narrow your values to the five or six that are most important. Finally, see if you can choose the one value that is most important to you.

Step 3: Specify Contributions. Make a list of the ways you could make a difference. In an ideal situation, how could you contribute best to the world in general, to your community, to your family and friends, and to your internship employer or future employers?

Step 4: Identify Goals. Spend some time thinking about your priorities in work and the goals you have for yourself. Make a list of your personal career goals. These may be short-term (up to three years) or long-term (beyond three years); it is up to you.

Step 5: Write a Mission Statement. Based on the first four steps and a better understanding of yourself, begin writing your personal mission statement. The following is a sample personal mission statement development for Melody, a young woman who is pursuing an internship and career in product development:

1. Past successes:

   Developed new features for stagnant product that resulted in surpassing sales goals.

   Collaborated as part of team that developed new positioning statement for product.

   Helped a local school for underprivileged children with a fashion show fund-raiser that was very successful.

   Increased turnout for the opening of a new local theater company through volunteer work in promotions and ticket sales.

   Theme: Successes all relate to creative problem solving and execution of a solution.

2. Core values:

   Hardworking and industrious

   Creative and intelligent

   Problem solver and decision maker

   Friendly and outgoing

   Family oriented

   Honest and compassionate

   Spiritual and healthful

   Passionate and contemplative

   Most important values: creative, analytical, compassionate

3. Contributions:

To the world, in general, and my community, specifically: to develop products and services that help people achieve what they want in life; to have a lasting impact on the way people live their lives.

To my family: to be a leader in terms of personal outlook, compassion for others, and maintaining an ethical code; to be a loving wife, daughter, and sister; to leave the world a better place for my family and friends.

To my internship employer: to be a positive example of my university and to develop a positive professional reputation in the industry by contributing to the internship organization as a self-initiated, innovative problem solver and dedicated employee.

To my future employers: to lead by example and to demonstrate how innovative and problem-solving products can be successful in terms of both fulfilling the needs of clients and generating profit for the organization.

To my friends: to always have a hand held out to them; for them to know that they can always come to me with any problem.

4. Goals:

Short-term: To begin my postgraduation career after successful completion of an internship with a progressive employer that allows me to use my skills, talents, and values to achieve success for the firm.

Long-term: To develop other outlets for my talents and to develop a longer-term plan for diversifying my life and achieving both professional and personal success.

5. Mission Statement:

To live life completely, honestly, and compassionately, with a healthy dose of realism mixed with imagination and the dream that all things are possible if one sets his or her mind to finding an answer; to pursue a career path in the fashion industry that allows me to live in accordance with my values and to create products that fill emotional and practical needs for my clients.

$\mathcal{F}$inal Thoughts

A personal mission statement is, obviously, personal; however, if you truly want to see how honest you have been in developing your personal mission statement, share a draft with people who are close to you. Ask for their feedback. Finally, a personal mission statement is not intended to be written once and then carved in stone. You should set aside some time annually to review your career and personal mission statement goals and make adjustments as necessary.

What Is a Poorly Written Personal Mission Statement?

A personal mission statement that is poorly written follows for your review:

> I aspire to be the very best in my field at what I do. I will make a habit of giving more than is expected. I will strive to understand others and deliver the highest level of service. I will have a career with the highest ethical standards. I will always be honest and forthright in all my dealings.

What is wrong with this personal mission statement? First, it is too general. It does not describe the writer's preferred, unique personal qualities. It has no personal or professional goals, plans, outcomes, or deadlines. An effective personal mission statement contains all these. One could apply this personal mission statement to just about anyone drawing a paycheck.

What Is an Example of a Well-Written Personal Mission Statement?

A powerful (albeit general, for the purpose of this text) personal mission statement follows:

> My purpose is to help my company double sales this year. I plan on accomplishing this goal by devoting one hour a week to learning a new skill in sales and negotiating offers and then applying what I've learned to the deals I'm currently involved in with my company. If I do this faithfully, one year from now I will advance in my career because my ability to increase sales for my company will be more valuable than it is now.

A more specific personal mission statement is illustrated next. Liz Tucker is a fashion designer by day and a certified mixed martial arts (MMA) instructor by night. As such, she aims to help people learn about everything linked to the sport of MMA. She does so professionally as a designer for the line Fighter Femme. The line is sold in specialty stores across the nation and through the company's Web site, which also contains information on MMA, including profiles on up-and-coming MMA stars, shopping tips, and MMA classes and gyms specifically for women. Liz's personal mission statement follows:

> I am a committed advocate for women interested in joining or currently participating in the sport of mixed martial arts. I will work to ensure that novices achieve the most positive first experience possible. This can include encouraging them to follow the careers of role models in women's MMA around the world, to buy the best sports apparel and equipment they can afford, to strive continually to improve their basic skills, and to recruit other women into MMA. I will use Fighter Femme's Web site as a vehicle, by encouraging people to submit stories of women progressing to the top ranks of MMA competition. A new profile will

Career Development Is a Process . . .

Step 1 (usually freshman year)

- If you have not declared a major or are unsure of a selected major, make an appointment with the Career Services Office to clarify your career goals by taking self-assessments and arranging job shadow experiences.

- Join a campus organization (preferably related to your major or career interest), and start developing skills that employers seek in employees.

- Research occupations. Talk to people working in jobs that interest you to learn about their education, experience, and skills. Learn *realistic* statistics on salary, where the jobs are located, and competition for jobs.

Step 2 (usually sophomore year)

- Find an *internship* or part-time job that relates to your career field and that will help you develop important communication and work-related skills.

- Make an appointment with your Career Services Offices to learn how to write résumés and job-search letters, search for full-time jobs or internships, and interview for jobs or internships.

- Continue researching career choices, learning what skills you need to be competitive, and working on developing those skills. Be realistic with your career expectations: learn what a realistic starting salary is; find out whether you need to relocate to start your career; discover if you need a graduate degree; explore whether you should expect keen competition for jobs—and how to be a strong competitor.

- Include information interviewing and job shadowing in your research on careers.

- Continue participating in campus organizations, and consider devoting some time to volunteer activities.

- Keep a portfolio of your work; explore the connection between your classroom

be posted each month. I will continue to design athletic apparel that fits, supports, and flatters the female MMA fighter—while assuring the best price/quality relationship possible. This year, four lines will be developed and marketed, rather than two, as in the past. To that end, I commit to doubling the revenues of Fighter Femme over the next two years and increasing the gross margin by 35 percent. I believe that personal and professional power comes through planning, confidence, strength, safety, and discipline—all characteristics of MMA. I will continue to encourage all MMA women to improve their skills so that they can adopt a well-rounded and balanced lifestyle.

knowledge (via assignments and projects) and the actual work world.

- Access internship postings using your university career center's online posting of full-time jobs, internships, and part-time/temporary jobs.

Step 3 (usually junior year)

- If possible, find a second internship for the summer. Study abroad? Intern with a different company?

- Continue participating in campus and professional organizations; assume leadership roles.

- Continue gaining experience in your field through internships, part-time or summer jobs, and volunteer experiences.

- Research employers who hire in your field; learn what they seek and where the jobs are located.

- Develop a network of contacts willing to be mentors or references for you; conduct information interviews with potential employers.

- Attend career fairs—those sponsored by your university as well as those sponsored by other organizations.

Step 4 (usually senior year)

- Update your résumé and other job-search material.

- Access job listings at your university.

- Register to participate in on-campus recruiting and to apply for jobs electronically.

- Improve your interviewing skills with practice interviews.

- Keep records of all employers you contact and date and method of contact.

- Do not wait until after you have graduated to start looking for a job. To the surprise of many job seekers, the search may take three to six months.

- Continue building your network of contacts. Use your participation in professional organizations and clubs to make connections with people who can provide you with job leads.

- Continue researching potential employers. Find out as much as possible about them, answering the question "Why are you interested in this company?"

Source: Career Center 2009. Missouri State University: Springfield, MO, 2009. With permission.

Next, develop a personal mission statement that includes your new step up the career ladder: your internship. This personal mission statement should incorporate your personal aspirations and values with your professional ones. Think about your goals, plans, outcomes, and deadlines as they pertain to you as an individual and as a professional. This will likely require focus, reflection, and several drafts but is well worth the investment of time and effort. After constructing your mission statement, your next job is to design a more detailed listing of your objectives and goals. Determine a time frame (e.g., six months, one year, three years) before you begin. Think about the responsibilities, tasks, and projects you discussed with your internship employer during and after the interview.

Setting Goals: Powerful Written Goals in Seven Easy Steps

The convertible is packed, and you are ready to go on your first-ever cross-country trip. From Madison Avenue in New York City to Rodeo Drive in Los Angeles, you are going to see it all. You put the car in gear and off you go. Your first stop is the Chanel Boutique on Madison Avenue in the Big Apple. A while into the trip, you need to check for directions because you have reached an intersection with which you are not familiar. You panic for a moment because you have forgotten the GPS. You search the car, but there is no map in the glove compartment. The heck with it, you say, because you know where you are going. You take a right, change the CD, and keep on going. Unfortunately, you never reach your destination.

Too many of us treat goal setting the same way. We dream about where we want to go, yet we do not have the map to get there. What is a map? In essence, it is a written word picture. What is the difference between a dream and a goal? Once again, it is the written word picture,

the plan. Goal setting is, however, more than simply scribbling down some ideas on a piece of paper. Goals need to be complete and focused, much like a road map.

The Seven Steps

1. Make sure the goal you are working toward is something you really want, not just something that sounds good. Goals should be realistic and consistent with your values.

2. One goal cannot contradict any of your other goals. For example, if your goal is to buy a $350,000 house, you will likely not reach that goal if your income is $35,000 annually.

3. Develop goals in the six key areas of life: family and home, financial and career, spiritual and morals, physical and health, social and cultural, as well as mental and educational.

On the accompanying CD-ROM there are two worksheets labeled as The Intern's Goals and Objectives: worksheet 1 and The Intern's Mission Statement: worksheet 2. Use these to further organize your thoughts.

Market Positioning

Just as you position yourself as a future fashion industry leader, a company positions itself to succeed in its industry. **Market positioning** refers to arranging for a product or product line to occupy a distinctive and desirable place,

4. Write your goal in the positive, instead of the negative. Work for what you want, not for what you want to leave behind. Part of the purpose in writing down and examining your goals is to create a set of instructions for the subconscious mind to carry out. Your subconscious mind is a very efficient tool. It does not determine right from wrong; it does not judge. Its true function is to carry out its instructions. The more positive instructions you give it, the more positive results you will receive. As thinking positively every day will also help your growth as a human being, you will not want to limit it to goal setting.

5. Write out each goal in complete detail. Instead of writing, "a new home" on your list, write, for example, "a 4,000-square-foot contemporary with four bedrooms and three baths and a view of the mountains on ten acres of land." Give the subconscious mind a detailed set of instructions. The more information you give it, the clearer the final outcome becomes. The more precise the outcome, the more efficient the subconscious mind can become. Can you close your eyes and visualize the home described above? Walk around the house. Stand on the deck off the master bedroom and watch the fog lifting off the mountain. Look back toward the huge walk-in closet full of designer clothes and shoes. Can you see it? If so, your subconscious mind can as well.

6. Make sure your goal is high enough. Shoot for the moon. If you miss, you will still be among the stars.

7. Write down your goals. Writing down your goals creates a road map to your success. The act of writing them down can set the process in motion. It is extremely important to review your goals frequently. The more focused you are on your goals, the more likely you will accomplish them. Sometimes, we need to revise a goal as circumstances and other goals change. If you need to change a goal, do not consider it a failure. Consider it a victory as you had the insight to realize something was different.

Source: Career Center, Missouri State University. Springfield, MO, 2009. Modified and reprinted with permission.

specifically in a certain market, specifically in the minds of target customers. When positioning itself in a market segment, an organization will identify all the competitive products and brands then used by customers. Successful organizations often seek out a marketing opportunity in which there is a substantial pool of customers and a low level of competition.

5.3   Describe any positioning strategies attempted by the internship organization.

_____

_____

_____

Market Repositioning

Market repositioning describes new activities a company implements to more effectively accomplish its objectives and goals. When a company repositions, it may eliminate divisions that are losing money, downsize by closing unprofitable locations, or change the management team. Box 5.4 shows the repositioning strategic plan of Donna Karan International from the perspective of its human resources vice president.

·§[BOX 5.4]§·

Repositioning and Redesigning Donna Karan International, Inc.

Redesigning the Company at Donna Karan

People are the most important asset, making Human Resources (HR) the most important function—no matter what the business. Find out the unique challenges faced by this HR leader— and some strategies for handling universal HR issues. Facing a challenge is one thing. Meeting it head-on is another. In 1997, New York City–based Donna Karan International experienced disappointing profits. As a young, fast-growing company, it had not always built its organization in the most profitable, efficient manner. Executives were forced to reevaluate the company's core operating groups' functions and relationships. Its new three-year strategic plan included a major downsizing driven by the reduction of the number of divisions from 13 to 6. Donna Karan also streamlined the company's senior management structure and made each of the six divisions fully integrated operating units.

Next, HR vice president Christina Nichols discusses how her department helped employees impact efficiency, cost savings—and raise company morale.

What factors drove the recent downsizing and restructuring at Donna Karan International, Inc.?
We're a very young company that has experienced tremendous rapid growth. When you grow very quickly, you don't always grow in the most profitable and efficient manner. So we made a difficult decision: to stop, evaluate what we've done, and readjust where necessary.

Which employees were the most impacted and why?
It's interesting. I've been with the company for almost six years and have been through a few other "downsizing" efforts. Typically there had been a target percentage to be cut in each division. This time around, however, the downsizing was driven by actual restructuring within divisions in an effort to impact efficiency and cost savings.

Another significant impact on the restructuring was our entrance into strategic alliances with other companies. This included the licensing

A model on the runway at DKNY's fall 2008 show in New York City.

of the company's beauty business to The Estée Lauder Companies Inc., DKNYjeanswear and activewear products to Liz Claiborne, and DKNY Kids to Esprit de Corps. The employees impacted were from all levels of our population.

What were the HR implications?
The restructuring process was draining to say the least! We were working with John Idol, our new CEO, trying to determine what the new structure would look like, trying to compile all the pertinent information for those employees who would be affected, coordinating outplacement services, and trying to coach management through the process. In the end, we managed to pull together as a team to make it happen successfully.

The aftermath of the restructuring process brings with it many new challenges. The employee population is dealing with the shock of losing co-workers, the stress of handling more responsibilities, and the uncertainty of their own job security. Responding to these concerns is difficult.

Unfortunately, companies can't offer anyone job security and yet, it's one of the most important issues to employees. I believe that deep down people knew this restructuring had to happen in order for the company to prosper, but that doesn't make it any easier to deal with the day-to-day issues. With the restructuring several months behind us, people are beginning to settle into their new roles and to re-emerge as strong teams.

What has HR learned in the process?
When we went through the restructuring process, we eliminated many jobs because of the decision to license various products. This was a fairly new

(continued on next page)

direction for the company. Forming strategic partnerships with the licensees has been an insightful process. You need to become the expert on the licensee's business so you can best educate the Donna Karan employees who will transition over [to working with them]. It's difficult to ensure that employees who transition to the licensee maintain the same level of compensation and benefits. It's a tough process because it doesn't end once the employees move over to the licensee's [work environment]. The role we play in this process already has evolved from working within the existing framework and facilitating the process to championing what's best for the employees.

Have you developed new programs, incentives, or work processes to ensure more teamwork and productivity?
A few months ago the company created several task forces to address our key business issues and to foster stronger teamwork between divisions. We currently have task forces for: human resources; strategic/business planning; creative planning; quality; and manufacturing/sourcing. The task forces have specific agendas and periodically present update reports. They've been successful in fostering teamwork.

The Strategic Planning task force has created the company's first formal strategic business plan. Each division now is responsible for creating its own mission statement, goals and initiatives that will ensure support of and contribution to the company's strategic plan. The Human Resources task force has been in the process of creating a corporate values statement. The preliminary work was done in the task force. Divisional meetings were conducted later to review feedback and to ensure people had a sense of ownership over the values. We haven't formally rolled out the values statement yet, but it's already starting to have an impact.

Which jobs have required additional training?
The immediate training needs associated with restructuring revolved around management. Before we actually went through the organizational changes, we conducted some brief sessions with the management teams to coach them on how to manage through the change. Frequently, the aftermath can be more difficult to manage than the actual restructure.

How has HR addressed morale?
We began face-to-face meetings with our CEO. That way, our employees can get to know him better and vice versa. We also began conducting regular update meetings with all our division heads.

Can you describe the corporate culture at Donna Karan International, Inc.?
Its corporate culture is difficult to characterize. It's demanding, rigorous, and challenging. It's also entrepreneurial, creative, rewarding, exciting, and energetic. It's an intense and committed environment. The people who work here put in 200 percent of themselves every day! In a word, it's passionate.

What has been one of your most recent innovations within human resources?
I would say it has been the creation of the team I work with in human resources. This is the most talented group of people I have ever had the fortune of working with and I'm a believer that you're only as good as your team. With all the changes in the company, from the arrival of our new CEO to the restructure, the goals and focus of the human resources department have radically shifted to remain aligned with the company's direction. We've positioned ourselves as strategic business partners with the divisions in the company. We've evolved from putting out fires and creating policy to well-rounded business partners.

Source: Sunoo, B. P. Repositioning the company at Donna Karan (1998). *Workforce* 77(7), 27–28.

5.4 Discuss repositioning strategies developed by the internship organization. If the organization has not repositioned itself, provide an example of a company that has successfully repositioned, and describe its specific strategies.

_____

_____

_____

5.5 As an exercise to maximize the internship experience, take the specific goals and objectives you clarified for your position as an intern and compare these with the objectives and goals of the business organization. How do the company's plans fit with your internship plans?

_____

_____

_____

The Company Image

Market positioning and repositioning activities can impact a company's image. What is a company image? Begin this analysis by answering the following question: What visions, feelings, and thoughts come to mind when you think of Wal-Mart, Kmart, Big Lots, or Sears? Next, think about Prada, Chanel, Dior, and Louis Vuitton. The mention of each company name probably calls to mind some distinctive thought, feeling, or vision, whereas Sally's Imports (a store you are probably not familiar with) does not. That is because each of the eight companies has created a distinguishable company image.

A **company image** is the combination of the thoughts, feelings, beliefs, opinions, and visions people have about a company and its products. It is what others think and feel about the company, not what the sales literature and sales staff say. Consequently, even the smallest of companies should be aware of and do whatever is appropriate to promote its image. The following describes two image characteristics:

> **A simple and complex concept**—Company image is both a simple and complex concept. How can that be? It is simple because successful companies create images that are easily described and recognized by their

Figure 5.2 Fendi's strong company image and logo allows customers to easily identify its products. (See also Figure 5.4.)

target audiences. It is complex because it takes many discrete elements working together to create an image. Some of these include advertising, marketing communications, publicity, location, price, and product positioning.

Marketplace identity—Company image is identity in the marketplace. It is important to note that a competitor may have the same image as another company. For example, think about two specialty apparel chains that operate in the same region. Both may have an image of offering quality products at reasonable prices. The customer may feel equally comfortable in stores of both chains, think they hire competent and friendly people, and appreciate each enterprise's contribution to the community. Because of this similarity, a customer may choose which store to frequent based upon location alone.

Company image, however, can differentiate a company from its competition. For instance, two apparel store chains may both offer quality products at reasonable prices. However, one chain might not be as clean or brightly lit as another. Its employees might not be as helpful and friendly. The customer may choose the clean, brightly lit, friendly store because of these image attributes alone.

Does every company have an image? Interestingly, a company has an image even if it does not undertake any activities to try to build one. Customers have thoughts, feelings, beliefs, and opinions about a company and its products and services, even if it does not advertise, distribute fliers, pass out brochures, or issue press releases. The following items will quietly, yet actively, create a company image. Although image is created by more than this list of items, reviewing this list will give you an idea of how the simplest of things may leave an indelible impression.

- The company logo. Does it evoke the desired thoughts and feelings in the target audience?

- The Web site. Is it wild and filled with colors, or is it conservative and designed with muted colors?

- Product packaging. Do products from the same line look like they come from the same company?

- The look of business cards, letterhead, and invoices. A look is created with color, paper, quality, and font choice.

- The appearance of the business. Window displays are, in effect, advertisements for people passing by. Web site opening pages also create that "walk-by" impression.

- The location and hours of operation of the business.

- The interaction between customers and employees in person, on the phone, and over the Internet.

- The way the phone is answered.

- The way employees are dressed. Are they wearing trendy looks, reflective of the brand? Are they dressed conservatively or "unadorned," to become a backdrop or support the brand?

5.6 What is the image of the internship organization? Describe it in terms of the items in the previous list.

_____

_____

_____

Importance of a Company Image

Company image sets the stage for how receptive a target audience is to the company's messages. For service businesses, image takes on an even greater importance because the company's human resources are essentially the company's raw material—machinery, inventory, and product all rolled into one. An extreme example will help make this point. A wardrobe consultant who wears an outdated suit that does not fit properly to a meeting with a potential client will not create an image that projects fashion taste and knowledge, causing the client to think twice about working with this consultant.

Some people confuse reputation with company image. Reputation is only one component of an overall image. For example, a company may have a reputation for always delivering quality products on time; but company image also includes the quality of its presentation materials, advertising, and pricing, among other variables.

5.7 What is the reputation of the internship organization in the community? the region? the industry?

_____

_____

Company Image and Positioning

It is impossible to discuss the concept of a company image without including its relationship with both product and market positioning. Following are descriptions of each concept as it relates to image:

Product position—The attributes of a product that differentiate or position it among competing products. For example, Prada offers a premium product in the world of footwear. Its shoes are tailored with high-quality, rich materials and can demand a premium price. Prada is not, however, the only premium footwear resource. Therefore, its product position among premium shoes is less unique than its product position among all footwear alternatives.

Market position—The attributes of an entity (for example, a store, business, or person) that differentiate or position it among competing entities. For example, Wal-Mart offers thousands of products, each with its own product position. As an entity, however, Wal-Mart holds a market position among both discount retailers and department stores in general. Both product and market positions influence a company's image but are not the only components of it. Customer service, hiring practices, advertising, marketing materials, and many other factors combine to create an overall company image.

5.8 Describe the internship organization's image as it relates to the product line and market positioning.

_____

_____

Company Image and Marketing Communications

Company image can make marketing communications efforts more or less effective than they would be on their own. **Marketing communications** is an umbrella term referring to all the activities a business undertakes to "talk" to its target market, including printed marketing brochures and other marketing messages, advertising, sales promotions, publicity, and public relations. For example, if a local retailer has a long-established history of having low prices, and that is its competitive advantage, an advertising campaign focused on the quality of its products may not be as effective as the same type of campaign for a retailer with an established reputation for high-quality products. Company image and marketing communications are interdependent. This means that company image influences its marketing communications, which in turn influence company image. When a company uses its company image as the foundation for all marketing communications, it achieves consistency. Consistent messages reinforce each other. Creating messages consistent with the company image will:

- maximize marketing dollars;

- support sales and sell products;

- attract quality vendors, dealers, and employees (they have to be "sold" on the company, too);

- satisfy investors; and

- clear the way for new product introductions.

5.9 Describe the company image communicated by the internship organization through its marketing communications.

_____

_____

Creating a Company Image

A company image is an intangible item—you cannot touch it or feel it. However, it is as important, if not more so, as the raw materials and machinery that fashion uses to make tangible products. Established company images can be changed and shaped through planned, consistent marketing strategies. Creating a company image is similar to gardening. You can do nothing, and most likely something will grow, from flowers to weeds. Conversely, you can carefully plan and tend a garden to make any number of landscapes, such as a rock garden, a flower garden, or a water garden. Just as certain plants complement each other to create a pleasing whole, your marketing strategy, communications, and product and market positioning should work together to create the image desired.

5.10 Analyze the internship organization and its products and identify which are the same and which are different from those of key competition. With your internship supervisor's approval, you might survey customers to learn what image the company's target audience currently holds. (It is important to view the internship organization from the perspective of its customers and prospects, not yours.) If possible, find out what competitors and competitors' customers think about the internship organization. Based on the feedback you have gathered, develop a plan to change or to continue to support the company image through all its communication efforts.

_____

_____

_____

Image Variables

There are a number of variables to consider when establishing or changing a company image. The following list of variables was adapted from http://www.onlinewbc.gov/docs/market/mk_co_image.html:

- **Marketing communications**—Brochures, advertisements, product packages, and business cards should reflect a consistent image. For example, a children's party planning service might create materials that look fun and youthful by using bright colors and cheery images.

- **Pricing strategy**—A company may use the "cost-plus-profit" formula as the best method for setting prices for products and services; however, a desired company image has an impact here, too. Does the company want to be the price leader with the lowest price in town? Or, does it want to focus on exceptional customer service at a slightly higher price?

- **Sales strategy**—Gimmicky, high-energy sales pitches work well for some products or services but do not fit a sophisticated company's image, for example. Sales strategy and tactics should align with the company image.

- **Customer service**—Customer service policies, such as merchandise return policy, impact image. Nordstroms is famous for its "we'll take anything back" policy. Company legend tells of an employee that gave a customer a refund for returned auto tires—though Nordstrom does not sell tires. Through its policy, Nordstrom has created an image that it will do anything to please its customers. Customer service policies should be consistent with the desired image.

- **Publicity**—Are publicity efforts focused on publications that match the desired image? For example, the owner of a luxurious boutique would focus publicity efforts on magazines such as *Town and Country*, rather than publications appealing to bargain shoppers.

- **Promotions**—Promotional events in which the company participates should match its image. For example, if the company offers wedding planning services, it might sponsor or participate in a wedding gown fashion show.

5.11   Describe how the following image variables work together to create successfully or ineffectively a consistent image for the internship organization: marketing communications, pricing strategy, sales strategy, customer service, publicity, and promotions.

_____

_____

_____

The mission statement, goals, and objectives of an organization create its personality or image. Sometimes, conflicting images may result. For example, a manufacturer or retailer may believe the company is offering fashion-forward merchandise and excellent customer service. The consumer may perceive the merchandise as conservative and customer service as inadequate because of a lack of alterations or delivery. The community may view this business with high regard as it contributes generously to charities. It may be difficult for the organization's management to perceive objectively conflicting consumer and community perceptions.

5.12   Discuss the internship organization's personality or image as it is perceived by the people employed within the organization; consumer it serves (its target market); and people working in this industry—people employed by vendors and services used by the company.

_____

_____

_____

The Company Location

Every business owner has heard it: "The three most important keys to a successful business are location, location, and location." Location certainly can play a significant role in the success of a company, particularly for many retail stores.

The definition and significance of a business location have changed considerably with the advent of e-commerce and the growth of mail order sales. The definition of business location is no longer confined to the geographical position of the company's headquarters, manufacturing plants, or retail outlets. **Business location** refers to the physical site, the destinations to which catalogs are mailed, or the company's Web site and Internet links, whether the business is a manufacturing, service, or retail operation.

Before examining actual location factors, the company often prioritizes the qualities most necessary to the success of the business. For example, the company selling product lines through catalogs or online may need offices and shipping and warehouse space. In this case, the factors of visibility, competition, neighbor mix, and image will be less important to the company than choosing a storefront location where all the business's sales can take place. Location is a multifaceted factor in business planning. It has entirely different meanings to manufacturers, e-commerce and mail-order retailers, and product development firms.

In this section, location factors are first examined in terms of tangible buildings, such as "brick-and-mortar" stores, manufacturing facilities, and warehouses—from regional to state and city levels. Next, the decisions the company makes in terms of a physical site for the business are explored. Location and visibility on the Internet are explored in Chapter 8. The location decisions for many fashion businesses begin with the geographic location of the company's headquarters.

The Region

A preliminary decision for business location is where to position the physical site of the company headquarters, facilities, and retail outlets, if applicable. Choosing a location is essentially a matter of selecting the place that best serves the needs of the business's target market. For some companies, the general location for the business is limited to the area where the company's owner chooses to live. Conversely, the location selection may begin with a broad regional search that is systematically narrowed down to a state, then a city, followed by a specific site.

5.13   Where is the internship organization located? Where are its headquarters, manufacturing facilities, and branch operations?

_____

_____

_____

_____

5.14 Were the sites of the business's operations selected according to convenience (e.g., the owner's residential city) or through research?

_____

_____

_____

_____

An important characteristic in selecting a location is evidence of a significant population that fits the business's target market. Rising disposable incomes and a stable economic environment are also preferred qualities. Access to suppliers, low operating costs, and an adequate and affordable labor pool are other preferable factors. In addition, a low level of competition from similar businesses in the region is important. In some cases, climate will impact the choice of location.

5.15 In terms of the regional location variables discussed previously, as well as others you identify, what are the key factors that impact location choices for the internship operation?

_____

_____

_____

_____

The State
After the company zones in on a region, the next step is to select a state. Every state has a business development office that recruits new businesses to that state. Although the offices providing this information will try to make this location look good, they are also excellent sources of demographic, political, and economic facts that can be assessed objectively. Some of the key issues the company examines are state laws, regulations, taxes, and any incentives or investment credits that the state offers to businesses locating there. The prospective workforce is also evaluated in terms of the quantity and quality of the labor supply, wage rates, and the union or nonunion bias of the state. Proximity to suppliers, such as apparel, gift, or home furnishing market centers, as well as sales representatives for merchandise lines, is a critical factor. Finally, the company evaluates the general business climate of the state.

5.16 Was the state in which the headquarters of the internship organization is located specifically selected? If so, what resources were used to research a preferred location?

_____

_____

_____

5.17 If the internship organization has numerous locations, describe why and how these additional sites were selected. Be sure to specify where the additional sites are located.

_____

_____

_____

The City

The assessment of a city as a location candidate for a company begins by analyzing the population in terms of its demographics. These include growth trends, family size, education, age breakdowns, gender proportions, income levels, job categories, religion, race, nationality, and population density. **Population density** refers to the number of people per square mile in a given area. It is an important characteristic to the success of businesses that rely on high-traffic volume.

Another factor that is assessed when selecting a city for a business location is competition: the number and locations of competing firms; competitors' offerings in terms of quality, price, and selection; and the success and failure rates of competitors within the city. Studying the size of the market for the business's products and services, as it relates to the number and types of competitors, helps determine whether the company can capture a market share large enough to earn a profit.

5.18 Describe the city in which the largest site of the internship organization is located. Discuss the population density and level of competition in the city.

_____

_____

_____

The Site

For some fashion businesses, the site of the company's facility is important. A home furnishings retailer, a residential design firm, and a vintage clothing store are examples of business types for which the facility may be best located in one of five basic site areas: the central business district, neighborhoods, shopping centers and malls, outlying areas, and at home. The **central business district** is the historical center of town—the area where downtown businesses were established early in the development of the city. **Neighborhoods** are locations in which residential areas are heavily concentrated. **Shopping centers** are centers and malls that provide the customer with "one-stop" shopping. They are classified as follows: neighborhood shopping centers, community shopping centers, regional shopping malls, and power centers. A **power center** is an area that combines the drawing potential of a large regional mall with the convenience of a neighborhood shopping center. Anchored by large specialty or department store retailers, these centers frequently target affluent baby boomers who desire selection and convenience. Although they still account for the majority of retail sales in apparel and soft goods, malls have declined in popularity over roughly the past two decades. "Sameness" and "staleness" are two of the adjectives used by shoppers to describe the reasons for this downslide.

Other fashion businesses may not require a site with customer traffic. A production plant, a freelance design firm, the product development division of a corporation, or a theatrical costume company, for example, may decide that the best site is distant from shopping areas. Lower costs, more space, greater accessibility, and fewer zoning restrictions may make the less visible site more appealing.

Figure 5.3 Through his Comme des Garçons store, the designer Rei Kawakubo pioneered the first shopping outpost in the Chelsea section of New York City, following an influx of art galleries into the then run-down industrial area.

5.19 Describe the location site of the internship organization as it relates to the terms above. You may not be interning for a fashion retailer. Think about a Web retailer in terms of an Internet community or a fashion magazine in terms of the firm's headquarters, the publishing house, and the locations where most of its magazines are actually sold.

_____

_____

_____

·⊰[BOX 5.5]⊱·

Choosing the Best Business Location

Too many would-be entrepreneurs become so excited about launching their new business ventures that they fail to invest the necessary time in finding the right location. But as your company's image and its location are closely tied, finding the right place to set up shop can be critical to your success. If you are in retail (product or service), think about the location of the business from your customers' point of view. For example, a large retail space in an industrial area may be affordable, but may not attract enough business. On the other hand, if your business involves manufacturing, wholesaling, or selling strictly over the Internet, then selecting a location will not hinge on customers visiting your business.

Here are some tips to make choosing the best location for your business a little easier:

- **Know your business.** Understanding the needs of your business is the first step in finding a location. Will customers visit your location? Do you anticipate walk-in business, or will customers call for appointments? Does your business make use of natural resources? How are your goods delivered? Does your business involve chemicals or excessive noise that might fall under zoning restrictions? Make a list of your business-specific needs.

- **Find your customers.** You need to identify who your customers are and how you can best meet their needs. If you are moving a business operation into a new city or rural area, find out as much as possible about population trends there. The U.S. Census Bureau provides plenty of helpful data on population trends and statistics. You can also contact local and state agencies for their input. When you have gathered as much information as possible, start creating your own demographic profile. Once you know who you're trying to reach, you can determine where you're more likely to find customers. For example, if you're opening an after-school center, you'll want to open it in an area that not only has many families but also has a high number of two-income households. Good research will help you find such a location.

- **Get a flavor of the community.** Before deciding to set up shop somewhere, investigate the community. Read some of the local newspapers. Visit the library and do some research on the history of the place. Speak with other small business owners in the area. Ask them if their business is succeeding and if they think your business would do well there. Try to find out how receptive the established business community is to new businesses that come to town.

- **Scope out the competition.** For some businesses, this may not matter. Five Internet businesses could be in the same building and nobody would ever know it. However, if you're opening a retail business, a restaurant, or a service-oriented operation, you'll want to know how many similar businesses are located nearby. Some communities feature areas with several similar businesses, such as the diamond district in New York City, with dozens of jewelry stores on one particular block. In other cities and towns, you may not want any competitors in the immediate area. The key is to determine whether you can gain enough of a market share. Do a competitive analysis, and if you scope out competitors,

see if you can gain a competitive edge by offering something your competition does not. If you're moving into an area with stiff competition, make sure you have enough resources to hang in there while you make a name for yourself.

- **Consider traffic and accessibility.** These factors will be more important to some businesses than to others. If your business does not have customers driving to your location, then traffic and accessibility are an issue only for your employees. But parking, foot traffic, automobile traffic, and sidewalk accessibility are all important things to consider.

- **Assess the building.** Before signing any kind of lease or purchasing agreement, ask yourself some important questions about the condition of the space you're considering. How old is the building? How old is the roof? Is everything up to code? Has the electrical system been improved lately? Can it handle your technological needs?

- **Balance cost with other factors.** Obviously, the cost of the location is important to consider, but be sure to look at the big picture as well. For example, no matter how attractive the price of a site might be, if your customers can't get there easily, or if the infrastructure can't support the necessary wiring for your Internet company, your business probably won't last very long. Spending more on a good location will probably pay off in the long run with lots of business.

Source: AllBusiness.com, Inc., 1999–2009.

The Customer's View of Location

Think about the location of the business from your customers' point of view, keeping image in mind. Is the location easy to access? What is the aesthetic appeal of the exterior? Does the interior of the building allow for the necessary elements of the business (e.g., interior displays, dressing rooms, restrooms, inventory receiving and storage, offices)? If the type of business and its target market are high-end and exclusive, the location should match. In contrast, if, for example, the company sells fraternity and sorority T-shirts to a university clientele, then a less expensive location adjacent to the campus may be a prime location. The location must be affordable. The cost of the location, whether a purchase or a rental, is obviously important to consider; however, the big picture is more significant. For example, no matter how attractive the price of a location is, if customers cannot get there easily, the business is in trouble from the start. Before signing any kind of lease or purchasing agreement, there are important questions to ask about the condition of the space being considered, the age of the facility and its components (e.g., the roof, the heating and air conditioning units, the electrical system). Bring in an inspector to learn if everything is up to code and if the building can handle the technological needs of the business.

If you are opening a retail business, you need to know how many similar businesses are located nearby, as well as how many new businesses are planning to open in the area. Some cities feature areas with many similar businesses, such as Rodeo Drive in Los Angeles, with dozens of fashion specialty boutiques in a few particular blocks. The question to ask is, "Can my business gain enough of a market share to generate the planned profit?" Complete an analysis of competitors to see if the business can gain a competitive edge by offering something your competition does not. If locating in an area with stiff competition, new business owners must have enough resources to survive while making a name for themselves.

Think about traffic and accessibility from the customer's viewpoint. Think about parking, foot traffic, automobile traffic, sidewalk accessibility, weatherproofing, and the mix of businesses in the area. Observe the customer traffic on various week and weekend days and evenings, noting which retailers' bags the customers are carrying.

Identifying the right location requires research, patience, and a multitude of decisions. It is one of the most significant factors related to a company's success.

5.20 Using the information in the previous box section, "Choosing the Best Business Location," analyze how effectively the internship firm's most recent location reflects, or does not reflect, these location tips.

_____

_____

_____

Location Checklist

There are a number of questions companies answer and prioritize when determining a location for the business. If the company is headquartered in a location separate from other parts of the business, then the following questions are answered and weighed for each site:

Target market—Is this location easily accessible by the prospective company's specified target market? Does this location meet the needs and desires of the target market?

Lifestyle preferences—Does the area fit the business's needs and the personal preferences of the company's owner and employees?

Image—Is the image of this location appropriate for the prospective business and its target market?

Compatibility with the community—Does the business's image fit with the character of the place and the needs and wants of its residents?

Neighbor mix—Is the assortment of neighboring businesses appropriate for the company and its target market?

Proximity to suppliers—Are markets accessible and shipping alternatives readily available?

Transportation networks—Are transportation alternatives available and cost-effective for both the company's consumers and suppliers?

Competition—Where are the direct and indirect competitors located in relationship to this location and the company?

Security/safety—Is the location secure for employees, customers, inventory, and facilities?

Labor pool—Is there an adequate number of qualified people available for employment near the business area? What are wage rates in the area?

Restrictions—Are there any city or county laws governing business sites that will impact this location?

Business climate—What is the overall attitude of customers, residents, and government officials toward this type of business? Are there any "blue laws" that prohibit business on Sundays? Are small business support programs, financial assistance, or incentives offered to businesses?

Services—Are services required for the company to make it accessible and affordable in this location?

Ownership—Is it more cost-effective to purchase or lease in this location? Is ownership an option?

Past tenants—Who were the past tenants in this location? What types of businesses were these? Why did they leave? Where did they go?

Space—Is the space adequate in this location? Is there room for growth?

History of the property—What is the history of this location in terms of past ownership and businesses?

Physical visibility—Is the location visible to the target market? Is visibility necessary to the success of the business?

Life-cycle stage of the area—What is the "age stage" of this area: emerging, growing, peaking, or declining?

Expenses—Will costs for this location fit within the company's budget?

Using Table 5.1, assess the site of the internship organization, and then answer questions 5.21 and 5.22.

Table 5.1
FACTORS TO CONSIDER WHEN SELECTING A SITE
Site:
Ranking scale: Least Preferable (1)　　Most Preferable (4)

Factor	Rank
Building exterior	—
Building interior (office and work areas, selling space, storage, traffic flow, parking)	—
Property taxes	—
Zoning	—
Maintenance needs and costs	—
Utilities needs and costs	—
Insurance requirements	—
Advertising and promotional expenses	—
Security	—
Signage	—
Parking	—
Vehicle traffic and speed limit	—
Image of nearby businesses	—
Proximity to customers	—
Proximity to suppliers	—
Area demographics	—
Population of trading area	—
Customer traffic	—
Economic conditions	—
Property investment potential	—
Costs of renovating facility	—

5.21 Did the internship organization build, buy, or lease a site for the business?

_____

_____

_____

5.22 Which factors were the most important? the least important?

_____

_____

_____

Designing Effective Fashion Spaces—Retail, Service, Publication, and Interior Design

The look of its exterior and interior clearly affects the success of a fashion business. Whether it is a manufacturer's showroom, an interior designer's office space, a fashion publisher's conference room, or a retail apparel store, clients develop opinions of a business even before they enter. They make assumptions about the image, price range, quality, and exclusivity of the product (whether tangible or service) inside the space simply by looking at its outside. The following attributes of a facility influence the opinions that customers form about it even before they enter it: exterior design, signs (e.g., logo and name), approach, and display windows.

The Exterior of the Facility

The expectation level of the customer is established outside the facility. Think about attending a party and seeing someone for the first time. As you walk toward this person and make eye contact, your opinion is quickly established even before words are exchanged. After you get to know a new acquaintance, initial opinions certainly may change but this takes some time. It is the same for a business operation. If the potential customers do not like the look of a business from the outside, they may never go inside to get to know the company better. The exterior should reflect the personality of the business, similar to the way clothing expresses the personality of its wearer.

The design of the exterior

The architecture of shopping malls has neutralized the impact of individual store architecture. Even when successful fashion stores are clustered in spaces as beautiful as London's Burlington Arcade or as unique as Les Halles in Paris, few shoppers remember the individual store's facade. Downtown businesses, outlets in strip centers, and freestanding factories have the opportunity to use exterior design as a tool to create a unique image. As customers approach a facility, effective architecture in terms of the surrounding environment can generate a powerful first impression. Physical fronts of facilities can represent attitude, price perception, value, and the target market through a combination of architecture, location, and signage. Urban Outfitters, Harrods, and Banana Republic are just a few examples of businesses that use these tools to project their images.

5.23   Describe the design of the exterior of the internship organization. Is the design how you believe it should be? If so, why? If not, what changes would you make?

_____

_____

_____

Logos and signs

Today, in place of eye-catching facades, the exterior image of a business is often communicated primarily by the name and design of its logo. There are some interesting messages that may be communicated to customers through signs—or their absence. Some designer companies, for example, have no significant signs, except for plaques at the entry. These exclusive businesses allow the building itself to communicate the company's image. In addition, they are sending the subliminal message that the smaller the sign, the more exclusive and higher priced the merchandise. Most department stores in downtown locations have their names on marquees or in large illuminated letters on the facade. Freestanding factories more often use a logo or graphic and name combination. Each variation creates a different perception of image and, subsequently, price.

5.24   Describe the exterior signage used by the internship organization. What is your assessment of the external signage choices?

_____

_____

_____

Approach

As customers approach the business, even before they walk up to the receptionist, speak to a company representative, or see the product line, they become aware of automobiles in the parking areas and the grounds and common areas as well as people moving to and from the entry. Through these variables, the customer quickly develops a perception about the location. For example, an image of prestige may turn to concern about safety when panhandlers are seen begging or security persons are walking the grounds. The clothing and carriage of fellow consumers tell specific stories in areas such as exclusivity, price expectation, and fashion leadership.

5.25 Describe the approach to the facility of the internship organization.

_____

_____

_____

Windows

The last piece of visual stimuli communicated to the customer before entry is the window. It is here that the balance of the final prejudgment is made. The visual experience before entering carries the most weight in the consumer's mind. Windows must have an overall consistency with the merchandise of the business. The size and number of windows should correlate with the

Figure 5.5 Designed by the American architect Peter Marino, the 10-story Chanel boutique is located on the elite Chuo-dori Avenue in Tokyo, Japan. The glass facade is embedded with 700,000 light-emitting diodes. The first of its kind, the facade of the building becomes a giant screen displaying custom-designed animations at night.

type of merchandise sold by the retail operation. Think of Bloomingdale's and how it projects a fashion-forward and creative image through the large display windows that surround the building. Compare this vision with that of Tiffany's, whose exterior features small windows at eye level: tertiary windows designed to present beautiful jewelry. Consider the large display windows in many of the showrooms located in a trade mart. How many buyers stop to review a sales rep's lines after being tempted by an attractive window?

5.26　Describe the exterior windows of the internship location.

_____

_____

_____

The Interior of the Facility

The goal of a fashion business planning its location space depends on the type of business. For many fashion firms, the goal is to create an environment that will entice the customer to buy. The size and layout of the facility, the colors of the decor, the displays, the fixtures and mannequins, the lighting, and even the placement and look of the cash desk come together to create the visual environment that can make or break a business (Figure 5.6). To the manufacturer, the goals of planning interior space are to maximize productivity, to ensure the safety of its workers, and to expedite the making of the product.

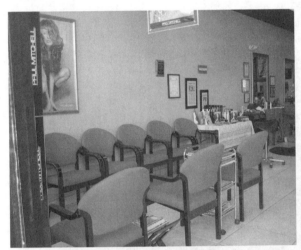

Figure 5.6 The SmartFixtures salon transformed its facility to make it more open and visually appealing.

The size of the product area

For the purposes of this text, we will talk about space in terms of the area allocated to the company's product (Figure 5.7). For example, if the internship business is a manufacturer, space would be designated for producing, storing, and shipping the product line. If you are interning with a magazine publication, space would be dedicated to editorial offices, conference venues, and sample

Figure 5.7 It is important to keep the company's product in a designated area.

⸱⸱ᢀ[THE FASHION INTERN]ᢀ⸱⸱

rooms. In this case, the product is the publication and all it takes is to put it in the consumers' hands. When retail customers see a spacious department, they often think of higher prices and exclusivity, as well as excellent customer service. A planned balance of merchandise, display, and wide aisles helps to project a desired image and to maximize sales.

5.27 Describe and define in square footage the product space allocated by the internship organization.

_____

_____

_____

Layout

Layout is the arrangement of the facilities in a business. The ideal layout contributes to efficient operations, increased productivity, and higher sales. **Retail layout** is the arrangement and method of display of merchandise in an operation that the consumer visits, such as an apparel store, a manufacturer's showroom, or a textile supplier (Figures 5.8 and 5.9). A business's success depends, in part, on a well-designed floor plan. A retail layout should pull customers into the business and make it easy for them to locate merchandise; compare price, quality, and features; try on the merchandise, if applicable; and, ultimately, make a purchase. Moreover, the floor plan should lead clients past displays of other items they may buy on impulse.

The effective layout of a manufacturing operation, however, should maximize productivity, minimize wasted space and employee time, and streamline the manufacturing process—all with the employees' safety in mind.

Space value refers to the value of each square foot of space in a retail store in terms of its generating sales revenue. Typically, the farther away an area is from the entrance, the lower its value. Space values also decrease as distance from the main entry-level floor increases. Selling areas on the main level and near the entrance are referred to as prime selling space. They contribute a greater portion to sales than do those on other floors because they offer greater exposure to customers than either basement or higher-level locations. Some businesses, however, work to offset lower space values through the layout placement of successful departments. For example, if a retail operation specializing in floor coverings is known for its unique imported tile selection, the tile department may be situated in the back of the facility on a platform level. This way, customers can see the tile selection upon entering the store, yet must walk through the other departments to get there. If customers come into the business for specific products and have a tendency to walk directly to those products, it also benefits retailers to place complementary products in their path. In essence, customers are tempted by seeing more merchandise to make more purchases.

Figure 5.8 A signature retail layout: Urban Outfitters store interior.

Figure 5.9 A grid retail layout: Wal-Mart Supercenter, in Beijing.

··⌘[THE FASHION INTERN]⌘··

Effective layout in business emerges from in-depth knowledge by the company of the target customers' buying habits. In a retail store, observing customer behavior can help identify the "hot spots" where merchandise sells quickly and the "cold spots" where it may sit indefinitely. A plotted pattern that is created from observing the movements of random samples of shoppers in the store is called a **tracking plan.** The tracking plan charts the flow of customer traffic and the places where customers tend to touch merchandise, pick it up, and buy it, as indicated on a floor plan of the store. The tracking plan is used as a reference when thinking about the design of new spaces as well as adjusting stock content by area. It is an excellent and inexpensive method used to maximize the sales potential of floor space.

5.28 If the internship organization is a retail business or wholesale showroom, indicate how the physical layout maximizes space values. Has a tracking plan been developed?

_____

_____

_____

5.29 If the internship company is a publisher or e-tailer, describe how space values are used in terms of, for example, the opening page of a Web site or the back cover of a magazine.

_____

_____

_____

Layout plans

Some fashion businesses have generated significant increases in sales by intentionally directing customer traffic patterns. These businesses use the placement of a department or the design of aisles within the operation to increase the customers' exposure to the merchandise assortment. A business may create a circular traffic pattern that requires the customer to walk around the business from entrance to exit. Another traffic pattern designed to make the customer circulate throughout the operation is formatted similar to a bicycle wheel with aisles, like spokes, attached to the circle or outer rim. In either case, the customer must pass through a number of departments before leaving the business.

Fashion organizations often use the following three basic layout patterns: the boutique, the free-form, and the grid (Figure 5.10).

Figure 5.10 Diagram of layouts for retail businesses.

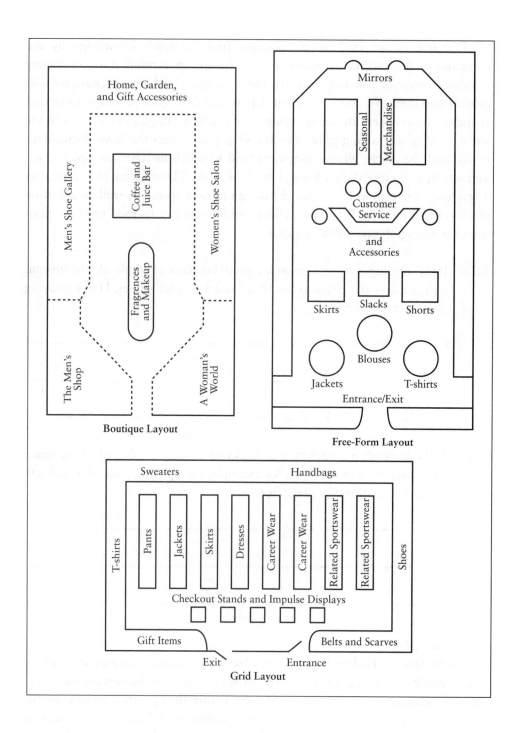

Boutique Layout

Free-Form Layout

Grid Layout

Boutique layout—Divides the business into individual shopping areas, each with its own theme. This allows the company the freedom to create new departments based on seasonal merchandise trends, featured designers, and customer lifestyles.

Free-form layout—Displays of varying shapes and sizes are arranged in a random fashion. The resulting image is relaxed and friendly and has been shown to increase the number of impulse purchases customers make.

Grid layout—Displays are arranged in a rectangular fashion so that the aisles are parallel. This creates a formal and organized environment especially appropriate for self-service operations.

5.30 Sketch and describe the layout of the interior of the business location of the internship organization. Identify the fixtures and furnishings. Name the type of layout, if applicable.

_____

_____

_____

Interior display elements

The customer's eye focuses on displays, as they tell the customer the type of merchandise the business sells. Merchandise displays are often referred to as "silent sales associates" because they market products and impact sales. There are a number of ground rules upon which visual merchandisers base their decisions. First, it is easier for the customer to focus on one display, rather than on a rack or shelf of merchandise. Second, open fixtures of merchandise can surround the focal display, creating an attractive and merchandise-specific selling area. Third, retailers can boost sales by displaying items that complement each other. For example, men's ties may be displayed near dress shirts to encourage multiple sales. Fourth, spacious displays provide shoppers with a better view of the merchandise, generate an expansive image, and reduce the likelihood of shoplifting. Finally, company owners must remember to separate the selling and nonselling spaces of a store (see Figures 5.11 and 5.12). Prime selling space (e.g., product displays, client meeting rooms, showroom floors, presentation rooms) should not be wasted on nonselling functions, such as storage, office, or receiving operations.

5.31 Describe the interior display elements of the internship organization. If applicable, indicate these elements on the layout diagram in Figure 5.10.

_____

_____

_____

Figure 5.11 Diane von Furstenberg's New York City flagship store and showroom.

Figure 5.12 The designer Yeohlee in her studio and showroom.

Lighting

Effective lighting has two main purposes. First, it enhances the merchandise selection. Second, it allows employees to work at maximum efficiency. A jewelry store retailer, for example, has lighting needs specific to its repair department, as well as lighting needs associated with its display cases. Proper lighting is evaluated by what is ideal for the job being done. Lighting is often an inexpensive investment, considering its impact on the overall appearance and operation of the business. Just as layout, color, and the other interior characteristics generate an image for a business, lighting, too, contributes to a business's image. A dimly lit business place conveys an image of untrustworthiness. An effective combination of natural and artificial light can give a business an open and cheerful appearance.

5.32 Describe and evaluate the lighting choices made by the internship organization.

_____

_____

_____

Fitting rooms

For an apparel store, the fitting rooms play a significant role in the sale of merchandise. Fitting rooms are usually regarded as nonselling space and, subsequently, are often pushed to a small, dark corner in the back of the store. Fitting rooms, however, are often the place where customers actually make their buying decisions. The effective fitting room is spacious, well lit, clean, convenient, and pilfer proof. There should be adequate places for hanging the merchandise. Mirrors should provide an accurate image and be accessible to the customer. Three-way mirrors that provide a back and front view of the customer may be intentionally positioned outside but adjacent to the fitting rooms. This placement encourages the customer to come out of the dressing room, wearing the garment in which she or he is interested. When the customer exits the fitting room to take a look in the mirror, the salesperson has the opportunity to assist with alterations, accessories, or alternative merchandise. The space should be comfortable, yet the retailer must minimize the opportunity for shoplifting in the fitting room. For example, tables with floor-length cloths or overstuffed chairs provide places for shoplifters to hide hangers. The location of a fitting room is also important. It should be situated away from exits and near sales personnel to assure privacy and service for the customer, without compromising merchandise security.

5.33 If the internship organization is a service or retail operation that provides fitting rooms, describe them. If applicable, suggest ways to improve the fitting rooms in terms of merchandise security and customer service.

_____

_____

_____

Checkout area

The checkout area, or cash/wrap desk, should be strategically located so that it is visible to the customer from all vantage points. Also, the checkout area can serve as a security point when it is placed near the entrance or exit. The area should be clearly identified, organized, and well lit. It should be outfitted with all the equipment and materials needed to smoothly process the sale. For example, the computer terminal, cash drawer, and telephone should be installed at the checkout area, in addition to materials such as tissue paper, bags, and credit card supplies.

5.34 Describe the checkout area of the internship operation, if you are interning with a retailer.

_____

_____

_____

5.35 Describe the reception area if you are interning for a manufacturer, museum, magazine, design house, or similar nonretail company.

_____

_____

_____

5.36 Describe the opening page of the Web site if you are interning in the e-commerce sector of the fashion industry.

_____

_____

_____

5.37 How is the company's image projected through this sublocation of the business?

_____

_____

_____

Mission Impossible?

Aiden is a junior in college majoring in fashion design. He has secured an internship position with a sportswear manufacturer in Quebec, Canada. Aiden is thrilled to receive on-the-job training as an assistant to the designer, as well as the opportunity to earn an income provided by the internship's summer salary. Because he is earning college credit for the internship as part of his degree program requirements, he is required to complete an internship workbook. To fill out the workbook, he will have to analyze the total company and document his work responsibilities as an intern.

A section of the workbook requires Aiden to inquire about the firm's mission statement. He schedules an appointment to meet with the sportswear company's owner, Jay Smith, to discuss this topic. Much to his surprise, Mr. Smith informs Aiden that the company executives have never formulated a mission statement. "However," he continues, "this is the perfect time to develop a mission statement and it is an ideal project for you." Aiden is hesitant and a little overwhelmed by the challenge, but agrees to develop a mission statement proposal by the end of the following week for Mr. Smith's review.

Aiden begins by analyzing the criteria that provide the foundation for a mission statement:

1. A description of the existing business

2. An analysis of the customer

3. The customer's perception of value

4. An understanding of potential business opportunities

With Mr. Smith's authorization, Aiden meets with the company's designers, its operations manager, a few of the sales representatives, and several buyers of the company's key retail accounts. His goal is to collect their views of the business and its ultimate customer, the person who actually wears the line.

Based on these interviews, Aiden determines that all parties agree on just one factor: they concur that the company produces active sportswear for male and female amateur and professional athletes who primarily participate in running, aerobics, and cycling. Aiden is perplexed by the variety of opinions he gathers from the different constituencies of the sportswear firm. It seems that each person he asks has a unique perspective on the company's product line and target market. The sales representatives indicate that the company's customer is more interested in quality, durability, and comfort than in fashion trends. The designers state that forward styling, color selection, and fit are most important to the company's clientele. The retail buyers have yet another view of the ultimate consumer—they believe that price is the most significant reason customers buy the line. Although quality and fashion-forward styling are important to the buyers, they like that the retail prices of the line are equivalent to or just below the prices of competitive lines.

As Aiden begins to draft a mission statement for Mr. Smith, he believes he has gathered more questions than answers.

1. Develop a mission statement that reflects the information Aiden has collected and that addresses the criteria necessary to formulate a mission statement.

2. What additional sources can provide information needed to construct an accurate mission statement for the company? What additional information is needed?

Market Repositioning

Lily's is a specialty store in Atlanta, Georgia, that carries bridal wear and special occasion apparel for women. The retail operation is located in a section of town that is undergoing dramatic changes. The neighborhood has recently been rehabilitated primarily through two sources of funding: (1) city funds designated to renovate its historic buildings and (2) the investments of local contractors interested in developing a new, fashionable residential area. Old brownstone structures have been converted to elegant townhouses, and storefronts have been restored to reflect the illustrious historical past of the locale.

As a result of the physical and economic improvements in the area, a new residential population has emerged. Young, single executives and career couples are relocating to this part of the city, bringing with them a higher expendable income than that of past consumers. Previously, the area attracted low-income customers from the heart of the city and had little consumer traffic from the more prosperous residents living outside of the close proximity of the city. Now, there is a "live-in" clientele with money to spend. The merchants are thrilled with the changes taking place in their neighborhood shopping district.

In the past, the owner of Lily's, Joyce Gillespie, has been very concerned with the pricing of the merchandise carried by the store. Because the previous customers were extremely cost conscious, Joyce located goods from budget to mid-priced special occasion and bridal wear vendors. She often purchased off-price and close-out goods to provide her customers with the type of merchandise they were seeking at affordable prices. Presently she is rethinking her merchandise assortment because she believes that this is the ideal time to trade up, to carry a higher-quality, higher-priced product mix. She could offer more exclusive styles and more personalized services. However, Joyce is concerned that it may take some time to attract the new, more affluent clientele. She worries that she should not totally alienate her current customer base.

Trading up her merchandise assortment will require a huge amount of changes. Joyce anticipates that the store will need some remodeling and that she will need to locate new vendors that carry a higher level of bridal and special occasion goods. Joyce also determines that she will have to reevaluate her promotional plans, focusing on style and selection rather than price. She will need to identify the advertising and promotional vehicles that will most effectively reach the new clientele. As she studies all of the challenges involved with changing her previously successful business, Joyce questions whether she should maintain her existing operation, rather than reacting to the recent changes in her shopping area.

If you were the owner of Lily's, would you maintain your business as it has operated successfully since its start-up?

If not, what would you do to adapt to the changing environment in your business area?

CHAPTER SIX

 # The Nature of the Organization

Objectives

- To classify the legal form of ownership of the internship organization

- To examine the type of organization the internship represents

- To categorize the products, nonstore selling, and types of services offered by the internship organization

- To identify the departments classified by function, within the internship company: operations, merchandising and management, human resources, marketing, research and development, and production

- To understand the communication channels of a business

What Is the Nature of the Organization?

In subsequent sections, each of the eight classifications of organizations will be discussed. The intern should be able to describe the internship organization as it relates to each classification system. All organizations in the fashion industry can be categorized by the following:

1. Legal form of ownership

2. Type of organization

3. Product offerings

4. Extent of nonstore selling

5. Types of services offered

6. Departments by function

7. Organizational structure

8. Communication channels

It is important to note that some classifications may overlap. For example, the intern at JCPenney may identify the company as a department store chain that also operates a mail order catalog business and is corporately owned. Similarly, Lands' End is a direct merchant of traditionally styled clothing for the family, soft luggage, and products for the home. What is a direct merchant? A **direct merchant** works directly with fabric mills and manufacturers, eliminating the markups of middlemen. The direct merchant can pass the savings on to customers, who shop directly with them from home or office or order by phone, mail, fax, or the Internet. Direct merchants ship purchases to their customers, which often makes shopping simpler, faster, and more convenient. Lands' End can be classified as a direct merchant, an Internet retailer, a factory outlet operator, *and* a catalog operation. In addition to its primary catalog, *Lands' End,* the company publishes catalogs for women's plus sizes; menswear; children's wear, from newborn to preteen; school uniforms; the home; and business outfitters (corporate sales).

Legal Form of Ownership

A business may be classified under three types of legal ownership: sole proprietorship, partnership, or corporation. In a **sole proprietorship,** one person owns a business and assumes personal responsibility for its debts. In a **partnership,** two or more people invest their time and money in a business and maintain liability for its debts. As specified in the partnership contract, the partners agree on how the business is to be operated, the amount of time each partner will devote to it, and how profits and losses will be shared. In addition, the partners

Figure 6.1 The fashion designer Ralph Lauren and Roger Farah, the president and CEO of Polo Ralph Lauren Corporation, at the Polo headquarters in New York City.

determine what will happen if one of them decides to leave the business. Within a **corporation,** stockholders invest in a business, but do not necessarily share in management decisions. Major decisions are made by a board of directors, whereas daily operations are conducted by executives and employees of the organization. Stockholders have limited personal responsibility for the firm's debts, as determined by the amount of their investments.

6.1   Describe the internship organization's legal form of ownership. Indicate the legal name of the firm, its location (including headquarters and branch divisions), and its auxiliary divisions, if applicable.

_____

_____

Types of Organization

Organization of businesses may take several forms. The terminology describes much about the business: a global chain may be under ownership of a group; a sole proprietor may operate a department store; a corporation may operate several design and manufacturing divisions. Knowing the industry language opens the door to truly understanding companies in the fashion world. Organizations may be classified as follows:

- **Global, national, regional, or local**—Where company headquarters, branches, factories, offices, and so on, are located.

- **Chain operation**—Multiple outlets operating under common ownership. The major functions of the business are often controlled by a central headquarters.

- **Ownership group**—A parent corporation that owns divisions of a business.

- **Factory outlet**—A manufacturer choosing to operate its own businesses, eliminating middlemen, and maintaining absolute control of the distribution process. For example, manufacturers may own and operate retail stores selling their discounted merchandise such as those run by Coach and Polo Ralph Lauren.

- **Single unit**—A business that has one outlet, often owner-managed. Boutiques ("little shops," as translated from French) are examples of very specialized single-unit operations. They focus on a particular merchandise classification, often carrying a unique selection of goods.

- **Leased departments**—Arrangement in which a company rents space to another company for a rental fee or a percentage of the lessee's sales or both.

- **Franchise**—A manufacturer, wholesaler, or service company that sells a smaller firm or individual the right to conduct a business in a specified manner within a certain period of time. The franchisee uses the franchise organization's name, logo, advertising, merchandise sources, and methods of operation in exchange for a fee or a percent of sales, or both.

- **Consumer cooperative association**—An operation in which the actual consumers own shares. These consumer-owners determine business policies, but actual operations are conducted by a manager and employees.

- **Department store**—A retailing business that features hard lines, such as home furnishings and electronics, and soft lines, such as apparel and accessories. Department stores usually employ 25 or more workers. Department stores with several units can also be classified as chains. A department store may carry higher-end goods, budget merchandise, discount inventory, or a combination of these.

- **Discount and off-price**—Firms that sell merchandise at below-market prices. Many emphasize self-service to reduce overhead and, subsequently, maintain lower prices.

- **Specialty**—Retailers or manufacturers that sell or produce a specific classification of merchandise. They are also called limited-line companies.

6.2 Describe the type of organization represented by the internship company using the classifications listed in this section.

_____

_____

Product Offerings

Type of goods offered refers to the organization's product, whether it be an object, a service, an activity, or an idea. Product classifications, branding, packaging, and labeling are different variables that must be considered when analyzing the product. These criteria are examined in Chapters 7 and 9.

Extent of Nonstore Selling

Nonstore selling methods refer to those retailing activities that do not require a physical facility yet are viable components that contribute to the productivity of the organization. For example, the owner of a lingerie boutique may develop a party plan for presenting the company's merchandise in the consumer's home. A specialty store may produce a catalog to mail to current and prospective customers. Nonstore selling methods are categorized as follows:

- Direct selling
- Party plans
- Mail-order retailing
- Telephone selling
- Internet selling
- Television selling

The Home Shopping Network illustrates nonstore selling via television. The Internet provides new opportunities for nonstore selling by retailers and manufacturers in nearly all product categories.

6.3   Describe the nonstore selling techniques used by the internship organization. If none have been implemented, and it is not a nonstore business, such as an e-retailer, explain why nonstore selling techniques are not applicable, or suggest types of nonstore selling that may improve the profitability of the internship organization.

_____

_____

Types of Services

Some organizations sell a service rather than tangible goods. Typical services sold include the following:

- Public relations

- Rentals (e.g., visual merchandising furnishings, props)

- Repairs (e.g., alterations)

- Custom work (e.g., one-of-a-kind apparel)

- Personal services (e.g., wardrobe consultation, special events coordination, wedding planning)

Formal attire and costume rental, custom sewing, and fashion show production are examples of services sold by fashion industry firms. Whereas some businesses are totally service oriented (e.g., a resident buying office), others may provide some services for a fee (e.g., alterations).

6.4   Describe the range of services sold by the internship organization. If no services are offered by the organization, explain why they are not applicable, or suggest services that may increase profits.

_____

_____

Departments by Function

Most specialty and department stores are organized according to primary business functions. Many apparel manufacturers, fashion forecasting services, magazines, and other fashion businesses are organized in a similar manner. Figure 6.2 illustrates the departmentalization of a company by function. Functions in

Figure 6.2
Departmentalization of a
company by function.

Operations
Maintenance, security, shipping supplies, and delivery services

Finance and Accounting
Control of expenses, income, and revenue, information
technology systems, and credit

Merchandising and Management
Buying, pricing, and selling of goods
Merchandise planning and control
Customer service

Human Resources
Employee recruitment, retention, education, motivation, and benefits
Health and safety

Marketing
Public relations, promotion, advertising, publicity, and special events

Research and Development
New product development and improvement of existing products, product testing,
costing, analysis or competition, and forecasting of trends

Production
Planning of output, present and future
Cost monitoring

Scheduling
Determining efficient methods of manufacturing

a company will vary with the type of business. For example, all manufacturers
will have production as a department within the company, whereas fewer retailers will have this department.

Merchandising marketing and **management** include responsibility for all
the activities involved in buying and selling merchandise. The **public relations**
area is concerned with all nonpersonal selling activities, including sales promotions, advertising, and publicity. The major activities of **operations** are the
maintenance of the business facilities, purchasing of supplies and equipment to
operate the business, and security. **Finance and accounting,** simply defined, are
the procedures put in place to run the money part of the business. This division is responsible for monitoring the firm's financial status through accounting,
information technology systems, credit and collections, budgeting, and inventory control. In many businesses, operations, finance, and accounting are combined into one functional division. The **human resources** area is responsible
for overseeing the company's employees. Finally, the **research and development**

area takes responsibility for the organization's work in developing new products or updating and improving existing ones. Some companies call this function design; others refer to it as product development. **Production** and **scheduling** are functions of manufacturers. Although small, independent businesses perform many of the same functions as large retailers, their organizational structure is often simpler, as each manager is often responsible for several functions. Next, each of the above functions will be discussed.

Operations

The operations area regulates the day-to-day functions of the business—from receiving new merchandise to following up on the customer's purchase. An effective operations division facilitates three major activities of the organization. First, it communicates and coordinates the activities within the business. Second, it monitors merchandise receipts, returns, shipments, and shortages. Finally, it provides security for both products and people.

Activities related to the physical operation of the organization are often grouped together under the supervision of the company's manager, or director of operations. The major responsibilities of the operations manager are physical plant maintenance, purchasing of supplies and equipment, product distribution, and security.

Figure 6.3 Operations personnel regulate the day-to-day functions of the business—from receiving new merchandise to following up on the customer's purchase.

6.5   List the name, location, and responsibilities of the internship organization's operations manager.

_____

_____

6.6   Discuss the loss prevention philosophy of the internship organization. Most organizations indicate shortages as a percent of sales. For example, a company may plan to have a shortage of 3 percent annually. What is the firm's existing shortage percentage? Its shortage percentage goal?

_____

_____

6.7   Describe the physical or structural deterrents to shortages/losses used by the internship organization (e.g., security systems).

_____

_____

6.8   Discuss techniques used to discourage (1) employee pilferage and (2) theft by nonemployees.

_____

_____

6.9   Summarize techniques used by the organization to reduce employee clerical errors.

_____

_____

Finance and Accounting

Often under the supervision of a chief financial officer (CFO), or treasurer, the finance and accounting function is charged with the monitoring and safeguarding of the company's financial status. The CFO may delegate these responsibilities by grouping them into the following areas: (1) accounting, (2) control, and (3) credit and collection. Box 6.1 outlines the responsibilities of each area.

Responsibilities of Finance and Accounting

Accounting

- General supervising
- Paying bills
- Paying insurance and taxes
- Processing payroll
- Managing inventory
- Mitigating shrinkage or loss caused by theft or clerical errors

Control

- Monitoring and approving expenses
- Planning budgets
- Controlling auditing reports
- Compiling merchandise statistics and reports
- Processing new credit accounts

Credit and Collection

- Invoicing credit customers
- Supervising cashiers in credit office
- Overseeing charge accounts and credit purchases
- Authorizing vendor payments
- Collecting past-due accounts

6.10 List the CFO's or treasurer's name, location, and department and his or her procedures for the control function of the internship organization. In some companies this may be the responsibility of the business owner.

_____

_____

6.11 Discuss types of credit offered by the internship organization, if any.

_____

_____

6.12 Examine the use of computers in the finance and accounting function (e.g., inventory control, credit management, and payroll).

_____

_____

Merchandising and Management

Merchandising and management functions work together in the buying and selling of products with the consumer's wants and needs in mind.

Merchandising

The major responsibilities of personnel assigned to the **merchandising** function are to locate, purchase, and maintain the inventory offered for sale as dictated by the preferences of the consumer. The selection of products available for sale in a fashion operation is called its **inventory,** or **merchandise assortment.** The merchandise found in a fashion retail operation has been purchased either by the business owner, a buyer who is employed by the company, or a resident buyer who represents the retailer. In large operations the buying tasks are performed by specialists who have acquired specific knowledge in preparation for the buying function. In small operations the buying function may be one of many carried out by the company's owner.

Whether a manufacturer or a retailer, and whatever the size of the business, it is the purchasing of fashion merchandise, more than any other merchandise classification, that provides the greatest challenge. In some apparel and accessory operations, the majority of goods are considered to be **staple,** or **basic, items,** products that are in demand for extended periods of time and thus not subject to rapid style changes. In contrast, **fashion items** are items subject to seasonal and trend changes, frequently available in a wide range of styles, with a life expectancy that is relatively brief. Most fashion operations selling apparel or accessories as manufacturers or retailers feature a mix of fashion and basic items.

6.13   What is the proportion of fashion to basic products in the merchandise assortment of the internship operation?

_____

_____

Buyers are the individuals who determine the merchandise needs of departments, or sometimes entire companies, and who ultimately make the inventory purchases. The buyer's responsibilities include:

*   selecting and purchasing products;

*   pricing products;

*   assigning floor space for items or lines;

*   selecting specific merchandise for visual presentations and advertisements; and

*   managing or collaborating with personnel in various areas of the business, such as sales, receiving, advertising, and visual merchandising.

The most important task performed by the buyer is merchandise selection. This responsibility encompasses determining which goods are needed, calculating the size of purchases and from which companies goods should be bought,

Figure 6.4 Fashion designers show their clothes and accessories to buyers at the Henri Bendel store in New York City. The twice-annual "Open See" gives unknowns and newcomers a chance to have their items selected and sold at what is one of New York's most select and expensive stores.

recognizing when merchandise should be ordered for timely delivery, and negotiating prices and terms of sale. The textile buyer for an apparel manufacturer is focused on selecting the right fabrics to be used in production of the line. The buyer for a retail store or Web site is concentrating on selecting the right apparel or accessories for the customer to buy. From a planning perspective, the buyer projects sales and inventory levels by month, and, subsequently, determines the amount of funding to be spent on inventory.

6.14 Describe the written plans required before the buyer begins purchasing merchandise. Does the buyer need approval of a supervisor before making purchases?

_____

_____

After the merchandise arrives at the business, the buyer's job is not over. The buyer determines which products will be carried in depth and which will be stocked in smaller quantities. In retail operations those lines from manufacturers that represent the greatest proportion of inventory are called **key vendors**. Lines carried in smaller quantities are referred to as **secondary vendors**.

6.15 Discuss key and secondary vendors used by the internship organization. For each source, estimate its approximate percentage of the inventory.

_____

_____

6.16 List top-performing merchandise sources by merchandise classification. Note why each source is a high performer.

_____

_____

6.17 Approximately what percentage of the inventory is produced domestically? abroad? Give the manufacturing location(s).

_____

_____

6.18 How are new sources for merchandise selected? Who approves acceptance of a new source?

_____

_____

6.19 What factors does the buyer take into consideration when selecting a new merchandise source? If the internship sponsor is a manufacturer's representative, how does he or she select and solicit a new line to represent?

_____

_____

6.20 List and describe examples of new resources used by the firm.

_____

_____

6.21 Where are the merchandise sources located? Does the buyer travel to merchandise sources or meet with source representatives in the internship organization's offices?

_____

_____

6.22 List locations and dates of regional markets and trade shows attended by buyers of the internship organization. How do the various markets compare?

_____

_____

6.23 According to the categories below, analyze the product assortment of the internship organization that provides a framework for the firm's buying and selling activities.

- Fashion leadership

- Merchandise quality

- Assortment depth and breadth

- Exclusivity

_____

_____

Some of you are interning with a publisher, a fashion show producer, or a trend forecaster. Others may be working with a public relations firm, a manufacturer, or a retailer. No matter which career path you are on, all businesses have a management function as a key part of the organization. What is management? It is leading, planning, organizing, directing, delegating, motivating, and communicating in a supervisory capacity, with the goal of making the business and its employees successful.

The manager of a department within a business, or of the business as a whole, is the person who leads, coaches, and motivates employees to deliver outstanding customer service and, subsequently, make a profit for the company while growing the business. The best managers know how and when to motivate, recognize, and reward staff for superior work. Training, supervising, and scheduling employees are also part of the manager's responsibilities, as may be hiring and terminating personnel. Depending on the organization, these tasks may be accomplished by the manager alone or in collaboration with the human resources division. A manager enforces policies and procedures to ensure that the department or business is operating in accordance with company guidelines. A manager is often responsible for monitoring competitors' activities. Depending on the organization, managing the business efficiently may include ensuring that all departments and the employees within them are functioning effectively. Finally, a manager oversees the overall performance of the business or department, particularly in regard to budgeting and expenses as well as profit and loss.

Figure 6.5 Managers are supervisors responsible for leading, planning, and communicating with personnel for the common goal of making the business and its employees successful.

6.24   Describe the responsibilities of the manager(s) in your internship organization in the following areas:

    a.   Employees (e.g., hiring, training, communicating, reviewing, rewarding, scheduling, terminating)

    b.   Finance and accounting (e.g., payroll, inventory, accounting)

    c.   Promotion (e.g., advertising, public relations, special events)

    d.   Place of business (e.g., security, receiving and delivery of products, visual merchandising, business layout, supplies)

    e.   Other (e.g., monitoring the company's local or regional competition, representing the business in the community)

_____

_____

_____

_____

_____

_____

6.25 Identify the management personnel in your organization. List their titles, and describe the responsibilities of each. Diagram the organizational structure (i.e., management and employees) within your internship organization.

_____

_____

_____

_____

_____

_____

Human Resources

Human resources, the personnel division, is concerned with the activities needed to locate, motivate, and retain a productive workforce. The functions of the human resources division include:

• recruiting and hiring new employees;

• training and retraining current employees;

• working with personnel transfers, promotions, and discharges;

• establishing wage and compensation scales; and

• creating and managing employee fringe benefits.

6.26 How does the organization locate qualified applicants for managerial and nonmanagerial positions?

_____

_____

6.27 Describe the steps used by the internship organization to select position applicants, including any employment tests that are utilized.

_____

_____

6.28 Discuss training offered by human resources management for the organization's employees.

_____

_____

6.29 How is the demand for employees projected? Who is responsible for forecasting employment needs?

_____

_____

6.30 If the internship organization has an executive training program, describe how participants are selected and what the program covers.

_____

_____

6.31 Summarize types of discounts and benefits available to employees of the internship organization.

_____

_____

6.32 Describe the frequency and depth of employee performance reviews. Who directs them?

_____

_____

Marketing

This division is concerned with selling the company and its products. Major activities of the marketing function are public relations, advertising, publicity, and special events for the organization. Marketing is used to project the character of the organization to the consumer and to the greater community. Further explanation of the marketing function is given in Chapter 12.

Interview with Former Management Intern Tiffany Selby

When and where did you do your internship?

June through August, working 40 hours a week in a branch of Dillard's department stores.

How did you find and secure this internship?

I worked part-time as a sales associate for over a year in the Ladies' Contemporary Department while I was attending college. I built a good relationship with the store manager and discussed my future plans about continuing with Dillard's with her. We talked about an internship as well as post-graduation employment.

What did you do on the job?

I attended management meetings and learned all of the systems, such as creating employee schedules, making charge backs, processing payroll, and more. I was responsible for merchandising departments in both the men's store and the women's store, which are separate in my location. Merchandising departments included working with displays, signage, and floor moves; monitoring inventory; meeting buyers from the corporate and regional offices; instructing new-hire training classes; and sitting in on interviews.

What were the positives? negatives?

Everything was a positive experience. I learned so much as an intern and am still learning as part of the management team every day. All of my internship supervisors were very supportive and patient. The challenging part was getting used to not knowing where I may be working the next day—Men's Sportswear, Ladies' Shoes, Contemporary Apparel, wherever.

What is the biggest thing you learned?

How much it really takes to keep a store that size going! Also, I learned much about managing people and getting them to respect you, coaching them to be great associates. Most important, I learned that sales are the bottom line, and if your department is not meeting the sale goals, you better have an explanation as to why and a plan to turn it around.

Did your internship open a door to postgraduation employment?

Yes, I am currently an assistant sales manager at Dillard's. I was assigned to Ladies' Shoes for sometime, but as a result of the economy and subsequent cuts, I am now the sole assistant manager. I am just about everywhere and working in all departments. Let's just say I am thankful I have a job that I enjoy and I am learning a whole lot!

What is your advice for future interns?

Choose an internship that is challenging, even if it does not sound fun, glamorous, or flashy. You may surprise yourself. This is a once-in-a-lifetime opportunity. When you are looking for an internship, research, research, and research. Know your finances, and send your résumé to as many places as you can so that you have options.

What are your future plans?

My next step would be sales manager, and that would be great. I am still very interested in learning the buying side. The buyers for my store are in St. Louis, which is not too far. That may be next. . . .

6.33 In what way does the organization build a positive image and generate sales through its marketing efforts? If effective marketing examples are available, provide copies (newspaper articles, brochures). If advertising is not effectively used by the internship organization, create a marketing plan for the company.

_____

_____

_____

The final two functions, research and development and production, will be examined in Chapters 10 and 11. Next, a look at organizational structure is presented.

The Organizational Structure

The **organizational structure** defines the chain of command, communication, and authority within the business. It lets company personnel and those outside the company know who reports to whom and which employees are responsible for the various functions of the company. Figure 6.6 illustrates common organizational structures for both a small and a large retail operation. Figure 6.7 shows an organizational structure for a large apparel manufacturing company.

Small Retail Organization

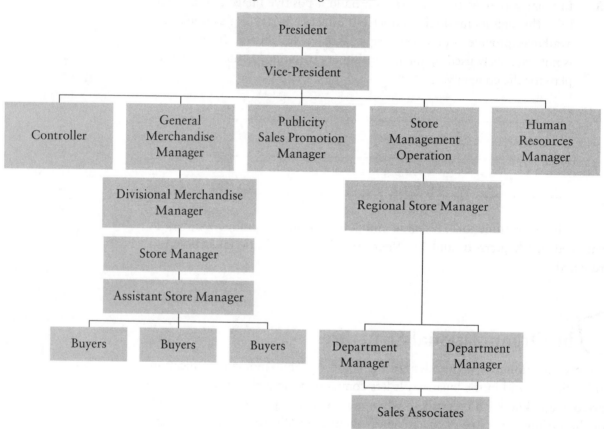

Large Retail Organization

Figure 6.6 Common organizational structures for small and large retail operations.

6.34 List personnel names and titles, and indicate job responsibilities for each position within the internship organization. If the organization's structure is not represented by Figures 6.6 or 6.7, develop a chart that shows the organizational structure. Illustrate the corporate organizational structure and branch organizational structure, if applicable.

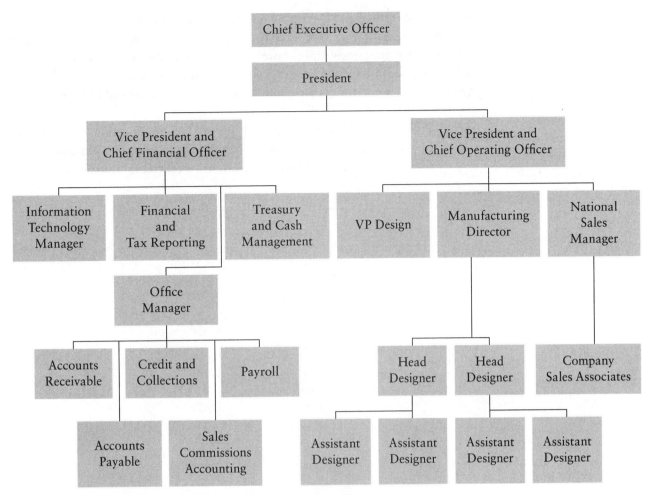

Figure 6.7 Organizational structure for a large apparel manufacturing company.

Communication Channels

Effective communication allows management to recognize employee and consumer wants and needs. Clear communication also enables employees to understand organization objectives, policies, and opportunities. One commonly used channel of communication is **downward vertical,** which is top-down communication between personnel in hierarchical positions, such as a written memo from a manager to employees. Another communication channel is **upward vertical,** bottom-up communication such as an e-mail message from an employee to a manager. Finally, **horizontal communication** represents messages between those in similar personnel positions, such as a conversation between managers or among employees.

Formal communication involves the use of employee handbooks, suggestion systems, newsletters, bulletins, meetings, and education departments (formerly called training departments) to transmit information. This is a good example of the downward vertical flow of communication. **Informal communication** refers to the use of vertical and horizontal lines for verbal communication. An unofficial communication network is referred to as the grapevine. **Grapevine** refers to verbal messages that frequently travel faster than messages sent through official channels. The disadvantages of the grapevine are that the information often becomes distorted and is not always disseminated to all parties who need to know.

6.35 Provide examples of formal and informal communication methods used by the internship organization. Diagram the examples to illustrate downward vertical, upward vertical, and horizontal communication channels.

_____

_____

Communication Channels

Diane Hunter is an intern in the accessories department in a branch store of Garland, a major department store chain. Ultimately, it is her goal to become an assistant department manager for this company after graduation. She is dedicated, hardworking, and enthusiastic and is well liked by her peers and by her supervisor, Mrs. Silverman.

Diane is conscientious about customer service within her department. If a customer is searching for an item that is not currently in stock, she immediately makes a notation of the requested item on the customer want list—a record of merchandise voids that will be forwarded to the accessories buyer. Diane will then write the customer's name and telephone number and the item in her personal customer book so that she can contact the customer when the merchandise arrives. It is Mrs. Silverman's responsibility to pass on the department managers' want lists to the buyer, John Andrew. Diane is anxious to build a customer following in an effort to increase department sales volume and her commission bonus and to make herself quickly and eminently promotable.

When the buyer, John Andrews, visits her branch store, Mrs. Silverman is not there. He mentions to Diane that he has never received a customer want list from her department and that he is curious about any specific items customers may be looking for that were not in stock. Diane looks surprised but does not respond to Mr. Andrews's comments. He notices that she is hesitant about answering his requests. Mr. Andrews quietly checks the customer want list notebook and notices that there are several pages of Diane's detailed notations in regard to unavailable merchandise that had been requested by customers. He realizes that this information would be quite helpful in determining which goods to send to the branch store.

Diane is concerned about the possibility of creating problems with Mrs. Silverman by mentioning to Mr. Andrews that the lists have been made, but have not been forwarded. She is surprised that these customer want lists are not being utilized because she recognizes that they are a worthwhile, if time-consuming, task. Diane is puzzled as to how to respond to Mr. Andrews's question about the want lists. She does not want to create conflict with her immediate supervisor, Mrs. Silverman, yet she realizes that her commission is dependent upon her sales volume. Her sales could greatly increase if she were able to fill her customers' requests. In addition, Diane recognizes that the performance evaluations of both Mr. Andrews and Mrs. Silverman will be critical in determining when and if she is hired as an assistant department manager position in the future.

The next day, Diane carefully reiterates to Mrs. Silverman his remarks about not receiving the customer want lists. Mrs. Silverman is apathetic and states that she is too busy to get all the departmental tasks completed. "Besides," she continues, "many of the customers have ridiculous requests, and Mr. Andrews doesn't have the time to follow up with them anyway."

If you were in Diane's position, what would you do?

I'd Rather Do It Myself

Jill Kolling is an intern in the merchandising and management training program of Dryer's, a large department store chain. She is a conscientious and ambitious intern who has aspirations of eventually becoming a buyer for Dryer's. Jill is enjoying the training program and has learned much about the company and the retailing business in general through its class sessions. As the training program comes to a close, the trainees are receiving the key assignments that will determine if they are placed in entry-level executive positions in the company's merchandising or management divisions at the close of the program.

The trainees are divided into groups of five persons each and given projects to complete as teams. Jill's team is charged with the development of a plan to reverse the declining sales in the children's wear department of the flagship store. It is an exciting yet familiar challenge for Jill because she worked as an intern under the manager of the children's wear department during much of her internship. The class of trainees disperse to begin work on the team projects.

During the initial meeting, Jill's team members find out that they simply do not get along. One of the members attempts to take charge and dominates the discussion. Two other trainees sit back and appear to be totally disinterested in the proceedings. The fourth member of the team plays devil's advocate and disagrees with every suggestion that is offered. Jill is both frustrated and worried. If the group does not receive a high score on this project, the team members will not receive placement in the merchandising or management divisions. Rather than receiving the preferred position of assistant store manager or assistant buyer, the trainees with just fair evaluations will only be assigned to the department manager positions. These trainees will have to work their way up to the entry-level executive positions after several positive six-month reviews.

In addition to the group score assigned to the project by the directors of the training program, the interns will receive separate scores for their personal contributions to their respective teams. The team members will individually submit confidential evaluation forms for each of the other members of their team. Jill is concerned that if she is seen as overly aggressive and controlling, her peer evaluations will portray her as an ineffective team player. Because the ability to work successfully with others is considered an important attribute for members of the company's staff, the peer assessments are a critical factor in the placement of the executive training program graduates.

Jill decides to prepare for the second meeting of the committee with a more positive attitude and an organized approach to the project. She constructs a list of suggestions to turn around the children's wear department's sales volume and develops pros and cons for each suggestion. She plans a strategy that will enable the individual team members to work effectively as a group. Jill decides that she will politely attempt to draw all of the team members into the discussion. She intends to solicit recommendations from each team member and alternate between taking the roles of leader and listener. Jill is looking forward to the next meeting because she believes it will be a productive session.

Designers select fabrics early in the product development cycle to form their collections, thinking forward to the next season. Here, the bold color combinations and animal prints reflect upcoming trends.
Courtesy of WWD.

COLOR PLATE 2

Plisse, quilting, and pleating techniques are applied to fabrics to define the comtemporary side of techno-forward fashion for spring 2011.

Courtesy of The Doneger Group.

Background image courtesy of The Doneger Group.

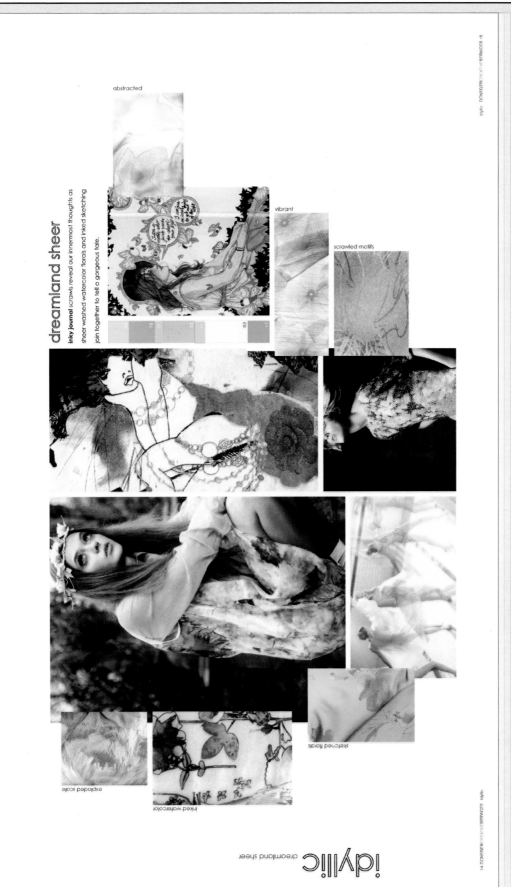

dreamland sheer

inky journal scrawls reveal our innermost thoughts as sheer washed watercolor florals and inked sketching join together to tell a gorgeous tale.

abstracted

vibrant

scrawled motifs

sketched florals

inked watercolor

exploded scale

idyllic
dreamland sheer

COLOR PLATE 3

Idyllic dreamland sheers is a theme inspired by nature and fantasy. This particular fashion forecast illustrates the theme through fabrics.
Courtesy of The Doneger Group.

COLOR PLATE 4

In this Design Workshop theme, the trend of Eclectic Artisan incorporates bright colors and mismatched prints with varying textures to inspire unique and artistic looks. Two variations of this theme are provided.

Courtesy of The Doneger Group.

COLOR PLATE 5

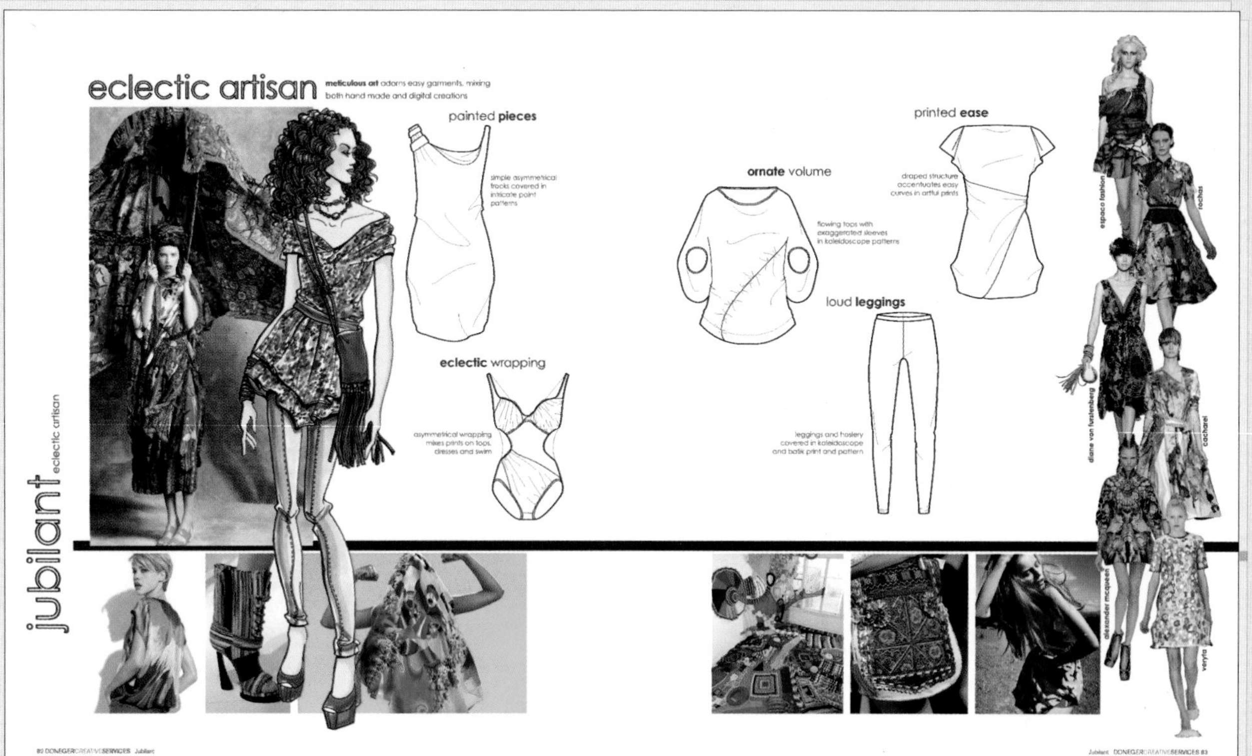

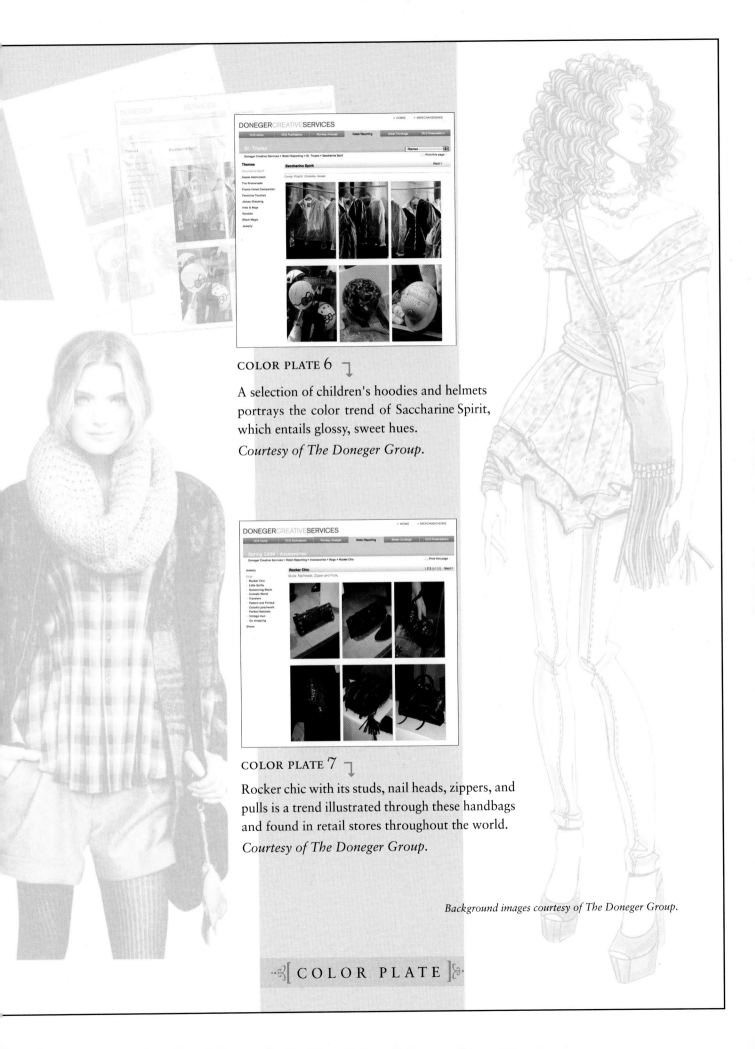

COLOR PLATE 6

A selection of children's hoodies and helmets portrays the color trend of Saccharine Spirit, which entails glossy, sweet hues.

Courtesy of The Doneger Group.

COLOR PLATE 7

Rocker chic with its studs, nail heads, zippers, and pulls is a trend illustrated through these handbags and found in retail stores throughout the world.

Courtesy of The Doneger Group.

Background images courtesy of The Doneger Group.

·ᗜ[COLOR PLATE]ᗜ·

COLOR PLATE 8

Blush is the common color theme among these designer runway fashions from Cacharel, Donna Karan, Givenchy, Doo Ri, and Calvin Klein.
Courtesy of The Doneger Group.

COLOR PLATE 9

Gucci's men's wear collection for fall 2010 is introduced in Milan, Italy, and has a common color theme.
Courtesy of The Doneger Group.

COLOR PLATE 10

Fashion innovation is not limited to Europe and North America. The Doneger Group takes viewers to Rio's runway scene for women's wear collections for fall 2010.
Courtesy of The Doneger Group.

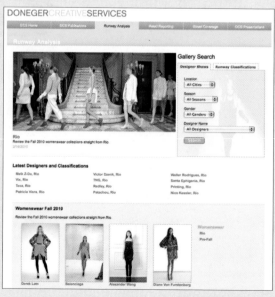

Background images courtesy of The Doneger Group.

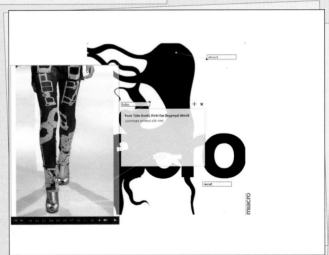

COLOR PLATE 11

A digital portfolio is a great way to showcase your work and creativity to potential clients or employers.

Courtesy of www.miacrodesign.com.

Through the channel of personal communication, Adriana Lima and Doutzen Kroes promote the new Vintage Victoria collection.

Courtesy of © Andrew Marks/Corbis.

Betsey Johnson's showroom is expressive of her company image with the use of vibrant colors.

Courtesy of Condé Nast Publications.

She is wrong! It is a disastrous rerun of the first meeting—the team members argue, sulk, withdraw, and eventually come to a stalemate. Nothing productive has been accomplished in two meetings, and the team has just one week to submit the final project. Jill is so upset that she is considering requesting permission from the training program directors to complete the project on her own. She feels that she simply cannot work with this group.

1. What would you do if you were in Jill's position?

2. If you were one of the program directors, and you found out about Jill's problem with this particular group, what would you do to remedy the situation?

CHAPTER SEVEN

The Customer

Objectives

- To analyze the consumer decision-making process

- To understand market segmentation as it relates to the internship organization

- To examine the multiple customer levels of some businesses

- To assess the buying motives of consumers targeted by the internship organization

- To identify the types, levels, and forms of service offered by the internship organization

- To discuss the responsibilities of customer service

- To explore sales techniques and methods of distributing the product to the customer

Who Is the Customer?

When examining the customer of the internship organization, it is important to recognize that there are two levels of customer: wholesale and retail. Some companies cater to both levels, such as the manufacturer who sells to retail stores and to consumers through a catalog or Web site. Other companies sell only to wholesalers or retailers. When answering the questions in this chapter, refer to the customer level targeted by the internship organization. A **target market** is a homogenous group of customers with similar characteristics, needs, and desires that a company has identified as its primary market.

Many successful fashion organizations have succeeded as a result of their ability to analyze, adapt to, understand, and anticipate their target market's wants and needs. The customer's background, emotional needs, habits, and values influence their spending patterns. The development of a solid strategy for pleasing requires constant evaluation of the changing customer and the ability to understand and influence the customer's behavior.

The Customer Decision Process

The buying process consists of steps the consumer goes through when deciding what, when, where, and how to make a purchase. The consumer decision process comprises the following steps:

1. Recognition of a need

2. Search for information

3. Evaluation

4. Purchase decision

5. Post-purchase reflection

7.1 Select a particular product of the internship organization to illustrate the buying process from the perspectives of the target customer and the sales associate, wholesale or retail.

_____

_____

_____

_____

Market Segmentation

Organizations that are interested in reaching special populations are concerned with **market segmentation,** the process of dividing the total market into smaller population sections that share similar characteristics. These characteristics include:

- demographics;

- psychographics;

- lifestyles;

- culture;

- social classes; and

- reference groups.

Organizations look for several things when segmenting markets. Consumer groups are chosen that are as homogenous as possible in their merchandise preferences, tastes, and shopping habits. A segment of the market with long-term potential that is not effectively served by competition is sought by organizations developing a market segment. Growing market segments include preteens and teens, plus-sizes, and baby boomers.

Demographics

Demographics refers to the breakdown of the population into statistical categories, such as age, gender, education, occupation, geographic location, income, household size, and marital status. Demographics can also be stated as statistics, numbers that describe a population according to categories such as average income, family size, or educational level.

Target demographics are the specific characteristics, such as age, income, and education, that are shared by a given population that a business aims to attract. Target demographics are founded on this simple proposition: people with similar demographic characteristics within a given region will purchase a similar range of goods and services. The bottom line is that a company, whether it be a manufacturer, a brick-and-mortar store, an Internet retailer, a fashion publisher, or a catalog operation, must carefully define its target customer. Target demographics are intertwined with image. Who its customer is reflects how other people see a business. Even the location of a business can give the customer an idea of its level of expected quality.

7.2   Identify the demographics of the internship organization's target customer.

_____

_____

Psychographics

Psychographics are qualitative factors that help predict a customer's willingness to spend income. These include interests, personality, and lifestyle.

Lifestyle

Lifestyle is affected by demographic background because age, income, and education greatly influence the way a person may choose to live. Lifestyle is the unique way of living through which a particular group of consumers sets itself apart from others. An analysis of consumer lifestyles requires the examination of social class, reference groups, and cultural influences.

7.3   Describe the psychographics of the internship organization's target customer.

_____

_____

_____

Figure 7.1 *Vanity Fair,* a Condé Nast publication, features celebrity and high-society event coverage, top-quality photography, and timely articles on high-profile people in the fashion news. The magazine targets a modern, sophisticated consumer who wants to keep up-to-date on the latest culture and fashion.

Culture

Culture and lifestyle are interdependent. **Culture** refers to the behavior typical of a group or class. The social meaning attached to a product within a culture is critical to assessing how the product will be accepted. Religious beliefs and nationality are key aspects of culture. The work ethic, the need for security, and a drive to purchase status symbols identified with success (such as designer apparel and fine jewelry) are considered characteristics of some cultures.

7.4 Describe the cultural influences of the internship organization's target customer.

_____

_____

Social Classes

Social classes are homogeneous divisions of families and individuals within a society. A social class division is determined by occupation, source of income, education, family background, dwelling type, and other variables. The most commonly applied labels for the class system are upper upper, lower upper, upper middle, lower middle, upper lower, and lower lower.

7.5 Identify the social classes represented by the internship organization's target customer.

_____

_____

Reference Groups

Groups who are influential in shaping the attitudes and opinions of people are known as **reference groups**. The family is considered one of the most influential of all reference groups. The person in a reference group who exerts the most influence on the purchase decisions of group members is called an **opinion leader**. Opinion leaders are found at all social levels and are selected to lead by their followers for several reasons. They are regarded as reliable sources of information and advice because of their expertise. They are highly visible to the group and are usually first to adopt new styles.

7.6 Describe the reference group of the internship organization's target customer.

_____

_____

Multiple Customer Levels

Some organizations cater to more than one customer level. For example, if the internship organization is an apparel manufacturer or a manufacturer's representative, the consumer can be profiled in two ways: the retail operation as consumer (the store that carries the merchandise) and the ultimate consumer (the person who ultimately uses the goods). Figure 7.2 illustrates one of Donna Karan's multiple consumer levels.

7.7 If the internship organization services more than one customer level, describe the consumer profile for each level.

_____

_____

_____

Figure 7.2 Donna Karan caters to multiple customer levels by producing ready-to-wear collections for her luxury market, DKNY for her bridge market, and her DKNYC line for better department stores. This example is from her DKNYC line.

Buying Motives

Buying motives are the reasons the customer will react to, or buy, a particular product. Buying motives are used to plan product lines, service offerings, and marketing strategies, such as sales techniques and advertising campaigns. A list of common buying motives is presented as follows.

- **Emotional**—Developed without logical thinking (needs such as love and vanity)

- **Rational**—Involve judgment and logical thinking (needs such as security and longevity)

- **Biogenic**—Relate to physical needs, such as warmth, hunger, and protection

- **Psychogenic**—Stem from psychological needs, such as the need to enhance the ego and show one's social status

- **Patronage**—Reasons why consumers choose one place to shop over another

7.8 Describe the buying motives used by the internship organization to appeal to the target customer and build sales. How are these buying motives communicated? For example, are national magazine advertisements used?

_____

_____

Customer Relations

Understanding the consumer allows the business to determine services that meet customer preferences. Customer relations are impacted by the services an organization offers and by how well it provides them. Types, levels, and forms of services vary with each type of organization in the fashion industry.

Types of Services

Businesses offer varying types of services, often reflecting the price ranges of their products. For example, a high-fashion boutique carrying expensive designer garments will usually offer a wide range of customer services, from alterations to home delivery. Some companies have become highly successful not only for quality products but also for a reputation of quality services, as illustrated in Box 7.1. In contrast, a discount retail operation, such as Sam's Club, will provide minimal customer services in an effort to maintain retail

Customer Service with a Smile

About Lands' End Service

Lands' End states, "Our goal is to please our customers with the highest levels of quality and service in the industry, along with an unequivocal ironclad guarantee." Lands' End operates on the principle that what is best for the customer is also best for the company. As a result, customers have learned to expect a high level of service. The following list of services was adapted from one that appears on the Lands' End Web site (http://www.landsend.com):

- Lands' End offers one of the simplest guarantees in the industry: "GUARANTEED. PERIOD." This allows customers to return items at any time, for any reason, for a full refund of the purchase price or a replacement.

- Toll-free phone lines for ordering and customer service are open 24 hours a day, 364 days a year.

- You think you've got mail. Lands' End receives more than 200,000 e-mails every year. Each e-mail receives a personal response, most within three hours.

- Gift cards and e-gift cards, available at landsend.com, arrive with a beautiful design to suit any occasion.

- Company phone representatives receive 70 to 80 hours of product, customer service, and computer training when hired, and 24 hours each year thereafter.

- To help customers with sizing questions, gift suggestions, and wardrobe coordination, Lands' End specialty shoppers are available 16½ hours a day (7:30 A.M. to midnight, Central Time).

- The company alterations staff will hem and cuff men's and women's trousers free of charge, and it adds only a day or two to delivery.

- Lands' End supplies customers with swatches of fabrics free of charge, on request.

- Lands' End offers replacement buttons, available for most products, free of charge.

- The company's Lost Mitten Club will replace any child's mitten lost in the same season as purchased at half the price of a pair, with free shipping.

- Most in-stock orders leave the Lands' End distribution center the next business day after they are ordered.

Lands' End logo.

prices below those of its competitors. At Sam's, the customer is not provided with dressing room facilities, packaging, or delivery. The bottom line is that the customer pays for the services offered by a business in one of two ways; either (1) the services are financed through the high markup margins reflected in the retail prices of the products or (2) sold as entities separate from the products, as in a fee charged for gift wrapping. Types of services to consider include:

- delivery;
- technical advice;
- discounts;
- after-sales services;
- replacement guarantee;
- credit;
- advertising services;
- promotional assistance;
- exclusivity arrangements;
- educational programs for customers;
- convenience of location;
- alterations;
- ease of contact;
- ease of payment;
- fixture availability;
- freight allowances;
- training of personnel;
- lay-away availability;
- special order availability; and
- reorder availability.

7.9 Which services are included in the customer service mix of the internship organization? Can you identify other customer services not included in this list?

_____

_____

Levels of Service

A business often predetermines the amount of service it will provide to its ultimate consumer when it identifies the target market and sets pricing. The level of service often varies with the type of business. For example, Payless Shoe Source offers a low level of service, whereas The Doneger Group offers an extremely high (or total) level of customer service for retailers, designers, and manufacturers. Figure 7.3 provides an illustration of a retail store in South America, offering a luxury level of customer service.

7.10 What level of service is offered by the internship organization? Is it adequate? How would you improve service offerings to increase the number of customers and, ultimately, sales revenues?

_____

_____

Forms of Service

Businesses choose to offer their varying level of services in many forms. Identical services can be provided in many ways. One apparel manufacturer may elect to send a merchandise coordinator to a retail outlet to set up displays, train sales personnel, and direct a trunk show. Another manufacturer may prefer to send direct mailers or videotapes featuring new lines to the retail buyer, rather than providing personnel to preview the lines.

Figure 7.3 A São Paulo socialite shop at Daslu, a massive boutique where only women are allowed to enter. Daslu is a shopping paradise for South America's high society.

7.11   What forms of service are offered by the internship organization?

_____

_____

Customer Service

Some business operations have an organized, separate department that has the primary function of servicing the customer. Others divide customer service responsibilities into several divisions, such as maintenance, credit, and adjustments. Finally, there are organizations that handle customer service responsibilities informally through management and often personnel who have direct contact with the customer.

Customer service department responsibilities include:

- customer complaints and adjustments;

- maintenance service;

- credit service;

- technical service; and

- information service.

7.12   What are the responsibilities of the customer service department within the internship organization? If there is no customer service department, who is responsible for handling this area? Discuss the responsibilities of the customer service department or representative from the previous list as they pertain to the internship organization.

_____

_____

_____

7.13   How are customer services, such as customer complaints and adjustments, technical, credit, information, and maintenance coordinated? By whom? Are these services used as tools to create consumer satisfaction and loyalty?

_____

_____

_____

Getting the Product to the Consumer

Sales and distribution are methods of delivering the product to the consumer. Selling techniques and methods of distributing the product from manufacturer to consumer are examined next.

Personal selling is a form of direct sales that consists of oral presentations to one or more prospective buyers for the purpose of making sales. A manufacturer's representative is employed for the purpose of selling. Electronic forms of personal selling are still rapidly increasing through the Internet and television.

The most common salesperson is the associate in the retail store; however, sales, or marketing, representatives are also employed by other segments of the fashion industry, including magazines, forecasting services, and display and equipment companies.

7.14 Describe the personal selling efforts of the internship organization. How many people are responsible for personal selling? Diagram the organizational structure of its sales staff, if applicable.

_____

_____

There exists a selling strategy that has been passed on from salesperson to salesperson for generations, although there are variations in the actual method. In some, the steps are in a different order; in others, two steps may be condensed into one. Basically, the techniques for selling are the same whether an idea, a service, or a tangible product is being sold. According to most, the eight steps to a successful sales transaction are as follows:

1. Gain the attention of the customer.

2. Establish rapport with the customer.

3. Find out what the customer's needs are through observation and active listening.

4. Explain how the idea/service/product will fill those needs by emphasizing its benefits.

5. Deal with the customer's concerns.

6. Gain commitment, and close the sale.

7. Try suggestive selling to make the "extra sale" of an additional product or service.

8. Reinforce the purchase decision, and thank the customer.

7.15 Have personal selling strategies in the internship organization changed over the past few years? Analyze current and future personal selling techniques.

_____

_____

Road sales is a term used to describe selling the product to the retail store buyer through sales representatives. **Sales representatives**, or manufacturer's reps, are employees who work on salary or commission, or both, and who sell the line to retail buyers in a specified territory, either at the buyer's location or during trade shows. They often focus on a specific merchandise classification or target market, such as women's sportswear or teen/tween customers. They frequently represent several lines that work well together, are noncompetitive, and can be sold to the same buyers. This type of salesperson is referred to as a **multiple line rep** or **independent rep**. The role of the sales representative is changing quickly and dramatically. As more and more retail companies move into product development, and as technology allows merchandise to be viewed online, the number of traveling sales rep positions is declining. Large manufacturers are employing **merchandise coordinators**, personnel who work for a salary, and possibly a commission, and who assist with the manufacturer's product line in the actual retail stores. The merchandise coordinator travels to retail stores carrying significant quantities of the manufacturer's product line. There, the merchandise coordinator works with the store's sales associates, refilling inventory, installing displays, providing training on new products, and assisting with customer events (e.g., fashion shows, giveaways, anniversary sales, and so on).

7.16 Does the internship organization use sales representatives or merchandise coordinators to represent the line to retail accounts? If so, how are they recruited, remunerated, and motivated? Where are they located? How are territories structured? Which trade shows are covered by sales representatives?

_____

_____

Channels of Distribution

A **channel of distribution** is the avenue selected for moving goods from producer to consumer. The primary channel of distribution for the fashion retail industry moves from the manufacturer to the retailer to the consumer. Some manufacturers, however, sell directly to the consumer through catalogs, Web sites, or factory outlets. An alternative, less often used channel of distribution in the fashion industry is the **wholesaler**. In this case, the manufacturer sells merchandise to a wholesaler, one that buys merchandise from a manufacturer and sells the goods to a company for subsequent resale to the consumer.

Conventional Marketing Channels

A **conventional marketing channel** consists of an independent producer, one or more wholesalers, and retailers. Each is a separate business entity, working to maximize its own profits. No one channel member has substantial control over the other members. Examples of conventional marketing channel levels are shown in Figure 7.4.

7.17 Which channels are used by the internship organization to move goods from producer to consumer? Why were these channels selected?

_____

_____

Distribution Channel Strategies

Distribution strategies include an intensive, exclusive, or selective number of intermediaries. The hosiery division of Hanes utilizes an **intensive distribution strategy**, selling its products to a specific type of retailer throughout the country. The company's goal is to make its product line available to as many different types of retail operations as possible, the objective of intensive distribution. Liz Claiborne uses a **selective distribution strategy**, choosing to sell its lines to specific, targeted operations. Escada, a German ready-to-wear firm, has chosen an **exclusive distribution strategy**, selecting preferred better stores because of the company's high-end price points and limited production capacity. In this case, an exclusive distribution strategy satisfies Escada's desire to make its high-quality, limited product available to a specific high-end clientele. Cost, control, and length of commitment should be evaluated when formulating channel design.

7.18 Discuss the channel design used by the internship organization.

_____

_____

Figure 7.4 Conventional marketing channels.

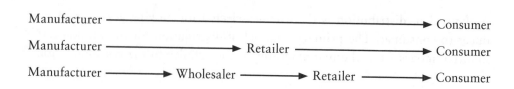

7.19 How does the internship organization select and motivate channel members?

_____

_____

Physical Distribution

Physical distribution describes the tasks of planning, implementing, and controlling the physical flow of materials and final goods from points of origin to point of use to meet the needs of customers at a profit. Some companies contract these activities to distribution firms. Other, larger companies maintain distribution centers that ship their goods, such as the Gap Distribution Center in Gallatin, Tennessee. Although this streamlines the distribution process, it adds to the cost of the product. The objective of physical distribution is getting the right goods to the right places at the right times for the least cost. The major physical distribution cost is transportation, followed by warehousing, inventory maintenance (keeping merchandise in stock), receiving and shipping, packaging, administration, and order processing. In short, physical distribution describes how companies store, handle, and move goods so that they will be available to the consumer at the right time and location.

7.20 How are the orders handled (order processing)? By whom? Are reorders handled differently?

_____

_____

7.21 Where are the stocks located (warehousing)?

_____

_____

7.22 How much stock is kept on hand (inventory maintenance)?

_____

_____

7.23 How are goods shipped (transportation)?

_____

_____

7.24 How quickly does the producer ship the product to the middleman? To the consumer? What is the **lead time**, the period between receipt of the order by the producer and receipt of goods by the consumer?

_____

_____

7.25 Using the information provided in this chapter, develop a profile of the internship organization's target customer(s). It may be simplest to describe each target customer as an individual, for example "a reader of _Fashion Teen_, Ashley, is a 16-year-old high school student residing in an urban area," and so on. You may also choose instead to describe the target market as a group, for example, "the target market of _Fashion Teen_ includes 13- to 18-year-old young women residing in households with average annual incomes of $70,000 to $100,000," and so on.

_____

_____

Customer Service

Maria Valdez has been hired this week as a customer service representative for one of the branch store units of a major discount store chain. Maria received a crash course in training for the position because the store management staff is always very busy. She was quickly shown how to operate the cash register, briefed on employee policies and procedures, and handed a store policy manual to read. Because she attends the local college as a full-time marketing student during the week, Maria works night and weekend shifts. As the store manager and assistant manager usually are not working during the evening hours, Maria is primarily learning the job on the job.

Because this particular weekday evening is very slow, Maria decides to use the time to review the employee and store policy manuals. After a few minutes, a customer approaches the customer service department with a large parcel. Several weeks ago, the customer explains, she purchased two Ralph Lauren bedspreads at the store. She indicates that the packages are unopened and that she has the receipt with her. She also has with her a copy of a newspaper advertisement in which a retail competitor is featuring the identical bedspreads at 30 percent off the price she paid for the items. The customer wants to keep her purchases, but she expects a refund on the difference between the competitor's selling price and the price she paid for the merchandise.

Maria has just finished perusing the store policy manual and is certain that there is no policy statement for this customer issue. She discusses the problem with several of the sales associates who have worked for the store for longer periods of time, but no one seems to know how to handle the situation. The customer is becoming impatient as Maria tries to locate assistance. After Maria asks her if she could return the next day to work with a member of the management staff, the customer becomes irate. She states that she has driven 90 miles to take care of this issue and then threatens that she will return the merchandise and never shop at the store again if the problem is not resolved to her satisfaction immediately.

As the only customer service representative currently in the store, Maria realizes that it is her responsibility to handle the customer's dilemma now. She questions whether or not she has exhausted all the possible resources. She realizes that she must resolve this situation immediately because the customer is becoming disgruntled.

1. If you were in Maria's situation, what would you do?

2. If you were the store manager, what would you do to prevent a similar situation?

Customers—Responding to Their Changing Needs

In the city of Savannah, Georgia, the downtown shopping district is a beautiful, historical, and lucrative area. There is a wide variety of restaurants, luncheonettes, hotels, and stores, including specialty apparel boutiques, gift shops, and more. The storefronts are edged with canopy-covered sidewalks and flower boxes, with metered parking spaces lining the streets facing the retail establishments. All these retail operations are sole proprietorships or partnerships; several are mom-and-pop shops that have been family owned for generations. A number of the retailers do not own the buildings in which their businesses are located. They rent the retail spaces from local businessmen who have owned the buildings for years. There are three colleges in the city that are within walking distance from the downtown business district. In addition, three strip centers are located on the perimeter of the city that feature some specialty stores as well as a few mass merchandise and discount operations.

In the past year, a large parcel of land on the south side of the city has been purchased by a retail mall development company. This will be the only enclosed mall in the city and will initially open with more than 100 retail operations, including major specialty store chains, national department stores, and boutiques, including sole proprietorships. Consumers in Savannah are excitedly anticipating the opening of the new mall. The local newspaper is filled with advertisements and press releases featuring the new

retailers and classified advertisements seeking management and sales personnel for the new mall stores.

Six months before the grand opening, the mall ownership group is promoting the opening of the new mall in a big way. Giveaways; promotional events, such as guest designer appearances, trunk shows, and fashion shows; and special discounts are featured in newspapers and magazines and in television advertisements weekly. Billboards announcing the grand opening of the mall have been erected at most thoroughfares. Local news shows are applauding the economic growth Savannah will experience as a result of the mall opening. The public relations efforts are effectively seducing the city's consumers to the mall.

Several months prior to the grand opening of the mall, the downtown merchants' association held a meeting to discuss the impact of the new competition on their businesses. Many of the downtown business owners were in a state of panic. Several stated that a number of their key employees were leaving, as they had secured new positions at the mall, leaving the store owners with vacant sales and management positions. Some of the other store owners said that their customers had mentioned the convenience of the enclosed mall and were anticipating its extensive parking and longer hours of business. A few of the downtown merchants were questioning whether they should renew their downtown leases or pursue reopening their businesses at the mall, although the monthly fees (e.g., rent, utilities, maintenance, promotion and commons fees) would be twice as costly, at a minimum. They discussed the extended shopping hours the new mall would offer customers, including Sunday openings. By the time the meeting came to an end, nearly all the downtown merchants were panicking about their new competition—the mall.

1. If you were the owner of one of these downtown businesses, what would you do to ensure the continuing profitability of your business?

2. If you were a real estate owner of a building leased by a downtown merchant, what would you do to ensure continuing revenue from your property?

CHAPTER EIGHT

The External Environment and E-commerce

Objectives

- To analyze the impact of the external environment on the internship organization

- To explore how the competitive, economic, social/demographic, political/legal, natural, and technological subsets of the external environment impact the internship organization

- To explore the growth and options in e-commerce in the fashion industry

Why Look at the Internship Company From the Outside In?

No organization operates in a vacuum. Events occurring outside of an organization can dramatically affect its life. There are a great number of outside influences on a business. These are referred to as the **external environment** and include competitive, economic, social/demographic, political/legal, natural, and technological influences. Because these influences cannot be controlled by the members of the organization, they are sometimes called **uncontrollable variables**. Although these variables are uncontrollable, management must be constantly sensitive to them in terms of how they affect the organization. For example, economic shifts can create changes in consumer spending, changes that can impact every level of the fashion industry. Anticipating and preparing for these changes leads to effective decision making.

Subsets of the External Environment

The external environment can be divided into smaller subsets. Figure 8.1 illustrates these subsets, which include the:

- competitive environment;

- economic environment;

- social/demographic environment;

- political/legal environment;

- natural environment; and

- technological environment.

Each of these environments affects organizations in the fashion industry, but in different ways and to differing degrees. The impact of the external environment depends on where an organization is in the channel of distribution and how an organization relates to its clients. We take a closer look at the competitive, economic, social/demographic, political/legal, natural, and technological environments in the following sections.

The Competitive Environment

Every organization faces competitors, sooner or later. An organization must identify and analyze direct competitors. **Direct competitors** are companies that provide similar products at comparable prices to a like target market. For example, Nieman Marcus and Saks Fifth Avenue can be classified as direct competitors. Successful companies must also recognize that there are indirect competitors trying to satisfy the customer's needs. **Indirect competitors** are

Figure 8.1 Subsets of the external environment.

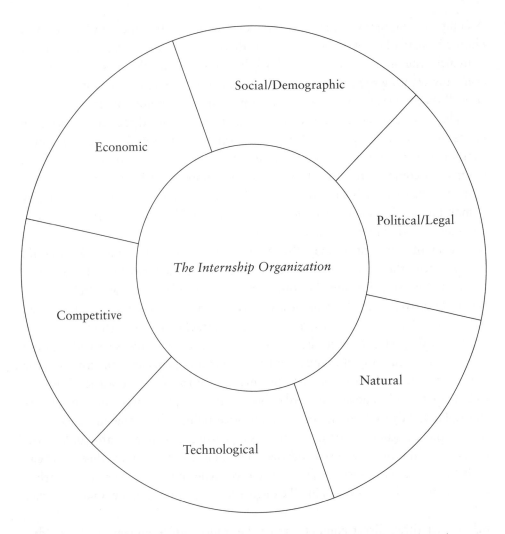

companies that provide different products at varying prices that may be purchased as alternatives by the target market. For example, the specialty store may directly compete with other local specialty stores; however, it may be indirectly competing with discount operations, mail-order catalogs, and department stores. Think about "high–low" dressing, in which the customer pairs designer jeans from a high-priced boutique with a T-shirt from a mid-priced department store and sandals from a discounter. It is a common trend in fashion consumer spending, one that makes all fashion retailers competitors of each other.

Market knowledge is as critical to the success of a fashion company as is customer knowledge. After all, the objective is to stand out from the crowd. A company cannot do that until it has examined what is out there at two different levels.

At the first level, the competition is any other company producing and/or selling a similar product at roughly the same price point, targeted toward the same customer or market niche. It is important for companies to be attentive to what direct competitors are doing, if only to refrain from duplicating their products or visual images. These direct competitors are clamoring not only to be the consumer's choice but to gain the wholesale buyer's attention as well.

A company competes at the wholesale level with any line the retail buyer may choose instead of it—whether that be the direct competition or a megabrand that convinces the buyer to carry it exclusively and drop all other brands. Ideally, a company wanting to grow will have such a great product and know its customer so well that the buyer or ultimate consumer cannot risk not having it.

The second level is less specific. Even if there is no direct competition in terms of another company with the exact same product and image, the fact is that any other place where the consumer may choose to spend money is also a company's competition. In a broader sense, competition is any other business vying for the consumer's retail dollars. This means that even though a company is making cute junior T-shirts, its competition could be a movie theater, a CD company, a hair salon, or a new restaurant.

Types of competition may change as retailing venues change. Who could have foreseen the huge growth of Amazon.com? As the face of retail changes, a company's product line may be competing with brands online, at different price ranges and from global companies. Consumers are less loyal to manufacturers or retailers these days, and there is no stigma attached to cross-shopping.

Cross-shopping refers to the customer's tendency to purchase a wide variety of products in an array of brands from any number of providers: directly from the manufacturer, in a resale store, at a flea market, or through a couturier. It is cool to buy smart. This tendency toward cross-channel shopping may cause merchants to display goods by lifestyle, rather than price point. The segmented moderate, better, and designer departments are disappearing, and lines with similar attitudes are being merchandised together. The new consumer mentality also puts added pressure on fashion business executives who must now be aware of price, quality, and look of products in all categories, not just one narrow market niche.

8.1 List three direct competitors of the internship organization. Next, differentiate these competitors from the internship organization. In which areas are competitors more successful? less successful? Why?

_____

_____

_____

8.2 List and differentiate six indirect competitors of the internship organization.

_____

_____

_____

Table 8.1
COMPETITOR SURVEY
1 = above average   × = average   2 = below average   N/A = not applicable

Organization _____

Address _____

Date/Day/Time _____

A. Location and Facilities
    1) Image of location _____
    2) Accessibility _____
    3) Parking _____
    4) General appearance of building _____
    5) Interior decor _____
    6) Maintenance/cleanliness _____

B. Product and Price
    7) Emphasis given to price _____
    8) General quality of product(s) _____
    9) Exclusivity of product line _____
    10) Services provided at no fee _____
    11) Private label goods carried _____
    12) National brands carried _____
    13) Amount of clearance merchandise _____
    14) General breadth of assortment _____
    15) General depth of assortment _____

C. Personnel and Customer Service
    16) Appearance of personnel _____
    17) Number of associates _____
    18) Ability of personnel to assist clients _____

D. Promotion
    19) Quality of advertising _____
    20) Quality of window displays _____
    21) Quality of interior displays _____
    22) Quality of promotional events _____

E. Comments

F. Additional Activities (as assigned)
    23) Describe the activity level of the organization at the time of your observation. _____
    24) Discuss the quality, availability, and cost of the organization's services. _____
    25) Profile the target market of the competitive business. _____
    26) What are your overall impressions of the company and its operations? _____
    27) Describe other observations: unusual happenings or events to gain a customer's attention. _____
    28) Based on these findings, is the competitor a threat or challenge to the internship organization? Should or can changes be made in the internship organization in light of the results of this survey? If so, what changes do you recommend? _____

8.3   Using a direct competitor, complete Table 8.1. If the internship organization manufactures a product line, it may be difficult to visit a competitor's showroom or production facility. Instead, a critique of the actual product line in a retail store may be the best solution. If you are unable to physically visit a location where the competitor's products can be viewed, look at the competitor's Web site, or review its catalogs and annual reports. It is not acceptable simply to state that the competitor is not accessible. Regardless of their geographic location or sector of the industry, knowing one's competitors is critical to success.

_____

_____

_____

Businesses are classified as being part of an open or closed competitive environment. An **open competitive environment** is a market in which there is a low level of competition; a **closed competitive environment** refers to a market that is saturated with a high level of competition.

8.4   Is the internship organization situated in an open or closed competitive environment? Explain and provide examples of well-known businesses in both an open and a closed competitive environment.

_____

_____

_____

The Economic Environment

A single organization has minimal impact on the general economic state of the world or the nation. An organization can do little about government policy decisions that, for example, may impact taxes paid by business owners or the minimum wage level for employees; however, these decisions will certainly affect the life of the organization. The important question is, how do changes in the economy and economic policy affect the internship organization? One cannot assume that a depressed economic environment will negatively impact all retailers, for example. General merchandise retailers may suffer under such circumstances, whereas others such as do-it-yourself retailers or resale shops may thrive as never before: small specialty stores with a loyal clientele and economically savvy store owners may survive an economic crisis, whereas large chain store organizations may lack the flexibility and customer patronage to keep their doors open.

8.5   Describe the current economic environment using data from recent publications on your internship organization's area of business (cite sources).

In what ways has the economic environment recently affected the internship organization? How does the economic environment affect organizations in this industry segment in general?

_____

_____

_____

The Social/Demographic Environment

Changes in population growth; shifts in geographical residence patterns; and attitudes about marriage and family, appropriate gender roles, and age-appropriate behaviors are all variables that make up the social/demographic environment. Of course, there are many others. A social shift that places a higher value on education and the arts may result in a larger market for a historical costume museum. An increase in the number of retirees devoted to playing golf may result in an apparel store's great success through the addition of a golf wear and accessories department. A trend toward smaller family size by two-income families may alter spending patterns and have repercussions throughout the industry from retailer to manufacturer and designer.

8.6   What changes in the social/demographic environment have recently affected the life of the internship organization? To what extent are the decision makers in the organization sensitive to these changes and their

Figure 8.2 Leisure markets, such as golf apparel, may see an increase in sales as America's large social demographic known as baby boomers approach retirement.

impact? In general, how have social changes affected businesses in your industry segment?

_____

_____

_____

_____

The Political/Legal Environment

Import quotas on merchandise manufactured in Asia, the prevailing attitude of the courts on acquisitions and mergers, a local community's change in laws regarding Sunday openings—these are only a few of the issues that constitute the political/legal environment in business. In addition, the current political environment has created an awareness of social responsibility. Replenishment of resources, implementation of global citizenship, and humane conditions for international labor forces are significant considerations in the world's workforce.

8.7 In what ways is the internship organization affected by the political/legal environment? In what ways are businesses in the internship organization's industry segment affected?

_____

_____

_____

_____

The Natural Environment

Most homeowner's insurance does not cover the elements that make the natural environment, such as wind and water. More subtle and more gradual are such environmental issues as the decline of textile production, which has caused the erosion of topsoil from prime agricultural land. Cold weather is generally believed to lead to depressed sales, but its effect is not just on the behavior of customers; the cold often leads to late delivery of merchandise as well. Concern over the world's supply of oil has had a dramatic impact on the production of most man-made fibers; the utility costs in factories and stores; and the price of fuel, which impacts how far customers are willing to drive to shop.

Figure 8.3
Demonstrators reproach
The Gap, claiming
the company exploits
workers in the third
world through low wages.

8.8 In what ways is the internship organization affected by the natural environment? In what ways are businesses in the internship organization's industry segment affected?

_____

_____

_____

_____

The Technological Environment

Technology has revolutionized all segments of the textile/apparel industry, from retailing and promotion to design and manufacturing. It has altered the way information is transmitted and used, how patterns are designed and graded, and how accounts are maintained. New materials aid costume restoration; new low-soiling carpets reduce cleaning expenses; new manufacturing equipment results in changes in labor costs; and faster, accessible communication devices make global business transactions a breeze. Technological advances affect businesses throughout the distribution channel.

The Internet has introduced a new world of fashion retailers, product developers, promoters, and more. E-commerce opened the door to customers from around the world to purchase products and services from new and established businesses at any time of the day or night. Products are designed in the United States, manufactured overseas, and purchased by the consumer—all online. Fabrics that change color with sunlight or body heat, that clean themselves or that cool and keep out ultraviolet rays, are speeding to the marketplace. It is impossible to predict what technology will bring to the fashion industry next, but it is important for businesses to be alert and open to technological advances.

8.9   In what ways is the internship organization affected by the technological environment? In what ways are businesses in the internship organization's industry segment affected?

_____

_____

_____

E-commerce

Technology and the consumer's limited time as well as desire for new products and immediate gratification have given birth to a new form of marketing: e-commerce. Today's Internet users, including customers, retailers, manufacturers, and suppliers, are computer savvy, with increasing reliance on e-commerce. Most businesses have added a Web channel of distribution to meet customer demand. Apparel consistently ranks among the top product categories sold online; however, the Internet is not just for selling merchandise directly to the consumer. In addition, the Internet has become an effective place to market products and brands.

Expertise in e-commerce strategies is best illustrated by those fashion lines that have successfully created profitable flagship Web stores for global consumers. Examples include DKNY, Lands' End, JLO by Jennifer Lopez, Phat Farm and Baby Phat, Rocawear, House of Deréon by Beyoncé, and Judith Leiber. The Internet has become a mass medium for public use, allowing for information searches, business transactions, and shopping. Whether a publisher, designer, or retailer, the Internet provides global exposure and potential sales from a worldwide audience. Figures 8.4 and 8.5 and Box 8.1 illustrate Internet success stories in fashion.

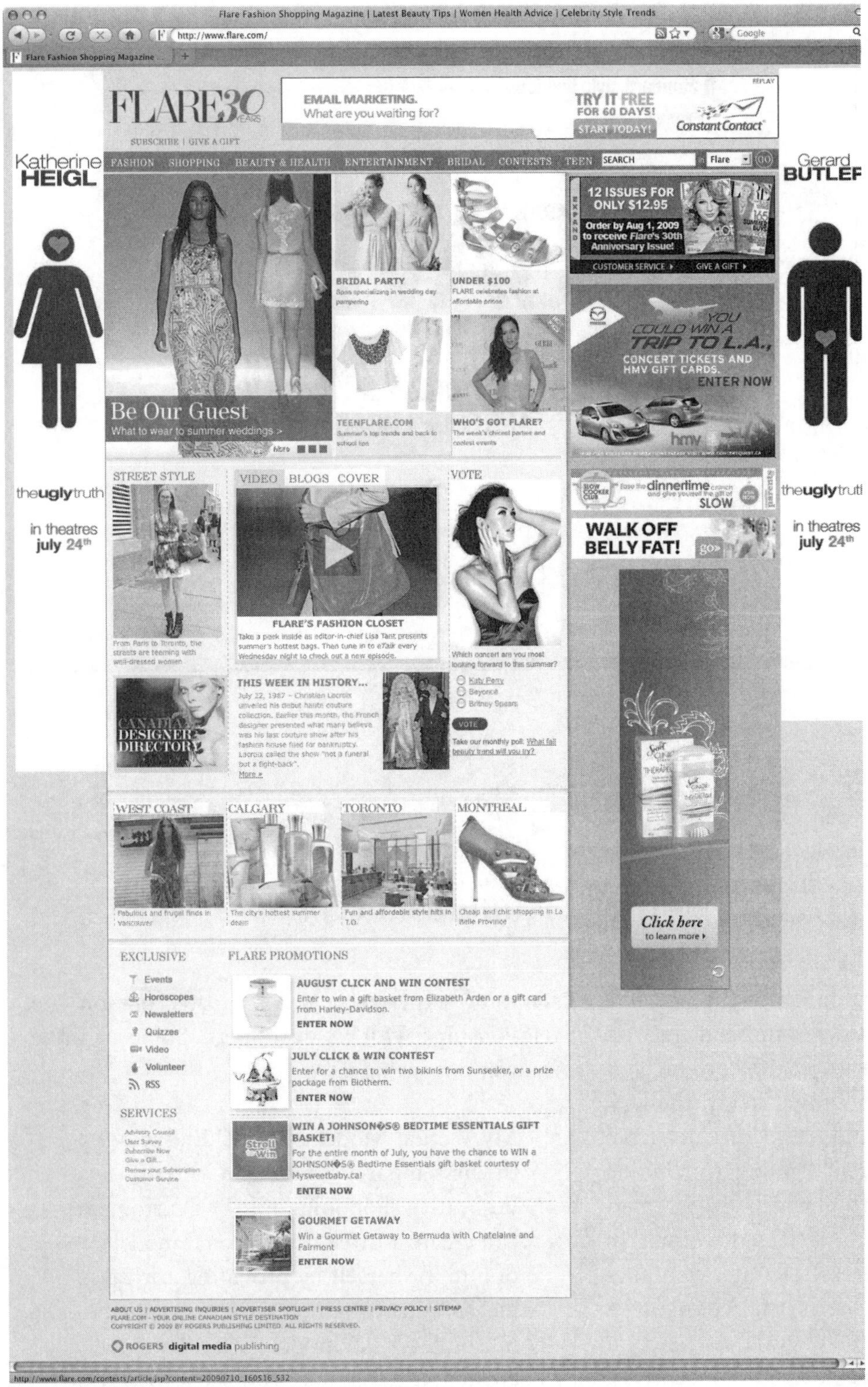

Figure 8.4 *Flare* magazine's Web site.

Figure 8.5 Standard Style's Web site.

··❦[B O X 8 . 1]❧··

The Lowdown on landsend.com

Lands' End was an early adopter of the Internet, launching its Web site (www.landsend.com) in 1995. Initially, the site featured 100 products as well as travel stories and essays. Today, the U.S. Web site offers every Lands' End product from all the company's different catalogs, including an overstocks section from which excess merchandise can be purchased at steep discounts. In addition, Lands' End offers separate Web sites for the United Kingdom, Japan, and Germany; a business outfitters Web site (www.landsend.com/businessoutfitters) provides company incentives, rewards, gifts, and group apparel.

Lands' End has been a leader in developing new tools and capabilities to enhance the online shopping experience and to foster one-on-one relationships with its customers. Some of these innovations include:

- **My Virtual Model**—Lands' End was the first apparel company to offer this innovative shopping tool. The customer can create a three-dimensional model of him- or herself by providing critical measurements, which are then applied to a personal virtual model. After the model is created, the customer can use it to "try on" items and outfits, to see how they will look. Outfits can be stored and recalled for later reference. When created, the model can also

Lands' End's Web site.

be used at other apparel Web sites in the My Virtual Model network and can be e-mailed to family and friends.

- **Lands' End Live**—This feature gives the customer the opportunity to "chat" online directly with customer service representatives while shopping at landsend.com.

- **Lands' End Custom**—This link provides custom-crafted clothing made specifically for the customer. He or she answers a few questions about fit preferences and body type, and the garment is individually tailored and delivered to his or her door in approximately two to four weeks.

- **Swim Headquarters**—For the customer looking for the perfect swimsuit, there are hundreds of options for every shape and style preference. For the customer with no time to browse, there are detailed listings of preferences to help one work with one's shape and anxiety zones. Many of the suits

also work with My Virtual Model so that the customer can see how they will look on her figure type.

- **Outerwear Headquarters and Outerwear Find and Compare**—This seasonal, easy-to-use guide to all Lands' End outerwear helps customers locate the perfect jacket, coat, or parka for all weather conditions. Customers can also select as few or as many items as desired, for an apples-to-apples comparison of prices and features.

- **Affiliate Network**—Other Web site operators can earn extra revenue by joining the Lands' End Affiliate Network and helping direct traffic to the Lands' End Web site. In exchange, they earn a percentage of every sale that results from a click-through to Lands' End from their sites.

Adapted from www.landsend.com

As today's customers have become accustomed to buying apparel at reduced retail prices, it is not surprising to find them shopping online for the lowest price. For retailers, the use of the Internet eliminates some of the traditional costs incurred by brick-and-mortar stores. For example, an online retailer can eliminate rent, mannequins, utilities, decor, security, and more. Those savings can be passed on to the online customer.

E-tailers can be classified according to many models, including click and mortar, distributed (or mall) storefront, auction, and members-only.

Click-and-mortar Model

Click and mortar is the term used to describe stores that have both a traditional brick-and-mortar facility and an online presence. Typically, these businesses recognize the advantage of offering at least some of their services or products exclusively online, as a supplement to the traditional storefront.

Storefront Model

A **storefront model** is a basic model for retailing online and is designed to simulate a brick-and-mortar store. These independent Web stores use **shopping-cart technology** and accept credit card charges through a secure server. This technology operates much like getting a shopping cart at the local market. As shoppers peruse the site, they select and place items into their virtual shopping carts. When the shopping trip comes to an end, the customer proceeds to the virtual checkout cashier to pay for the items. The latest shopping-cart technology allows customers the option of removing items if they decide not to purchase them, just as if they were hanging clothes back on the rack in the store.

Distributed or Mall Storefront Model

Distributed storefronts are also referred to as **mall storefronts** because they simulate the brick-and-mortar shopping mall. Various Web storefronts feature different kinds of merchandise, enabling customers to move from one store to another to purchase the things they want. In a distributed storefront model the customer can be electronically linked directly from the fashion apparel site to, for example, a home accessories Web site that sells bed linens, pillows, and home decorating books. This site may link to another offering home delivery of flowers and plants. By making strategic links to numerous Web sites, a distributed storefront model can be developed.

Auction Model

Think about eBay, and you will agree that the online auction model is a proven success. Part of that success comes from combining the excitement of bidding with the opportunity to get a real bargain without ever leaving home.

Figure 8.6 Members-only luxury shopping at Gilt Groupe.

Members-only Model

When a traditional retailer (e.g., Sam's Club) offers low prices, bulk packaging, and other services to members only, it can generate substantial income from membership fees. The goal of the members-only model is to build a loyal customer base that chooses the store facility or Web site, rather than shopping elsewhere (Figure 8.6).

8.10 Describe the e-models used by the internship organization. If there are none, select the model you believe would best build the internship company's business online, and support your choice.

_____

_____

_____

Crossing the Bridge to a New Market through Market Positioning

With much consideration the owners of a better designer dress company, Maggie Paris, are deciding whether to open a new division of the company, with specific interest in the bridge market. The bridge market caters to clientele who want designer looks at prices lower than those of the original designer line. Typically, bridge designer lines are one notch beneath designer lines. Bridge lines have more unique styling than contemporary misses' lines but are usually not as expensive as designer lines. The hierarchy, with regard to styling, price, and exclusivity, from highest to lowest, is haute couture, designer ready-to-wear, bridge, contemporary. A summary of the characteristics of a bridge line follows:

- The prices are a step higher than those of moderate apparel.

- The styling is more fashion forward than mid-priced apparel.

- The fabrics and construction details are lower in cost to produce than those of the designer lines.

- Many of the styles in the bridge lines are modifications of the most successful styles in the designer lines.

As many designer styles are knocked off by moderate-priced apparel manufacturers, several major designers have opened their own lesser-priced divisions and have created bridge versions of their own top-selling designer styles. Most important, the designer name frequently has status appeal to the consumer, in both a designer and a bridge line. The designer can thus use ego allure to generate substantial sales volume through the addition of a new product line and the subsequent recruitment of a new target market. Because Maggie Paris has been extremely successful in the designer dress market, the company's owners are eager to increase the firm's revenues by using the company's name and image to appeal to a new market.

The corporate executives are discussing the advantages and disadvantages of opening a bridge dress line. They examine the cost of producing and promoting a new line, the possibility of oversaturating the market with the designer's name, and the risk of losing designer line customers to the proposed new line. They analyze the number of bridge dress lines available in the market and the successes and failures of potentially competitive lines. Finally, the executives review the prospective sales volume that may be generated, the production capabilities of the firm's design staff and contractors, and the potential target market in terms of retail store accounts and ultimate consumers.

Maggie Paris's leadership team learns that the company does not have the manufacturing capabilities to produce an additional line; however, the team also discovers that it can obtain the funding to support a new division. At this stage the executives believe that they need to examine alternatives to a bridge line in order to explore all possible expansion opportunities.

1. If you were a member of the executive staff of Maggie Paris, would you recommend adding a new bridge dress division? Why or why not?

2. Would you advise an alternate means of increasing company revenues? If so, what are the alternatives you would propose, and which one would you ultimately recommend?

E-commerce

Wearable Products, Inc., is a progressive company that manufactures moderate to better misses' apparel. The line features classic designs with contemporary twists that appeal to the updated misses' customer who has a large expendable income. Examples of the line's hot sellers include: cashmere sweaters in the latest silhouettes, fitted man-tailored separates in worsted woolens, and knit silk T-shirts with dyed-to-match drawstring pants. The company owners are convinced that there is a new world of marketing opportunities available through the Internet. As a company that has built its reputation by leading on the cutting edge, the owners of Wearable Products, Inc. believe that they are following the pack because they have yet to establish an online presence.

They recognize that the Internet will provide instant access to millions of people around the world. The owners have researched the Internet and learned that the explosive growth thus far has been phenomenal; experts predict that the number of users will grow exponentially on into the next century. Although the owners believe that the Internet promises to be one of the most powerful business tools of tomorrow, they question where they will find the time and resources to "go E" and how the Internet could impact sales to their retail store clients. Through a workshop they attended on understanding and using the Internet, the owners learned that Wearable Products can be marketed to millions of potential customers for a minimal service provider fee. The owners believe that there may be a vast audience of consumers sitting in front of their personal computers, ready to purchase Wearable Products at retail prices, doubling their unit markup.

The company principals have definitely decided to procure an Internet on-ramp, to invest in a service provider membership, and to secure a national server. To generate new promotional ideas and to keep the entire team up to date on marketing opportunities, the executives intend to provide training for key employees in marketing and public relations on the Internet. Although the company team has yet to determine whether to sell at retail online or whether to promote the line, they believe that supplementing current promotional strategies with the Internet will provide a more forward approach (and possibly a more cost-effective one) to marketing in the future. The company owners are anxious to get started and up to speed—fast!

1. If you were one of the owners of Wearable Products, Inc., how would you begin marketing your company through the Internet?

2. Would you sell the product line via the Internet?

3. What are the advantages and disadvantages to retailing apparel and soft goods on the Internet?

CHAPTER NINE

The Product and Pricing

Objectives

- To identify the three levels of a product

- To analyze the various product classification systems and product terminology commonly used in the fashion industry

- To examine fashion products and the product life cycle, product lines, and product mix

- To examine branding decisions as they affect a product's characteristics

- To investigate the variables that affect pricing

- To understand how consumer demand and types of competition impact pricing

- To explore pricing strategies and price zones

- To identify markup and markdown pricing adjustments

What Is a Product?

A **product** is anything offered to a market for attention, acquisition, use, or consumption. It is capable of satisfying a consumer's want or need and may be an object, service, activity, place, organization, or idea. A product can be a dress, a pair of shoes, an image makeover, a promotional plan, a trend forecast, a fashion show production, and more. The product may be intangible or tangible. **Intangible products** are those goods that cannot be touched or held, such as a service or an idea. **Tangible products** are those that can be physically held. In this chapter, product levels, classifications, the product life cycle, branding, packaging, and pricing are examined.

Product Levels

There are many layers to a product, tangible or intangible. Think carefully about the reasons people buy certain services or things: perceived prestige or status (often created through promotion), a great warranty, or a beautiful gift box. These layers are referred to as the **product levels**. There are three levels of a product: core, formal, and augmented.

1. **Core level**—Represents the main benefit or service provided by the product.

2. **Formal level**—The product and its accompanying attributes including packaging, brand name, quality, styling, and features.

3. **Augmented level**—Incorporates such extras as installation, delivery, credit, after-sale service, warranty, advertising, and promotion.

Figures 9.1 and 9.2 illustrate the three levels of a product and how these levels can be used in marketing efforts, such as a magazine advertisement or a Web site product description. For example, MAC Cosmetics offers cosmetic items, such as lipstick and eye shadow, as core products. The lipstick tube and applicator, its packaging, the color assortment available, and the brand name are parts of the formal level of the product. Finally, the guarantee of customer satisfaction, the complimentary facial service, and home delivery via Internet purchases are elements of the augmented product level. If one is employed by a service-oriented business, the product *is* the service. A salon, for instance, may feature hairstyling, makeup application, esthetics, and nail services as its products.

9.1 Identify and describe three primary products of the internship organization, and diagram the levels of each of these.

_____

_____

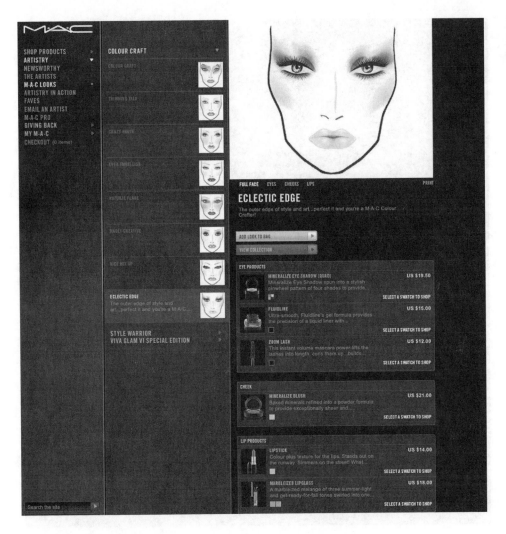

Figure 9.1 Levels of a product: core, formal, and augmented.

Product Classifications

Products in the fashion industry can be diverse in terms of use, frequency of purchase, shopping habits, and many other variables. Categories have been developed to segment and to clarify the differences and similarities in fashion goods and services. A discussion of general and specific product classifications follows.

Marketers have created **general product classifications**, which are groupings based on similar product characteristics that enable companies to develop marketing strategies for specific products. All products may be grouped into one of the three following classifications:

1. **Nondurable goods**—Tangible goods that are normally consumed in one or a few uses. Shampoo, nail polish, and facial cleanser are examples of nondurable goods.

2. **Durable goods**—Tangible goods that normally survive many uses. Apparel, jewelry, footwear, and fabrics are examples of durable goods.

Figure 9.2 Example of product levels incorporated into an advertisement.

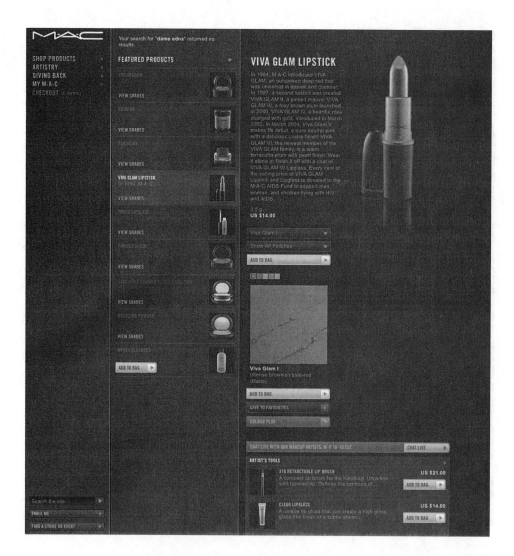

3. **Services**—Intangible goods, to include activities, ideas, benefits, offered for sale. Custom design work, alterations, and personal shopping are examples of fashion-related services.

9.2 Classify the internship organization's products as they relate to the categories of nondurable, durable, and service goods.

_____

_____

Specific product classifications have been developed to enable manufacturers and retailers to describe goods in terms of the customer's frequency of purchasing, shopping habits, and brand preference. Figure 9.3 illustrates the differences between convenience, shopping, specialty, and unsought goods. The list that follows describes these classifications.

	Customer Brand Specific	Price	Frequency of Purchase	Shopping Trip Distance & Time	Customer Service
Convenience	less	low	most	short	minimal
Shopping	↓	↓	↓	↓	↓
Specialty	more	high	less	long	maximum
Unsought	most	varies	least	varies	varies

Figure 9.3 Comparison of convenience, shopping, specialty, and unsought goods.

- **Convenience goods**—The consumer purchases these products frequently, quickly, and with minimum effort spent in comparison shopping (e.g., shampoo).

- **Shopping goods**—When in the process of selection and purchase, the customer compares similar products, or shopping goods, on the basis of quality, price, and style (e.g., a sweater).

- **Specialty goods**—A significant group of buyers habitually makes special purchase efforts for goods with unique characteristics or brand identification, or both (e.g., Seven jeans).

- **Unsought goods**—The customer does not know about these goods, or knows about them but does not normally think of buying them. Customers may be introduced to the product through advertising. Promotion is the key to selling unsought goods (e.g., the Snuggie fleece throw with sleeves).

9.3 List specific product classifications (e.g., convenience, shopping, and specialty) as they pertain to the internship organization.

Industrial products are products that are necessary to the manufacturing process. They are classified in the following two ways: (1) how they enter the production process and (2) how much they cost. They are separated into three distinct categories. The first is referred to as **materials and parts**, goods that enter the manufacturer's product completely, such as raw materials and manufactured materials and parts. The second category is called **capital items**, goods that enter the finished product partly, such as specialized equipment. The final category is referred to as **supplies and services**. These are items that do not enter the finished product in any form. They include operating supplies, maintenance and repair items, and services as well as business advisory services.

9.4 If the internship organization produces industrial goods, identify the product classifications. If not, provide examples from other companies.

_____

_____

There are a number of other product terms that are commonly used in the fashion industry. **Hard goods** refer to appliances, electronics, and home furnishings. **Soft goods** incorporate textile and apparel products, including accessories. Fashion businesses also refer to merchandise in terms of pricing, with **high-end goods** being at the top and **low-end goods** representing budget price points. These goods are the lowest priced in the merchandise assortment. What is classified as budget for one fashion business may be completely different in another. For example, Puma running shoes may be the lowest-priced, or budget, line at Saks Fifth Avenue, whereas Puma may be a high-end line at Macy's. **General line** refers to a wide variety of merchandise or to an inventory of great breadth. (Breadth is further discussed in the following sections.) A department store that features women's, men's, and children's apparel, as well as home furnishings and home accessories, is an example of a retail organization featuring a general line of merchandise. **Limited line** represents the other end of the spectrum. Limited line operations feature a particular product category with depth of selection. A limited line retail operation, for example, may feature men's furnishings, such as ties, belts, and socks.

9.5 Identify the products of the internship operation according to the following classifications:

Hard goods:

_____

_____

_____

Soft goods:

_____

_____

_____

High-end goods:

_____

_____

Low-end goods:

_____

_____

_____

General line:

_____

_____

_____

Limited line:

_____

_____

_____

The Product Life Cycle

An understanding of the product life cycle is essential for identifying a target market, pricing and promoting the product, and selecting distribution channels. The **product life cycle**, also referred to as the *fashion diffusion process*, is a model designed to identify the selling stage of a particular product by estimating its level of customer acceptance. As a product moves through its life-cycle, businesses can measure the opportunities for growth by analyzing life-cycle stages. This information is used to make decisions about whether to continue selling the product and when to introduce new, follow-up products. It is important that all fashion business executives, from manufacturing and retailing to trend forecasting and publishing, recognize the life cycles of not only their products but those of competitive products as well. The product life cycle includes the following:

- Introductory stage
- Growth stage
- Maturity stage
- Decline stage

Introductory Stage

The first stage of the product life cycle is the **introductory stage**. This is the time when innovative goods that appeal to fashion leaders, or trendsetters, are first offered. During the introductory stage, the focus is on marketing the new product to potential consumers. Effective advertising and promotion are used to educate and inform consumers about the new product and how it will satisfy their needs.

Growth Stage

The next stage in the product life cycle is the **growth stage**. A product enters the growth stage when a larger number of consumers begins to accept and purchase it. The product typically generates its peak sales volume as it moves through the growth stage. Typically, profits increase as the demand for the product increases. In the fashion retail industry, styles change, and change frequently. It is important for companies to recognize that in order for them to continue reaping the revenues from the success of a new product, consumers must believe this product is meeting their needs; failure to do so will result in a decline in sales. Successful companies have found a number of ways to meet the needs of consumers in the ever-changing fashion market. Some modify the product to make it appear new. Others find new uses for existing products. Still others develop entirely new products and use the target market's positive relationship with the company as an opportunity to introduce a new product or product category.

Maturity Stage

The next stage is the **maturity stage** in which the product is at either a peak or a plateau in sales. In this phase the product is mass-produced and mass-marketed. During a product's maturity stage, sales generally continue to increase, but typically at a slower rate than during the growth stage. The success of the product in the marketplace brings on the challenge of increased competition. Many times, in order to compete, prices must be lowered to hold market share, thereby lowering profit margins. During the maturity stage a company must work diligently to differentiate its product from similar products of competitors. Often, this is the time when services are added to the product mix. When the product enters the maturity stage, marketing know-how becomes most significant.

Decline Stage

As consumers lose interest in the product, sales drop off, and it enters the **decline stage**, the final stage of the product life cycle. At this point the product is often found in discount stores and on markdown racks. Some companies take advantage of this stage of the product life cycle by selling discounted merchandise at clearance prices to the consumer. There are retailers and wholesalers that specialize in buying and reselling products at the start of the decline stage. As sales steadily decline, profit margins become extremely low. The product is often a dead trend, unless someone develops a new twist, a new use, or a new image to revive its popularity.

Figure 9.4 illustrates the stages of the product life cycle.

9.6   Using a diagram of the product life cycle, identify the point where most of the internship organization's products are located.

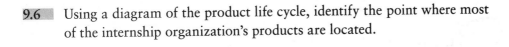

9.7   Next, choose a minimum of six products offered by the internship organization, and show their locations on a diagram of the product life cycle.

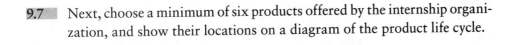

The Product Line

A **product line** is a group of products that are closely related because they function in a similar manner. In addition, they are sold to the same customer groups, are marketed through similar types of organizations (e.g., retailers, wholesalers, promotion houses, and so on), or fall within given price ranges. For example, Liz Claiborne offers several product lines, including a ladies' sportswear line, a jeans line, a ladies' dress line, a men's wear line, and a fragrance line.

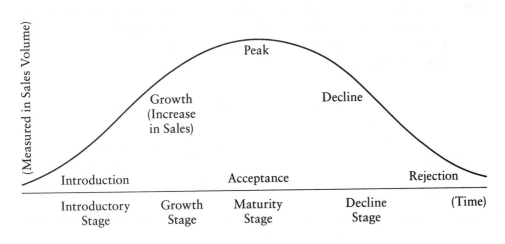

Figure 9.4 Product life cycle.

9.8   Identify the product line or lines featured by the internship organization.

_____

_____

_____

The Product Mix

A **product mix** is the set of all product lines and items that a particular seller offers for sale to buyers; it is also referred to as the product assortment. For example, Tommy Bahama's product mix consists of four major product lines: men's leisure wear; women's apparel; hats and ties; and licenses for watches, sunglasses, and so on. Each product line consists of several sublines. Men's leisure wear, for example, includes jackets, jeans, shorts, and shirts under the Tommy Bahama label. In fact, there are four subbrands within the company: _Relax_, cotton shirts to wear by the barbecue or pool; _Indigo Palms_, jeans that sell for around $100; _Island Soft_ silk and embellished shirts; and _T B 18 Golf_, clothes for the country club set.

Product mix **dimensions** describe the assortment of merchandise in detail. **Assortment** refers to the total number of items in the product mix. Words describing merchandise assortment include the following:

- **Breadth**—How many different product lines the organization carries

- **Depth**—How many variants are offered in each product of the line, such as sizes and colors

- **Consistency**—How closely related the various product lines are in end use, production requirements, and distribution channels

9.9   Categorize the internship organization's product lines, discussing the assortment and features of each. Within each product line, identify the product mix. Evaluate the breadth, assortment, depth, and consistency of the total product mix.

_____

_____

_____

9.10 How often does the internship organization introduce a new product (including a service for sale) or product line? Compare the depth, breadth, and assortment of these lines. What is the average number of styles or units in a new product line?

_____

_____

_____

$\mathscr{S}$easonality of the Fashion Industry

Seasonal patterns refer to distinct changes in activity within a calendar year. Seasonal patterns include changes in climate that influence apparel needs and holidays that affect consumer spending trends. For many types of businesses in the fashion industry, certain times of the year produce higher sales than others, thus affecting sales, cash flow, and profits. Although spring is the key season for prom and bridal gown manufacturers, the winter holiday months of November and December result in top revenues for many fashion retailers in other merchandise areas.

The geographic location of a retail operation also affects the seasonality of its merchandise. For example, retailers located in southern states with consistently warm climates will carry lightweight goods year-round. The National Retail Federation produces merchandising and operating reports that give statistical information on national retail sales, compiled monthly by the store type and merchandise classification.

9.11 Examine seasonality and its impact on the products marketed by the internship organization.

_____

_____

One of the most effective ways to anticipate seasonal factors is to develop an annual chart showing each month's percentage of sales based on the total year. These monthly sales projections are not firm or fixed; they are usually based on previous years' sales. Two location factors, climate and community, strongly influence the seasonality of merchandise and services. Both are difficult to predict; however, an annual chart provides a baseline for future sales and inventory planning.

9.12 Develop a sales chart for the internship organization by estimating the percentage of total sales by month for one year.

Branding and the Product

Branding has become an integral part of the fashion industry. (Branding is discussed as part of the product development and design functions in Chapter 10.) When a company investigates potential products or product lines for the business, branding is often a key consideration. Branding can significantly affect company image, customer identification with the business, and profit potential. Some brand names immediately conjure up images in the consumer's mind. When customers think about Gucci, Calvin Klein, or Polo Ralph Lauren, they envision a certain status. These brand names often transmit feelings of prestige, confidence, and success. This is exactly what the promotion department of these companies intended to do with their advertising efforts. Brands such as French Connection, Kenneth Cole (Figure 9.5), Benetton, and Moschino approach branding in an unconventional and sometimes rebellious manner. There are companies that want to be known as the "bad boys" of fashion brands. These firms intentionally go against tradition to generate a nonconformist image that makes them distinctive in marketing activities.

If branding is a decision the organization decides to make, the firm must decide if it will put a name, logo, or other identifier on its product. Even if the company is not manufacturing a product and is, instead, retailing product lines, the choice of brands carried reflects an image. Image is also impacted when a name for the business must be determined. An organization's name is essentially a brand name. Because branding can add value to a product, some companies prefer to be affiliated with an established brand through licensing, franchising, or naming the business to associate it with a particular brand in customers' minds. In other cases, a business may choose to design a completely new brand—*itself*.

Branding and the Customer

In his text *Strategic Brand Management*, Jean-Noel Kapferer writes, "Manufacturers make products; consumers buy brands" (p 83).

The most successful product developers do not just create product lines; they create brands as well. When branding a private label, developers create an image or personality for products. Image determines how the brand will be perceived, and it is developed to best attract the target customer. With the plethora of parity products on the market, image may be the only means of product differentiation. One important method of communicating image to the

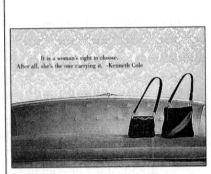

customer is advertising. Take a look at the jeans market. Although there are subtle differences between brands in fit, details, and denim washes and weights, most brands are selling a similar five-pocket jean. However, the advertising for Levi's, Diesel, Polo, Guess, and Arizona jeans differs drastically. Each brand has loyal customers who buy primarily because of image.

A carefully defined target customer will allow the brand to formulate an image and a product that will appeal to him or her. Because of the necessity of communicating a brand's image to the target market via advertising, the brand must decipher where the customer lives, works, and plays. This knowledge will help guide the brand's marketing.

A checklist for successful branding includes:

- An on-target, high-quality product
- A thoroughly defined target market
- A specific point of view or image
- An effective means of communicating a brand's image

What Drives a Brand?

There are two main approaches to the design of a line: design-driven or merchandising-driven. A **design-driven brand** is one that is led by a designer expressing his or her own artistic vision and personal sense of taste. This type of brand appeals to customers who relate to the designer's particular style and taste and includes most brands with designer names. A customer attracted to a design-driven brand may think, "If I were a designer, this is the type of clothing I would design." These apparel brands tend to be more original and creative but may lack consideration for the customer's comfort or actual wearability of garments, as do some designs by Viktor and Rolf or Rei Kawakubo. Design-driven brands also have the distinction of representing both a particular designer's viewpoint and a line of products. The personality expressed by the brand is usually an extension of the designer's personality. In the case of a brand like Ralph Lauren apparel and accessories, the brand has several faces: English gentleman, East Coast aristocrat, Western individualist.

Merchandising-driven brands, or "void-filling" brands, are those that do just that. These market-based brands search for a void in the market, or an underserved customer, and create a product to appeal specifically to that customer. Design decisions are based on careful monitoring of past sales and successes, in conjunction with customer wants. This type of brand takes direction from the customer by keeping in touch with him or her and customizing products accordingly. The customer's comfort is of utmost importance to this type of brand, though its products may not be too exciting. Many private brands are merchandising driven.

Brands must be sold in retail outlets that are appropriate for them. A retailer's brand must have a fashion image consistent with that of the customer it attracts. It is the responsibility of merchandisers at companies with both types of brands to make sure that the designed products add up to a marketable line.

9.13 Select a brand or label within the internship company, and describe its personality, the brand image, and whether it is merchandising-driven or design driven.

_____

_____

Branding Terminology

Companies must decide whether to put a brand name on products. Branding may add value to a product and can become an important element of the product marketing strategy. Branding terminology includes the following:

- **Brand**—A name, term, sign, symbol, or design, or a combination of these that is intended to identify the goods or services of one seller or group of sellers and differentiate them from those of competitors.

- **Brand name**—The part of a brand that can be vocalized.

- **Brand mark**—The part of a brand that can be recognized but cannot be spoken.

- **Trademark**—A brand or part of a brand that has legal protection because its owner has exclusive rights to use the brand name or brand mark, or both.

- **Copyright**—The exclusive right to reproduce, publish, and sell the material in the form of a literary, musical, or artistic work.

9.14 Describe and identify branding usage within the internship organization. If the internship operation does not directly use a brand name, select a product within its inventory for your response.

_____

_____

9.15 What brand sponsorship decisions have been implemented by the internship operation?

_____

_____

Packaging and Labeling

Packaging is part of the product's formal level. Packaging is defined as the activities of designing and producing the container or wrapper for a product. **Labeling** is part of the packaging and refers to the printed information that describes the product and appears on or with the package. Factors that have contributed to the growth of packaging as an effective marketing tool include convenience, value, consumer affluence, company and brand image, and innovational opportunity.

9.16 Discuss the roles of packaging and labeling as they pertain to the internship operation. For example, is the product put on a hanger, folded, tagged, or boxed? If the product is a service, how is it "packaged?" Is it presented through a storyboard, proposed through a PowerPoint presentation, or packaged in another fashion?

_____

_____

_____

Figure 9.6 Donatella Versace's limited-edition fragrance Gianni Versace Couture comes nestled in a handmade napa leather train case embossed with a Greek key pattern, a house signature.

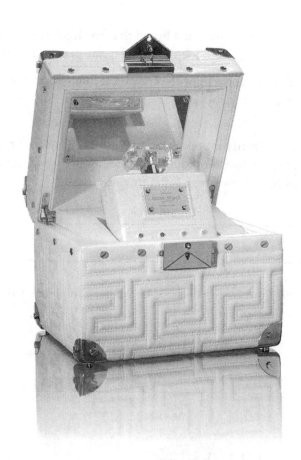

The Role of Pricing on the Product

Regardless of the organization's product and profit orientation, pricing is central to decisions that impact the product, the customer, and the organization. Usually, the price set for a product is intended to accomplish two purposes: (1) to cover all the costs associated with the product and (2) to provide some amount of profit. Normally, it is the user of the product who will completely pay the price; however, in some cases, the government may completely or partially pay it. For example, a city or state museum may be open for free some or all of the time because the city or state bears all or part of the costs of operations. Another illustration of this is a trade organization, such as Cotton Incorporated or the Wool Bureau, that offers "free" services, such as trend forecasting and fabric sourcing, to its retail and manufacturing clients. These services are subsidized by the trade organization's members (e.g., cotton and wool producers).

Pricing is a key factor for consumers when deciding whether to buy. To establish price, the company takes into consideration the following factors:

- Company expenses and overhead
- Planned markups
- Desired image

- Prices competitors charge

- Prices consumers will be willing to pay

Prestige specialty stores, such as Neiman Marcus and Saks Fifth Avenue, and designer boutiques, such as Chanel and Versace, use their image and exclusivity to demand higher prices. A Gucci key chain may actually cost as much to manufacture as one available at Wal-Mart, but the Gucci customer is willing to pay much more for the status name. Generally, pricing strategies are implemented to increase sales; increase profits, regardless of changes in sales; or maintain market share.

It is important to note that large retail companies can offer products at a lower price because of their quantity purchases and resulting product discounts. For many smaller businesses, price may not be an effective basis for competing because they cannot purchase the large amounts required for quantity discounts and private label buys. Also, most small businesses do not have a product development division. Often, they carry some of the same merchandise competitors do, at comparable prices. As a result, small companies must find other ways to differentiate their businesses. Developing special promotions, focusing on the quality of their product, or providing exceptional customer service may prove to be more cost-effective ways for them to compete.

Setting the Retail Price

The price of the product or service must take into account costs, customers, competition, and the market. Setting prices too high may result in a high profit margin but may also lower sales volume, reduce the customer base, and, ultimately, impact the company's future. Setting prices too low may limit profits and lead the consumer to believe the product lacks quality. Price often represents the value of the product for both seller and buyer. It plays a role in establishing an image of the product in terms of its value, and it determines profit margin. The image projected by a manufacturer selling designer apparel will be completely different from the image projected by a discount manufacturer. To consumers, price may distinguish the type of stores in which they shop. Price sends a message to the consumer about the quality and value of the product. The selling price should be consistent with the consumer's perception of the product as well as the marketing goals and the image the business wants to project.

9.17 Who is responsible for setting the prices on products the internship organization sells?

_____

_____

9.18 What image do these prices project to the consumer?

_____

_____

Variables in Pricing Decisions

Too often companies price their products based on an estimate or on what the competition is doing. An awareness of the price established by the competition is important, but other variables must also be taken into consideration. Scarborough and Zimmerer (2002) noted that the following factors should be considered when determining the price of a product:

- Costs of the product (or service) to include raw materials, labor, shipping, storage, and so on

- Market factors of supply and demand

- Sales volume potential

- Economic conditions

- Business location

- Seasonal fluctuations

- Psychological factors (e.g., "green" design and sustainable, recyclable products)

- Credit terms and purchase discounts

- Customer's price sensitivity

- Company image

- Competition

Other factors to consider include legal restrictions, the characteristics of the target markets, the number and characteristics of distribution channel members, standard trade practices in a particular industry, and purchasing habits.

9.19 Which three of the price variables listed above most directly influence product prices established by the internship organization? Why did you select these?

_____

_____

$\mathcal{L}$egal Restrictions in Pricing

Legal restrictions in pricing refer to the role and actions of city, state, and federal government in the establishment of prices. A primary concern of the government is price-fixing. The Robinson-Patman Act prohibits price discrimination to channel members unless the discrimination can be defended on the basis of savings to the seller. In addition, individual states may have laws that prescribe the minimum price for which a product may be sold. Also, consumer legislation, as illustrated by laws banning bait-and-switch pricing tactics, is developed to protect consumers. **Bait-and-switch** refers to the practice of advertising a low-priced item and then describing it as an inferior product in an attempt to sell the consumer a higher-priced item.

9.20 In what ways do the government and its laws affect the pricing practices of the internship organization?

_____

_____

9.21 Which laws have the greatest impact on the internship organization's pricing decisions?

_____

_____

9.22 How well informed are decision makers in the organization about the legal restrictions on pricing policies and practices?

_____

_____

9.23 Where would a company representative go to get legal information on pricing practices for management in your organization?

_____

_____

9.24   Generally, how much concern is given to the legal implications of pricing practices?

_____

_____

$\mathcal{P}$ricing Strategies

Two key pricing strategies are commonly used for products in the fashion industry: demand pricing and competitive pricing.

Demand Pricing

Demand is an important influence on pricing. Demand is referred to as elastic when changes in price affect demand. For example, when prices go up, demand often decreases. This reaction is elasticity.

There are a number of pricing strategies used to influence demand. A **loss leader**, for example, is a product offered at an extremely low price, thereby generating little or no profit and perhaps even a loss. Loss leaders are often used in advertisement to attract customers or catch their attention. A promotional pricing strategy is one that keeps prices to a minimum, despite the possible result that store services and physical space may suffer, in the belief that there are always some customers who care more about low prices. **Penetration pricing** is a strategy designed to capture a large share of the mass market by offering the product at a low price.

Psychological pricing refers to using odd versus even endings on retail prices. Psychological pricing assumes that buyers are more attracted to an odd numbered price (like $7.95) than to an even-numbered price (like $8.00) because the odd number implies a sale or bargain price. **Prestige pricing** assumes that customers infer a relationship between price and quality and will not buy a product if the price is too low. **Customary pricing** assumes that customers expect a certain product to be available at a certain price and that significant deviation in either direction from that customary price will result in decreased demand.

9.25   How does demand impact the pricing of the products offered by the internship organization?

_____

_____

9.26 Describe the internship organization's primary pricing strategy. Is it promotional, penetration, psychological, prestige, or customary, or a combination of these? What are the decision factors for pricing products the way the company does it?

_____

_____

9.27 To what extent is psychological pricing important to the internship organization? If psychological pricing is not used, why not? Is there a concern for the psychological response of consumers to price that is discussed informally in the organization, such as the overuse of price reductions or customers waiting to buy at sale prices?

_____

_____

9.28 Does the internship organization apply loss-leader pricing in its promotional efforts? Provide an example of this strategy from the internship company or another business.

_____

_____

Competitive Pricing

Competition, too, impacts price. If a company's prices increase while those of its competitors remain stable, customers are likely to move to the competitor. If, however, prices for everyone in the industry go up, and no competitor is offering a cheaper price, demand is more likely to remain stable.

Competitive pricing is a strategy in which an organization bases its prices on those of the competitors. It is important in this type of pricing to base figures on companies comparable in size and merchandise. Larger companies often buy in large volume, enabling them to have a lower cost-per-unit price. Retail prices may be set either above or below those of the competition. To price below the competition often requires the business to increase its sales volume and reduce costs. As a result, inventory needs to turn over at a faster rate. Therefore, the business must closely monitor its inventory. Pricing below the competition can bring about price wars in which competitors cut prices, too, leaving both businesses with the need to find alternative ways to generate profits.

9.29   In what ways does the internship organization apply competitive pricing strategies?

_____

_____

Pricing above the competition is possible when considerations other than price are important to the buyer. Manufacturers or retailers carrying exclusive merchandise, or brand names that are not readily available, may be able to price above the competition. Escada, Burberry, and Armani are examples of retailers that are able to price above the competition because of the exclusivity and prestige of their merchandise assortments. Companies offering exceptional customer service can also price higher than other stores.

9.30   Describe the competition of the internship organization as it impacts demand in terms of specialized products and pricing. Is the organization offering exclusive products that allow it to set higher prices?

_____

_____

Price Setting and Price Lining

Price setting and price lining are two other pricing strategies used by manufacturers and retailers in the fashion industry. **Price setting** is a technique to establish price on a product that is new to the market or selling to an elite group of buyers not sensitive to price. The product is marketed to be perceived as top quality and so must project a prestigious image. The product's higher price enables high promotion costs to be recovered quickly.

9.31   If the internship organization employs price setting, provide an example of this strategy. If not, provide an advertisement to illustrate the concept and discuss why the internship organization could or could not apply price setting.

_____

_____

Price lining refers to a marketing strategy based on a preferred customer price point. Using the price-lining strategy, the retailer stocks merchandise that will be sold at specific price ranges or price lines. The merchandise within each category will be similar in quality, cost, appearance, and other attributes. For example, a fashion retailer may buy sweaters from various name vendors and average the costs to price them all at $39.99 each, regardless of the wholesale cost. The retailer is using one price to promote the product or products effectively. One price allows the retailer to promote the merchandise with impact by simplifying the marketing message through a single retail price.

9.32 Provide an illustration of price lining as a promotional effort.

_____

_____

$\mathcal{P}$rice Zones

Successful companies are aware of the consumer's changing perception of value. Most products carry an acceptable price range, as opposed to one ideal price. **Price zones** refer to the ranges of prices that a customer will pay for an item. For example, the contemporary female customer between the ages of 18 and 25 may purchase beach sandals at Wal-Mart for $3.99 and evening sandals at Dillard's for $79.00. If she never pays less than $3.99 or more than $79.00 for sandals, then this is her price zone. Fashion retailers and manufacturers must determine the maximum price consumers are willing to pay, or the **price ceiling**. The minimum price that can be charged based on cost is known as the **price floor**.

9.33 Select a product marketed by the internship organization and specify the price ceiling and price floor the average customer of the organization will likely pay for the product.

_____

_____

9.34 Has the internship organization ever attempted to offer a product at a price above or below its price zone? If so, what were the results of this price shift?

_____

_____

arkup

Markup is the amount of money added to the wholesale cost of the product to establish the retail selling price. The amount of the markup may be determined by the type of merchandise sold, services provided by the business (such as free delivery), how often the product sells, the amount of profit the company wants to make, and what the competition is doing.

Fashion businesses offering a variety of products often find it effective to use a flexible markup policy. A flexible markup policy is one that allows the company to apply different levels of markup to varying merchandise classifications. For example, retailers carrying apparel lines frequently carry accessory lines to accompany the clothing. The initial markup on a line of belts may be different from that on a line of dresses.

9.35 Does the internship organization apply a standard markup percentage on its products? If so, what is this figure? If not, how are markup and the resulting selling price determined?

_____

_____

Markdowns

A **markdown** refers to a decrease in the selling price of an item. It is, simply put, a price reduction. Markdowns are a fact of life in the fashion industry because of changing fashion trends and seasons. Most companies establish a policy and procedures for taking markdowns. The policy may include what to mark down (e.g., merchandise that is more than 30 days old) and when to take the markdown (e.g., the first day of every month). The policy may also indicate how to take markdowns. For example, the buyer may determine that the first markdown will be a reduction of 30 percent off the initial selling price. He or she may decide that this price change will be noted on the merchandise ticket in red pen and that all markdowns will be entered into the computer, by department and vendor. Precise records of markdown amounts are necessary to generate an accurate inventory result. In addition, a detailed record of markdowns enables the buyer to determine which vendors provided the best sales and profit performance and which vendors should be eliminated from the merchandise mix.

9.36 Describe price changes, such as markdowns, made to move slow-selling or second-quality products.

_____

9.37 How often are price reductions taken?

_____

_____

9.38 What is the organization's markdown policy? If it does not have one, what would you propose as a markdown policy?

_____

_____

9.39 What is the common reduction percentage for a given period of time? For example, merchandise that has not sold in a 30-day period may be reduced by 30 percent off the selling price.

_____

_____

9.40 Where, how, and by whom is the decision to reduce a selling price determined?

_____

_____

Figure 9.7 Devoted bargain hunters can't resist sales on designer goods.

9.41 To what extent is standard trade practice important in pricing decisions? Is pricing calculated in a certain way because that is how companies in this industry do it?

_____

_____

$\mathcal{P}$ricing Guidelines

In *Writing a Convincing Business Plan*, DeThomas and Grensing-Pophal (2001) provide four guidelines that can be used in determining price:

1. **Know the full costs**—Research indicates that the management of new companies rarely understands the full cost of operating the businesses. The most effective method for understanding cost is to perform a break-even analysis for the business as a whole and for individual products/services or product lines. A company's break-even point is the level of operations at which revenue from sales and total costs (expenses) are equal. There is neither a profit nor a loss. By performing this calculation, the company can identify the minimum level of sales or activity required of the business to keep it in operation. The break-even point can be calculated in terms of either units or sales revenue. It can be calculated for a single product, a product line, or the overall operations of the business.

2. **Price, image, and goals are interrelated**—Pricing policy cannot be established in a vacuum. The selling price of the product/service should be consistent with the company's marketing goals, the image the organization is attempting to project, and the perceptions and expectations of the target market.

3. **Price, product differentiation, and market power are inseparable**—The ability to set price independent of competition depends on the degree of differentiation the product or service commands and the market power of the firm. The more difficult it is to differentiate the product or service from that of the competition, the more likely it is that the firm will have to accept the going market price. The same is true of market power. Larger firms and industry leaders have more flexibility in setting selling price than do smaller firms and industry followers.

4. **Price and nonprice perceptions are significant**—Although selling price is an important influence on consumer purchases, it is not the main reason consumers buy. More important are the ways price and nonprice considerations are perceived by consumers. In the fashion industry, consumers will take into account price, quality, exclusivity, and service. These areas are closely interrelated in the minds of consumers when they determine which fashion merchandise they will buy.

9.42 Using the pricing guidelines developed by DeThomas and Grensing-Pophal, analyze the pricing decisions made by the internship organization. How do they compare?

_____

_____

··❧[C A S E   S T U D Y   9 A]❧··

Choosing a Message—Price and the Product

"The price is what really matters," shrugs the young man leaning back in his chair with his feet on the table.

"No, I disagree," a tall woman in black quietly interjects, "it is the product image. It's status. I believe we should go for contemporary market appeal."

"You are both offtrack," another man remarks. "It is the fit of the merchandise that the customer truly appreciates."

A young woman dressed from head to toe in the line of the latest new designer interrupts: "I cannot believe that none of you recognize that it is the line's fashion-forward styling that makes it so appealing to the customer."

The promotional division of Black Dog, a well-known jeans manufacturer with an international retail distribution, is meeting to determine the corporation's fall campaign. The members of the promotional team are brainstorming the company's advertising approach to introduce the new fall line. The array of promotional concepts is diverse. Some are creative; others are more practical. Price, styling, fit, and prestige are among the central messages that the promotional staff

has recommended so far, with price most often cited as the significant variable. Additional ideas surface as Black Dog team members discuss the option of using a current issue as a promotional theme. Suggestions include economizing with style, purchasing "green goods" to protect the environment, and dressing up and down with an adaptable jean.

One member of the promotional team mentions that the campaign is an international effort, as the initial advertisements will be featured worldwide through major fashion magazines and the Internet. He believes that the corporation must express an international cultural awareness and appreciation of diversity. He continues by stating that some of the popular topics in the United States are not necessarily areas of concern or accord to populations abroad. The rest of the group agrees. They decide to take an alternative approach to using a current issue as the promotional theme for the global advertising campaign.

After some discussion, Black Dog's promotional team debates using a celebrity model, a film or music industry star, or even an animated

(continued on next page)

character as an advertising vehicle for the fall promotion. The team members examine the costs, exclusivity, and international appeal associated with each of these options. After several hours of brainstorming, the group agrees that each member will present his or her preferred promotional message and media recommendations at the group's meeting the following week.

1. If you were a member of the Black Dog promotional team, what message would you recommend for the fall campaign? You may choose not to agree with the team's preliminary decisions.

2. Who would you select to deliver the message? How would you get the message out globally?

Tommy Bahama Clothing Line Grows Up

A dozen Tommy Bahama designers, many of them drinking coffee, contemplate the 18 pairs of assorted shorts displayed in front of them during daylong preparations for a presentation of next fall's fashion line to salespeople from all over the country. Where their inspiration comes from is obvious.

Their inspiration is represented by a poster-size photograph propped on an easel next to the shorts. The picture is of Positano, a romantic Italian village perched above the Amalfi coast. "Our tried-and-true Tommy Bahama customer doesn't just travel to Las Vegas or Scottsdale, Arizona," said Joey Rodolfo, the company's chief designer of men's apparel. "He's a worldly guy. He goes there, puts his feet in the sand, and wears some great shorts and shirts."

The company targets men, and to a lesser extent women, who are between 35 and 55 years old and have an annual income above $150,000. It sells shorts for $80 and up, shirts for $200, and a $500 dinner jacket, among other things. Advertisements in *Wine Spectator*, *Esquire,* and *Cigar Aficionado* feature a handsome Italian man with salt-and-pepper hair and a roguish smile. "The Tommy Bahama lifestyle is a dream for men sitting in front of a computer screen," said Tom Hermann, a Tommy Bahama alum who is president of Redmond denim-line Jag Jeans. "It's Bob Marley kind of stuff—I close my eyes, and all of a sudden I'm on a tropical island under a palm tree."

Training Ground

Tommy Bahama is headquartered in Seattle, rather than fashion centers New York or Los Angeles, because of its relative proximity to apparel manufacturing sites in Asia, and because it has long been a training ground for clothing designers, said chief operating officer Doug Wood. Many of the company's designers cut their teeth locally at Nordstrom, Eddie Bauer, and Unionbay. (Rodolfo helped start Seattle sportswear company Cutter & Buck.)

In the 1980s, Tony Margolis and Bob Emfield, then in sales at Seattle's Generra, began to wonder what it would be like to plant themselves on the beach and never return to work. While vacationing on Florida's Gulf Coast, they pictured a graying guy who had more than enough money to live well without ever having to put on a suit and tie again. They named him Tommy Bahama. In 1992, they enlisted longtime clothing designer Lucio Dalla Gasperina, previously of Unionbay Sportswear in Seattle, to create the Tommy Bahama line.

Consisting mostly of silk Hawaiian-style shirts, it was sold at vacation resorts and upscale specialty stores for the first few years, until department stores such as Nordstrom and Neiman Marcus also began to carry it. Today, the company operates 70 Tommy Bahama stores in the United States—its first was in 1996 in Naples, Florida—and has nine licensed locations in Canada, Dubai, and Australia. Annual sales top $450 million.

Tommy Bahama for the most part has been on an upward trajectory, though it is coming off one of its toughest financial quarters since being bought by Oxford Industries, a publicly traded company in Atlanta, in 2003. Tommy Bahama has posted a slight decline in sales, citing waning consumer confidence and depressed home values in Florida, California, Arizona, and Nevada, where about two-thirds of its stores are. Tommy

(continued on next page)

Bahama is managing its inventory more cautiously to avoid the kind of price slashing that cuts into profits and runs counter to its upscale image, said Don Kerkes, president of the men's division. Also, it's introducing more expensive "price points" because the upper end of the market seems to be holding up, and for the first time has begun selling merchandise on its Web site. "There was a time when our woven shirts were right around $100," Kerkes said. "Today, our woven shirts are anywhere from $100 to $175, and they sell as well at $150 to $175 as they do at $100. Our customers certainly are willing to spend the money if the product is right." Tommy Bahama's challenge is to sell a sun-and-surf lifestyle at wine-and-brie prices.

The company oversees four brands under its namesake Tommy Bahama label: Relax, for "patio kings," or men who like to barbecue in their backyard by the pool (think cotton rather than silk); Indigo Palms, which sells jeans for $88 and up; Island Soft, a dressier, more expensive offering; and TB 18 Golf, for the country club set.

Many of the company's stores include white-tablecloth restaurants, where coconut shrimp, macadamia-nut-encrusted snapper, and piña colada cake are among the top sellers. The restaurants "romanticize" the Tommy Bahama brand so that the customers feel like they're not just buying a man's shirt but a whole lifestyle. Tommy Bahama's stores with restaurants ring up an average of more than $1,000 a square foot in sales annually, compared with a target of $800 to $900 at stores without restaurants.

Sales to Retailers

Sales to other retailers account for about 45 percent of the Tommy Bahama business, matched by sales at its own stores. Licensing fees make up the remaining 10 percent. Manufacturers pay Tommy Bahama fees in exchange for permission to sell products under the palm tree logo.

Licensed products run the gamut from furniture and ceiling fans to watches and sunglasses. Earlier this year, Tommy Bahama added another: Barbadian rum created with Sidney Frank Importing. Someday soon, Tommy Bahama might introduce vacation packages and possibly its own vacation resort.

Source: Martinez, A. "Tommy Bahama clothing line grows up." *The Seattle Times*, retrieved from http://seattletimes.nwsource.com/html/businesstechnology/2004088389_tommybahama23.html

1. Develop a product and pricing plan for the next five years for Tommy Bahama. What are the strengths and risks of this plan? Consider developing a SWOT (strengths, weaknesses, opportunities, threats) analysis.

2. Which new products or product lines do you recommend that Tommy Bahama add? Why?

CHAPTER TEN

Product Development and Design

Contributed by

Professor Kirsteen Buchanan
STEPHENS COLLEGE

Objectives

- To define and explore the history of product development

- To examine the types of product development businesses from the manufacturer to the retailer

- To understand the importance of product segmentation in creating a brand

- To analyze competition as it relates to product development goals

- To examine the activities of research and forecasting in product development

- To assess the merchandiser's job in product development

- To explore the steps of product development

What Is Product Development?

Product development is exactly what it sounds like: creating and manufacturing a product from start to finish. Chapter 6 examines the functions of a company; the research and development function is, in essence, product development. This is not a new process. Manufacturers in every industry, from fashion to airplanes to household appliances, have always engaged in product development. However, beginning in the 1980s, it became popular for retailers to develop products of their own instead of simply selling a collection of other manufacturers' brands. The Gap, for example, used to carry a variety of casual brands, such as Levi's. Now its stores carry only Gap-branded merchandise, which is designed and developed in-house. Product development may be the function of one department or a division within the organization (e.g., Macy's, Inc.) or the mission of the entire company (e.g., Liz Claiborne, Inc.).

Why Move into Product Development?

There are three main reasons why retailers moved into the business of developing their own products or lines of products:

1. **Satisfying the customer**—To be able to fulfill specific customer demands

2. **Fashion exclusivity**—To project fashion images unique to their particular companies

3. **Profit**—To make more money on each item, by going directly to factories instead of buying from manufacturers

In the beginning, retailers ran into several problems while developing their own products. There is a long tradition in the fashion business of knocking off the hot, or successful, designs offered by the competition. A **knockoff** is simply a copy of another style, either detail by detail or with a few small changes. Although it may not be the case today, retailers were historically known for compiling their private label lines as collections of knockoffs. Because many of them were knocking off products that were already on the market, many of their private label products lacked fashion newness. Retailers also had to take responsibility for most fit problems. Another hindrance was that many overseas factories required that retailers open letters of credit to pay for goods, thus tying up large amounts of the retailers' dollars in advance of shipping.

As retail-driven product development matured, retailers began to build their own highly skilled design and merchandising teams to prevent some of these problems. Large retailers are now major employers of designers, technical designers, print and textile designers, sourcing specialists, merchandisers, quality controllers, pattern makers, trend forecasters, and colorists. As a result, it is important for all fashion students to know about the product development process. Because buyers and planners have also become an integral part of product development, they must be cognizant of the product development cycle and design terminology as well.

Some major retailers do not try to develop products in certain specialized apparel categories because they are too precarious or too dependent on major brand names. According to Burns and Bryant (1997), private label products are most appropriately developed in the following categories:

- Moderate and entry price point

- Basic apparel

- Easy-fit apparel

- Categories with weak or no competing major brands

Many stores prefer to leave development of highly specialized apparel, such as swimwear, or categories that require major advertising investments, such as cosmetics, up to the major brands. Because styling on basic products makes it difficult to tell a major brand from a private brand, stores are safer with this type of merchandise. A retailer takes a big risk, however, when trying to develop trendy or high-fashion merchandise.

10.1 What is the main category of product that the internship organization develops (e.g., women's apparel, cosmetics, luggage, and so on)?

_____

_____

10.2 Why did the internship company first begin creating its own products?

_____

_____

Types of Product Development Businesses

In the fashion industry, there are three key types of businesses:

1. **Manufacturers**—Companies that create, produce, market, and distribute lines of apparel on a continual basis. This can be done by a *designer* with his or her own company or by a company *employing designers*. Manufacturers can own their own factories or can use contractors to construct their products. Examples include: Jones New York, Anna Sui, and Kellwood.

2. **Contractors**—Domestic or offshore factories that make and finish goods. Contractors usually do not design or distribute the goods. Examples are Hill Knitting Mills and Shishi City Fengcheng Garment Company, Ltd.

3. **Retailers**—Entities that sell products to the ultimate consumer, including the vast range of brick-and-mortar stores (e.g., department stores, mass merchants, specialty stores, boutiques, discount stores, and off-price stores) as well as catalogs and online stores. Almost all national retailers currently engage in some form of product development.

Retail Product Development

Before examining the product development process in detail, it is necessary to examine the general types of items that have evolved as retailers have become more involved in the customizing of products. Following are types of product development that may be implemented by retailers:

- **Retail label**—A label with the retailer's name on it, such as Neiman Marcus or Saks Fifth Avenue. A retailer may negotiate with a manufacturer to put its label on a group of items instead of, or in addition to, the manufacturer's label, although the retailer may not have anything to do with the design or development of the items. Some of the items carrying a store label may be **exclusives,** or items that only one retailer carries. In some cases, a retailer could negotiate to be the only one in a geographic region to carry a particular item or the only one in the country to carry a particular color. In these instances, the label may read, for example, "Burberry Exclusively for Neiman Marcus."

- **Private label**—A name owned exclusively by a particular retailer, such as Copper Key at Dillard's.

- **Private brand**—A name owned exclusively by a particular store that is extensively marketed with a definite image, such as Target's Mossimo brand or the Macy's INC brand.

- **Direct market brand**—A brand that is both the name of the store (usually a specialty store) and the name on the label. Examples include Ann Taylor, Express, and Banana Republic.

Manufacturer Product Development

The main business of most manufacturers is designing and developing their own lines; however, with the advent of retail product development, many have found it harder to compete. Therefore, manufacturers have begun to develop a variety of other products besides those in their signature lines. New types of product development at the manufacturing level include private labels and licensees.

As noted previously, manufacturers may design, develop, and construct items specifically for one retailer as a private label. This is especially seen at manufacturers specializing in highly technical or very inexpensive sorts of apparel.

Authentic Fitness, for example, develops swimwear for Wal-Mart. Some manufacturers sell only private label merchandise. They may even develop seasonal lines that they showcase in a showroom, but items are sold only on an exclusive basis, with fairly substantial minimum orders per style. A private label manufacturer will typically take a smaller markup than a manufacturer selling its own line.

Licensees are manufacturers that have paid for the right to use a designer's, celebrity's, or character's name and to develop lines under those names. Some licensees include Phillips-Van Heusen (Kenneth Cole New York), The Levy Group (Betsey Johnson outerwear), Kellwood (XOXO), and Estée Lauder (Donna Karan Cosmetics). Licensees typically must receive approval from the licensor on the design direction of the line but are responsible for financing all line development, marketing, and sales of the products. Therefore, close communication is necessary between licensee and licensor in order for the look of the product and advertising to remain consistent, especially if the brand has a number of licensees.

10.3 Does the internship organization conduct product development? If so, describe the product categories being developed. Under what labels does the company develop products? If not, select private label lines offered by a well-known retailer to answer the questions.

_____

_____

_____

Creating a Brand: Product Segmentation

Upon deciding to develop any sort of product, a company must first determine exactly what it wants to make. Developers will select a general product category, such as women's sweaters. They then must narrow the focus. The fashion market is extremely segmented, with each brand filling its particular niche. It is not enough simply to decide to create a line of women's sweaters because that is far too broad a category to allow for effective line development. Instead, the product developer may narrow its focus and elect, for example, to create contemporary sweaters for fashion-forward customers in misses' sizes 4 to 14. Companies focused on brands usually make a specific product type created for a particular size range appealing to a customer with a unique taste level who is willing to pay a certain amount of money. All these factors intertwine to provide a unique product profile. Product segmentation components include product, price, size, and taste level categories. As an illustration, Figure 10.1 shows the product segmentation categories for women's sportswear.

Figure 10.1 Product segmentation categories.

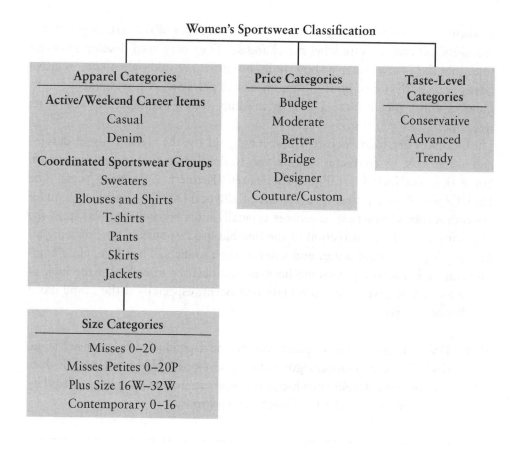

Women's Sportswear Classification

Apparel Categories

Active/Weekend Career Items
Casual
Denim

Coordinated Sportswear Groups
Sweaters
Blouses and Shirts
T-shirts
Pants
Skirts
Jackets

Price Categories
Budget
Moderate
Better
Bridge
Designer
Couture/Custom

Taste-Level Categories
Conservative
Advanced
Trendy

Size Categories
Misses 0–20
Misses Petites 0–20P
Plus Size 16W–32W
Contemporary 0–16

10.4   Select one of the internship company's brands, and describe the product components that blend to make the brand unique: product, price, size, and taste level categories.

_____

_____

The Merchandiser's Job in Product Development

The merchandiser's responsibilities vary widely, depending on company requirements. In a nutshell, **merchandisers** work with product development teams to decide what to make and then organize and control the entire product development process. Merchandisers are responsible for the development of balanced, marketable, profitable, and timely product lines. In some companies the merchandiser oversees the design function and may serve as a liaison between the design and sales departments. Merchandisers create the initial line plan and project target wholesale costs by analyzing sales from previous seasons, fashion trends, and customer wants. Merchandisers work closely with designers on seasonal themes and guide them on the development of cost-effective, marketable styles. Merchandisers may also have responsibilities in the sourcing and marketing functions. **Sourcing** refers to locating the suppliers and manufacturers for a product. The hallmarks of a good merchandiser are excellent communication, thorough market knowledge, decisiveness, organization, a keen fashion sense, strong analytical skills, creativity, and an astute marketing instinct. The successful merchandiser is continually cognizant of the market environment and the target customer.

> Successful merchandisers must have a comprehensive understanding of the companies' market and products. This knowledge requires in-depth research and analysis of a company's target market. The merchandiser's ultimate objective is to provide the "right" *p*roduct at the "right" *p*rice in the "right" *p*lace using effective *p*romotion to obtain a high percentage sell-through at retail. To achieve these four "Ps" of marketing, a merchandiser must focus the efforts of the design department on developing products that meet the needs of the target market. (Rosenau & Wilson, p. 88)

Typical merchandising tasks may include the following:

- Market research; tracking market trends; attending trade shows and markets

- Fashion forecasting

- Meeting with retail accounts

- Attending consumer focus groups

- Shopping the competition

- Scouting fabric and trim markets

- Analyzing past sales and market trends

- Strategic planning, including developing the merchandising calendar and line plan

- Developing design concepts along with the designers

- Developing cost estimates for the new line

- Participating in, and giving direction on, the line presentation to the sales department

- Production authorization: choosing and quantifying which styles will actually be produced, sometimes prior to sales

- Sourcing

- Fostering a creative environment so that designers can do their best work

10.5 Describe the unique qualifications of the merchandiser. What experience and skills are required for the job?

_____

_____

_____

10.6 What are the keys to success for a good merchandiser?

_____

_____

_____

10.7 Discuss the merchandiser's job responsibilities.

_____

_____

_____

10.8 What is the career path if one wants to become a merchandiser?

_____

_____

_____

Planning for Product Development

Strategic planning is the key to successful product development. Upon deciding to develop product, a smart company will articulate its general vision, taking into account social, political, and economic conditions. Each department in the company will create an action plan to reach the company's goals. Strategic planners will specify a target market, a marketing mix by product categories, company resource allocations, and anticipated sales and profit results (Rosenau & Wilson, p. 2001).

The number of seasons, or product offerings per year, can vary greatly, depending on the company. Some companies prefer to have goods flow into the retail operations on a biweekly or monthly basis, continually offering the customer fresh products. Others find this constant flow prohibitive and stick to a traditional four- to six-season line release. Additional seasons make planning and strict attention to deadlines even more critical.

Integral to a company's action plans for upcoming seasons are a number of calendars. The **marketing calendar** includes line preview and release dates by season; start and end shipping dates; and weekly or monthly sales plans; and weekly or monthly shipping plans. The **merchandising calendar** is the product development team's schedule. Its goal is to deliver the right product (e.g., style, quality, and price) at the right time. When creating a new line, developers carefully plan how often they want goods to flow into the retail operation. When the delivery schedule is completed, a calendar is created by working backward from in-store delivery dates, listing all tasks in the product development cycle, with deadlines for each. The resulting calendar may require that developers work on different phases of several seasons at the same time. Delay at any point can jeopardize an entire season. The merchandiser must be constantly aware of the development progress as it relates to the calendar.

Next, the merchandiser develops a detailed **line plan**. The line plan shows the number of styles in the line, the number and general types of fabrics to be used, colors per style, anticipated stock-keeping units, and approximate target costs. The line plan gives designers guidelines from which to work and focuses their efforts in a distinct direction, while taking into account fabric and yarn minimums and lead times.

A **sales forecast** is created by key merchants, in conjunction with sales personnel and a review of past sales. It includes projections of sales by category, style, color, and size, based on historical data and statistical analysis. This information may be used to place preliminary fabric orders and to block out production time in factories. For retailers, it is used to project the amount of money to be spent on new merchandise.

10.9 Who at the internship company gives the initial direction or decides the general product categories to be developed?

_____

_____

_____

10.10 How is it decided how much importance to place on certain items?

_____

_____

_____

10.11 Attach or scan a merchandising calendar and a line plan from a previous season, if available.

_____

_____

_____

10.12 Describe a situation in which a deadline on the merchandising calendar was missed and the consequences.

_____

_____

_____

The product developer considers several factors when putting together a line or seasonal collection of groups of styles. Next, these factors will be examined: line composition, line structure, and line balance.

Line Composition

Whereas retailers sell directly to the ultimate consumer, manufacturers really have two levels of customer: the retail buyer and the ultimate consumer. A consumer will be drawn to the line because of color, style, price, touch, quality, fit or size, or care. This attraction is known as **line appeal**. A buyer or merchant may be drawn to a line because of image, line structure, sales presentation, knowledgeable salespeople, customer service, trunk shows, in-store merchandising opportunities, price or value, advertising assistance, and opportunities for retailer education.

Manufacturers must develop their products to be attractive to both levels of customer and market differently to each level. Some manufacturers open retail stores so that they are able to communicate directly with the consumer and not have to rely on their retail accounts for communicating accurate feedback. In any case, product developers will carefully balance their lines to have maximum appeal to their target markets.

Line Structure

Often, a designer-priced line is called a **collection** and comprises several groups of styles. Each group on the line may be based on a small selection of fabrics and developed around a unified color story and a theme. Though several groups may be shown at once to a particular market, they may be delivered at staggered times.

There are two types of lines: item lines and coordinated group lines. An **item line** is a selection of only one type of item, organized around groups of fabrics and showing a range of silhouettes. Dress, suit, and coat lines are item lines.

In sportswear, item lines include T-shirt, sweater, and jean lines. **Coordinated group lines** are found primarily in the sportswear and related separates markets. Each group is built around a coordinating fabric and includes items that may be mixed and matched to form a variety of ensembles. In apparel they are often referred to as related separates and are frequently shipped as a group.

10.13 Discuss the grouping of products within the internship company. Does the company divide groups by theme?

_____

_____

_____

10.14 How many groups are in a seasonal collection?

_____

_____

_____

10.15 Is the line an item line or a coordinated group line?

_____

_____

_____

Line Balance

Lines should be focused. **Line balance** ensures that lines have enough variety to make it hard for the customers to choose just one thing—they should want to buy everything. Fashion companies tend to segment product lines into varying percentages of the following types of items. Although some of these terms are explored in Chapter 9, they are presented as follows, as they fit in the product development process:

- **In-stock basics**—Items that are always carried and that change minimally. These items have a long selling life and are in demand season after season. Examples are white cotton T-shirts and five-pocket denim jeans.

- **Core basics**—Basic items in fabrics that are carried every season in colors that may change slightly. Fabrics can also change with each season, for example, corduroy in fall and linen in spring.

- **Fashion items**—Styles that are very current and in demand for a short amount of time. They may come in a limited color range. Examples include leather pants, stretch twin sets, and leggings.

- **Key items**—Not-too-trendy but not-too-basic fashion items that are the must-haves for the season, offered in many colors or a variety of fabrics. These items are usually advertised and carried in-depth. Examples are rib-knit V-neck sweaters and boot-cut corduroy pants.

- **Trendy items**—Items that are very exciting but that are carried minimally as customer acceptance is being tested; items that pull the customer into the store. Often these are impulse items showcasing a wild fashion color, a unique fabric, or a very fashion-forward silhouette. Examples include T-shirts with rhinestones, circle-quilted jackets, and printed velveteen pants.

Manufacturers may specialize in lines including one or a few of these categories, whereas retail product developers may include all the categories in their lines.

Product developers must also include balanced ratios in their lines of:

- tops to bottoms;
- hard pieces to soft pieces (e.g., denim to silk);
- knits to wovens;
- short sleeves to long sleeves;
- variety in necklines and body lengths;
- fashion colors to basics; and
- prints to solids.

The goal is to make it difficult for a buyer to choose just one item in the line to the exclusion of others.

Choose a specific group or collection and analyze it, attaching or scanning a line sheet, look book, or sketches, if possible. If you are interning in design or product development, choose a product line your company creates. If you are interning for a retailer or publisher, select a line the internship company features.

10.16 What percentage of items are basic items, key items, fashion items, or trendy items?

_____

_____

_____

10.17 What is the top-to-bottom ratio?

_____

_____

_____

10.18 What percent of items is devoted to hard pieces? to soft pieces?

_____

_____

_____

10.19 What were the top-selling colors and sizes in the group? Why do you think this was so?

_____

_____

_____

Product Development Steps

There are a number of steps taken when developing a line, though the details may change depending on the type of product, whether the line is to be produced overseas or domestically, whether the line is a private brand or a manufacturer's brand, and if the company has an in-house sample department. An example of a full in-house product development division is that of The Doneger Group, as illustrated in Box 10.1 on page 291. Following are the general steps for developing a product line each season:

1. Inspiration and market research: Last year's numbers are analyzed and product categories decided.

2. Trend forecasts and line planning: The company decides what it believes in. Color stories are decided.

3. Fabric and trim research and selection: Prints are designed.

4. Concept development: Storyboards are created. Designs are sketched. Sample fabrics and trims are ordered. Labdips (dye approval swatches) are requested.

5. Merchandising meetings: The line may be edited from sketches.

6. Specifications: Specs are written, and technical packages are compiled.

7. Sourcing: Prototypes and preliminary costing are requested.

8. Patterns and first samples: These are produced by a sample room or contractors. Often as many as twice the number of designs are made than will actually be needed. Factories advise on costs.

9. Samples: Samples are fitted, edited, and adopted into the line during a line review. The fitting process continues until the sample is approved or dropped. Costs and details are negotiated. Quantities may be discussed and orders placed at this time, depending on factory lead time.

10. Sample line: The sample line for sales representatives is produced. Private brands may require only a meeting sample. Costs are finalized. Photo and production samples are requested. Line sheets are developed. (A **line sheet** provides information about the products being sold. Often, it includes an order form for retail buyers to use.)

11. Sample marked up: If it is for a manufacturer's line, the sample is marked up to allow for profit, sales commissions, overhead, marketing, advertising, customer service, store markdown money, and so on. The line is sold by the company sales representatives during trade market weeks and on the road to retailers. Manufacturers may wait for orders from retailers before placing orders for fabrics or contracting with factories.

12. Private brand sales: If for a private brand, the styles will be "sold" internally to buyers who quantify the purchase. Quantity may be an integral part of cost negotiation, or it may be determined when specifications are originally given to factories.

13. Fabric and trim: Production fabric and trim are ordered as soon as the factories receive orders.

14. Manufacturing: Production goods are manufactured.

15. Shipping: Goods are shipped to the manufacturer and packed to ship to its retail customers or are shipped directly to the retailer if for a private brand.

16. Receipts: Goods are received by the retail accounts.

Fashion is a deadline-driven business. It is critical that deadlines not be missed at any step of the development process because this could ultimately result in goods being delivered late and sales being lost. Typically, the bigger the company, the more meetings will be held to discuss each step in the development process. Editing and adoption require input from a number of interested parties, including designers, merchandisers, sales managers, and company executives.

mesh separates

Figure 10.2 Line sheets.

miacro CaCo₃

www.miacrodesign.com

style: talc-t
color: chalk / flint
description: long sleeve top / hand dyed
content: 80% nylon 20% spandex
msrp: $150
wholesale price: $68

style: talc-l
color: chalk / flint
description: legging / hand dyed
content: 80% nylon 20% spandex (band 85/15)
msrp: $150
wholesale price: $68

style: truck-t
color: lime / chalk
description: long sleeve top / hand printed
content: 80% nylon 20% spandex
msrp: $150
wholesale price: $68

style: truck-l
color: lime / chalk
description: legging / hand printed
content: 80% nylon 20% spandex (band 85/15)
msrp: $150
wholesale price: $68

style: snails-t
color: carbon / tannic
description: long sleeve top / hand printed
content: 80% nylon 20% spandex
msrp: $150
wholesale price: $68

style: snails-l
color: carbon / tannic
description: legging / hand printed
content: 80% nylon 20% spandex (band 85/15)
msrp: $150
wholesale price: $68

style: twilight-t
color: blood
description: long sleeve top / hand dyed
content: 80% nylon 20% spandex
msrp: $150
wholesale price: $68

style: twilight-l
color: blood
description: legging / hand dyed
content: 80% nylon 20% spandex (band 85/15)
msrp: $150
wholesale price: $68

style: topo-ct
color: tannic / blood / carbon
description: long sleeve top / hand printed
content: 80% nylon 20% spandex
msrp: $150
wholesale price: $68

style: topo-cl
color: tannic / blood / carbon
description: legging / hand printed
content: 80% nylon 20% spandex (band 85/15)
msrp: $150
wholesale price: $68

style: topo-qt
color: flint / chalk
description: long sleeve top / hand printed
content: 80% nylon 20% spandex
msrp: $150
wholesale price: $68

style: topo-ql
color: flint / chalk
description: legging / hand printed
content: 80% nylon 20% spandex (band 85/15)
msrp: $150
wholesale price: $68

blood | clay | tannic | calcite | chalk | carbon | flint | lime

organic separates

miacro CaCo₃

style: bones-f
color: carbon / chalk
description: funnel neck top / hand printed
content: 97% organic bamboo 3% spandex
msrp: $150
wholesale price: $68

style: cracked-f
color: flint / chalk
description: funnel neck top / hand printed
content: 97% organic bamboo 3% spandex
msrp: $150
wholesale price: $68

style: ooid-cf
color: clay / carbon
description: funnel neck top / hand printed
content: 97% organic bamboo 3% spandex
msrp: $150
wholesale price: $68

style: millipede-f
color: blood / carbon
description: funnel neck top / hand dyed
content: 97% organic bamboo 3% spandex
msrp: $165
wholesale price: $75

style: ooid-qf
color: calcite / lime
description: top / hand printed
content: 97% organic bamboo 3% spandex
msrp: $150
wholesale price: $68

style: metallurgy-fd
color: flint
description: funnel neck dress / hand dyed
content: 97% organic bamboo 3% spandex
msrp: $225
wholesale price: $102

style: millipede-ld
color: blood
description: long sleeve dress / hand dyed
content: 97% organic bamboo 3% spandex
msrp: $250
wholesale price: $114

style: pitch-l
color: carbon / blood
description: long sleeve top
content: 97% organic bamboo 3% spandex
msrp: $150
wholesale price: $68

style: metallurgy-l
color: flint / chalk
description: long sleeve top / hand dyed
content: 97% organic bamboo 3% spandex
msrp: $185
wholesale price: $84

style: (1) surface (2) undergrowth
color: (1) calcite (2) carbon
description: long pant w/ gusset
content: 100% organic cotton twill / (bamboo band)
msrp: $350
wholesale price: $159

style: x
color: flint / chalk
description: reversible tunic dress / hand printed & dyed
content: 100% organic cotton twill
msrp: $350
wholesale price: $159

style: flowstone
color: carbon / clayalk
description: reversible tunic dress / hand printed & dyed
content: 100% organic cotton twill
msrp: $350
wholesale price: $159

style: (1) blind (2) haze
color: (1) carbon (2) calcite
description: hooded vest / self lined
content: 97% organic bamboo 3% spandex
msrp: $225
wholesale price: $102

www.miacrodesign.com

Figure 10.3 Order sheets.

mıacro CaCo₃

nylon mesh separates

leggings

style	color		s / m	m / l	total quantity	wholesale $	msrp $	total cost $
sinkholes-cl	tannic beige					68	150	
snails-l	carbon black					68	150	
talc-cl	flint grey					68	150	
talc-ql	chalk white					68	150	
truck-l	lime green					68	150	
twilight-cl	blood red					68	150	

long sleeve tops

style	color		s / m	m / l	total quantity	wholesale $	msrp $	total cost $
sinkholes-cl	tannic beige					68	150	
snails-t	carbon black					68	150	
talc-ct	flint grey					68	150	
talc-qt	chalk white					68	150	
truck-t	lime green					68	150	
twilight-ct	blood red					68	150	

mıacro

organic bamboo jersey

hooded vests

style	color		s / m	m / l	total quantity	wholesale $	msrp $	total cost $
blind-hv	carbon black					102.27	225	
haze-hv	calcite cream					102.27	225	

reversible hooded scarves

style	color		s / m	m / l	total quantity	wholesale $	msrp $	total cost $
millipede-rhs	blood red					56.82	125	
quicklime-rhs	calcite cream					56.82	125	
salamander-rhs	carbon black					56.82	125	
salamander-rhs	clay brown					56.82	125	

pencil skirts

style	color		s / m	m / l	total quantity	wholesale $	msrp $	total cost $
millipede-ps	blood red					56.82	125	
quicklime-ps	calcite cream					56.82	125	
talc-ps	carbon black					56.82	125	
salamander-ps	clay brown					56.82	125	

miacro CaCo₃

organic bamboo separates

funnel tops

style	color	s / m	m / l	total quantity	wholesale $	msrp $	total cost $
bones-f	carbon black				68	150	
pitch-f	carbon black				62	135	
cracked-f	flint grey				68	150	
metallurgy-f	flint grey				75	165	
millipede-f	blood red				68	150	
ooid-cf	clay brown				68	150	
ooid-qf	calcite cream				68	150	

long sleeve tops

style	color	s / m	m / l	total quantity	wholesale $	msrp $	total cost $
bones-l	carbon black				79	175	
pitch-l	carbon black				68	150	
cracked-l	flint grey				79	175	
metallurgy-l	flint grey				84	185	
millipede-l	blood red				79	175	
ooid-cl	clay brown				79	175	
ooid-ql	calcite cream				79	175	

miacro

organic bamboo jersey

dresses - funnel

style	color	s / m	m / l	total quantity	wholesale $	msrp $	total cost $
millipede-fd	blood red				102.27	225	
metallurgy-fd	flint grey				102.27	225	

dresses - long sleeve

style	color	s / m	m / l	total quantity	wholesale $	msrp $	total cost $
millipede-lsd	blood red				113.64	250	
metallurgy-lsd	flint grey				113.64	250	

organic cotton twill

shorts

style	color	s / m	m / l	total quantity	wholesale $	msrp $	total cost $
surface-s	chalk white				136.36	300	
undergrowth-s	carbon black				136.06	300	

pants

style	color	s / m	m / l	total quantity	wholesale $	msrp $	total cost $
surface-p	chalk white				159.09	350	
undergrowth-p	carbon black				159.09	350	

10.20 Describe the development process of one product in particular and the key personnel involved in its creation.

_____

_____

Research and Forecasting

Large companies deliberately calculate the fashion image they want to project for the upcoming seasons. The fashion director or merchandiser creates formal trend forecasting reports, color stories, and seasonal themes, which are presented to all design and development staff members. This helps ensure the creation of consistent looks across all departments. **Forecasting** is the process of identifying fashion trends, interpreting them for a particular customer or market, and communicating them to designers. A forecaster is a type of market researcher who must know the customer inside and out. The forecaster's responsibilities include:

- gathering information from diverse sources;

- analyzing current events, looking for common denominators, and projecting possible scenarios for the future; and

- anticipating when the customer is ready for a change.

The forecaster is adept at gathering data but must also be able to sift, analyze, and organize that data. In many companies the merchandiser is also the forecaster.

Forecasters, product developers, and designers must continually research the customer, the product, and the market. **Consumer research** involves finding out everything about the customer's characteristics and behavior by analyzing demographics and psychographics. **Product research** involves anticipating the sales potential of new products, recognizing how lines are structured, identifying preferred product design and characteristics, and determining which items must be included in the line. Product research also involves developing better-performing fabrics or design and improving manufacturing techniques. It includes an understanding of fit and comfort for the customer. **Market analysis** is the study of general market trends. It can be divided into long-range forecasting and short-range forecasting. **Long-range forecasting** refers to researching economic trends related to consumer spending patterns and the business climate by looking into the future. **Short-range forecasting** applies to one particular company and refers to the type of planning a company does to advance its goals in the near future. Short-range forecasting is also called sales forecasting because it requires analyzing numbers from past seasons and strategizing new activities for growth. Fashion trend forecasting fits under the category of short-range forecasting as well.

The Doneger Group

History

Founded as a buying office by the late Henry Doneger, in 1946, The Doneger Group has evolved as a leading resource to the retail, manufacturing, and auxiliary communities of the fashion industry by consistently building its fashion and merchandising expertise. Today, under the direction of Henry's son, Abbey Doneger, The Doneger Group has maintained its heritage, while strategically growing its business through the addition of new services and acquisitions to best support the growth and strategic initiatives of its clients, and the direction of the industry.

Merchandising

Henry Doneger Associates (HDA), the foundation of the company's merchandising divisions, offers retailers extensive advisory services, seasonal merchandising direction, and current business and market analysis in all classifications, sizes, and price levels for women's, men's and children's wear.

HDA International provides information, sourcing, and product development opportunities to international retailers from a range of U.S.-based manufacturers and importers. Services include comprehensive market coverage, personalized merchandising consultations, strategic product planning, and access to an extensive network of business resources.

Carol Hoffman, a division of The Doneger Group since 2001, advises women's specialty retailers in the contemporary, better, bridge, designer, and couture markets. This division provides extensive market coverage in all classifications of sportswear, dresses, outerwear, suits, accessories, and lingerie.

Price Point Buying uncovers off-price merchandise in women's, children's, and men's apparel and accessories. This division is dedicated to providing retailers with outstanding buys, allowing them to build sales and increase profits.

Directives West is Doneger's West Coast merchandising consulting arm, providing clients with extensive retail and street coverage, insight into the West Coast lifestyle as it relates to fashion and consumers, and market analysis in the categories of contemporary, better, junior, moderate, accessories, men's, young men's, and kids. Founded in 1982, Directives West became part of The Doneger Group in March 2008.

Tobé, best known for The Tobé Report, one of the industry's most respected fashion publications for over 80 years, became a division of The Doneger Group in 2005. Tobé provides highly strategic thinking on top-level issues and long-term positioning. Concentrating on consumer-based business and trend intelligence, Tobé reviews the retail and wholesale markets, focusing on retail analysis, market direction, the impact of pop culture and the media, and relevant fashion-related events, to identify trend lines in consumer behavior.

Fashion Direction is provided to complement and support the company's market intelligence. A select team works closely with the creative and merchandising teams to offer perspective on seasonal trends and influential design concepts, as they evolve and are applied to the buying and merchandising process.

Trend and Color Forecasting

Doneger Creative Services, DCS, offers a broad range of products and services in keeping with

(continued on next page)

the direction of the industry. DCS Creative Directors cover the apparel, accessories, beauty, and lifestyle markets in the Women's, Men's, and Youth categories and communicate their analysis through printed publications, online content, and live presentations.

The well-respected team of creative directors is the strength of Doneger Creative Services. DCS has the finest talent in forecasting and analyzing fashion trends, all with a discipline for focusing the intelligence on the application to business.

The Doneger Creative Services trend and color forecasting product line takes a unique approach to the traditional trend-forecasting offering. Products and publications are developed in continuum, addressing color, merchandising, and classification trends as they evolve from concept to creation. The Doneger Group's creative intelligence is researched, reported, and archived to track trends as they emerge and develop, creating a useful resource for clients at all stages of development:

- Researches worldwide shifts in the marketplace to determine macro trends in business, fashion, and consumer lifestyle.

- Analyzes and identifies key style trends based on color, fabric, silhouette, and design influence/mood.

- Advises clients on merchandising concepts, color and trends, key items, and business opportunities specific to their business.

- Publishes seasonal color forecasts, trend analysis, and beauty reports, an online reporting service including global runway, retail, and street coverage.

Through the **Margit Publications** division, Doneger Creative Services offers clients the opportunity to purchase the Pantone Color System, European fashion magazines, and a number of complementary, specialized trend services.

Customized Projects

Doneger Consulting delivers bespoke projects from The Doneger Group's comprehensive industry insight and perspective. Doneger Consulting leverages on The Doneger Group's industry expertise, including merchandising information at retail and wholesale, trend and color forecasting, and product development. With this broad foundation of market intelligence, Doneger Consulting readily identifies unique business opportunities and develops them to the individual clients' business needs and objectives.

- Lifestyle profiling: identification of lifestyle trends across categories; new concepts relating to consumer experiences; insight into related style industries and lateral markets.

- Industry analysis: in-depth examination of particular segments of the industry; comprehensive retail reporting including assessments of merchandise assortments, brand positioning, and growth opportunities.

- Customized color and trend research: individualized analysis of merchandise trends, color stories, and delivery flow; presentation of relevant cultural influences and consumer profiling.

- Product line creation: development of seasonal color palettes, materials and style direction; identification of essential items and product opportunities; product design and development including key fabrications and finishing details.

Doneger Online Services

The Doneger Group has a technology platform that gives clients immediate access to the research and development of market, business, and industry intelligence. The company's technology initiatives are focused on delivering emerging trend concepts, runway analysis, photographic coverage of the streets and stores by city, and extensive market coverage by category in an easy-to-use format.

Technology is used in all areas of the company to support day-to-day activities with clients, and to customize information and ideas in merchandising, product development and branding for specific clients. The Doneger Group merchandising and creative experts consistently communicate research, analysis, and opinions on all areas within The Doneger Group business through the Doneger Web site at www.doneger.com:

- Printed publications can be downloaded.

- Runway images are catalogued.

- Market product can be viewed; features keep clients up-to-date on issues of fashion and lifestyle.

- All major trade events are covered.

The Doneger Group.

- Extensive fashion reporting on streets and stores throughout the world is presented.

- Business intelligence and emerging concepts are discussed.

10.21 If the internship organization has its own trend forecasting department, discuss its structure and the unique qualifications of the employees in this department. If there is no forecasting department, who at the internship organization is responsible for deciding the fashion direction of the company?

_____

_____

10.22 How is trend research done?

_____

_____

10.23 How is trend information communicated to product development personnel? Attach or scan a sample of an internal fashion trend communication.

_____

_____

_____

The Designer's Job

A designer is a creative person who is curious about a wide variety of subjects and is able to juggle many tasks at the same time. This curiosity can translate into excellent market research and fabric and trim sourcing abilities. A designer is a trend forecaster in his or her own right, with a feel for what the customer will be ready for next. A designer must be adept at synthesizing a variety of fashion influences while retaining garment marketability and fulfilling customer wants and needs. An important designer trait is the ability to compromise. Designers must balance the desired fashion look of a garment and the highest possible quality standards with cost that is desirable to the target customer.

Following are typical designer tasks:

- Shopping the retail market for design ideas and knowledge of the competition; buying samples

- Shopping the fabric, yarn, and trim markets

- Attending trend forecasting meetings

- Developing color palettes and colorways

- Determining styling direction and creating concept boards or storyboards

- Shopping the print market and buying print paintings

- Sketching garments by hand or on the computer

- Recoloring garments or prints

- Designing embroideries, screen prints, appliqués

- Writing specifications

- Corresponding with factories or in-house sample departments regarding drapes, patterns, and garment construction

- Attending fit meetings

These tasks, of course, vary depending on the type of company for which the designer works. Larger companies may assign some of these tasks, such as writing specifications or developing color palettes, to more specialized personnel, such as technical designers.

10.24 Describe the unique qualifications of the designer, in terms of experience, personal characteristics, and skills.

_____

_____

_____

10.25 What are the designer's job responsibilities? Describe a typical day.

_____

_____

_____

10.26 What are some of the designer's favorite fabric, trim, or print resources?

_____

_____

_____

10.27 What experiences, education, and personal characteristics does the designer look for when hiring an assistant?

_____

_____

_____

10.28 What should be included in a portfolio when applying for an assistant designer position?

_____

_____

_____

The Design Process

The design process refers to the conception of a style, including its inspiration or theme, color palette, fabric selection, silhouette, and fit.

Inspiration

After a fashion company as a whole has decided the general trend direction it will take for an upcoming season, the designer can begin work on the line. **Inspiration** is based on influences that direct or guide a company. Most designers prefer to gather additional inspiration by shopping fashion-forward stores; exhaustively scanning all types of magazines; visiting museums, galleries, and libraries; attending movies and plays; or traveling. Designers may visit trend forecasting services if any are subscribed to by their companies. While this gathering period is happening, designers are also viewing all the new fabric and print lines. Sometimes they will do this at large fashion shows, such as Premiere Vision or the International Fashion Fabrics Exhibition. Designers may also request fabric research from offshore factories. Through this process, designers usually find a few, possibly unrelated, items that inspire them to develop a design concept and take a particular approach to the line.

Fabric and Color Stories

During the research and inspiration process, the designer will be drawn to certain fabrics and will ultimately compose groups of fabrics to be used for different style groupings. At the same time, he or she will develop color stories. The group concepts will incorporate information from the trend forecasts and from past bestsellers. Each group will usually be based on a fabric suitable for the season, to be offered in several colorways, plus fancies (e.g., prints, patterns, textures) for fashion items. Fabric stories should be balanced to allow for the mixture in each group of hard pieces and soft pieces, basics and fashion items. Because the primary variable that impacts garment cost is the price of the fabric, the production and sourcing staff may have input on final fabric choices to make sure chosen fabrics will allow them to meet their target costs. The merchandiser may have a great deal of input into the fabric and color choices as well, sometimes dictating them in the line plan.

Styling Direction

Group concepts are developed that synthesize theme, silhouette, color, and fabric. Storyboards may be created for review by key executives, to be approved before proceeding further.

Style Development

Upon establishing group concepts, designers begin sketching individual styles. They usually have a particular silhouette in mind that epitomizes the fashion trends for the upcoming season and may repeat versions of this silhouette throughout the line. Some styles may be completely original, but sometimes designers will adapt styles from actual garments found on shopping expeditions or in magazines. Most

Figure 10.4 The designer's inspiration backstage at Giambattista Valli's spring 2008 runway show at Espace Jardins du Louvre, in Paris.

Figure 10.5 Style development illustrations and sample cards in Dominique Sirop's atelier.

lines include at least a few **carryovers,** or bestsellers from a previous season. The designer must be careful to include important basics and to balance each group with the help of the merchandiser. Generally, 20 to 50 percent more styles are designed for the line than will actually be sold. Many companies ask for estimated costs from factories before samples are made, so styles can be either dropped or adjusted when the line is still in sketch form. Making product samples is quite expensive, so the merchandiser will generally try to keep the number under control. When a complete group of styles is finalized, all the sketches are placed on a line sheet so that the group may be seen at a glance.

Product Specifications

Product specifications refer to measurements, construction, and component guidelines. For example, product specifications for a blouse may include the type of interfacing, the size and source of the buttons, and the width of the collar and cuffs. At some companies, designers write specifications themselves; at others, this task is delegated to technical designers. **Prototypes** are first samples, requested from in-house sample rooms or from factories. As soon as prototypes are complete, precosting may be done to determine if styles will be cost-effective. Certain construction or design details may be adjusted for more optimal costing.

Fittings

When prototypes are received, designers and production staff meet and fit the garments on fit models. It is the objective of the development team to maintain a consistent fit for the brand, while taking into account the evolution of the fashion silhouette.

Editing and Merchandising

While the fitting process progresses, frequent line review meetings are held to finalize the line. The development team makes sure that the groups stay in fashion focus; that styling is consistent; and that, once again, the best possible product is being offered. Styles are dropped, added, or adjusted to ensure each group has the best possible composition. Costs are reviewed as well, and details are modified so that garments hit the target costs. Top executives usually attend the meeting for final line adoption. This is when each style is evaluated in relation to the original line plan, and the line is viewed with an eye toward a powerful sales presentation. By this time the line may have approximately 10 percent more styles than called for in the line plan. The line will be edited during the final adoption process so that it meets the line plan.

10.29 Using a collection from the internship organization, list the steps in the development process of this group.

_____

_____

_____

10.30 What was the inspiration for this group?

_____

_____

_____

10.31 Which styles were carryovers, or repeats, and which were new? How many styles were in the initial group, and how many were finally adopted?

_____

_____

_____

Figure 10.6 The designers Mark Badgley (at left) and James Mischka demonstrate a fitting on the model Denise Muggli at the Badgley Mischka headquarters, in New York.

Color and Labdips; Prints and Strikeoffs

Colors and patterns are constantly changing in the fashion industry. There is a special language to describe this area of product development. The following is a discussion of some of these industry buzzwords.

Labdips

As soon as the colors and fabrics have been determined, the company must decide whether any of the colors will be custom dyed for any of the fabrics. If so, original color standards must be sent to the dyeing mills or fabric companies so that dye formulations may be created. The mills will send **labdips,** or swatches of dyed fabric, to the product development team for color approval prior to dyeing large yardages of fabric. Organizing and approving labdips may consume a significant amount of the designer's or colorist's time.

Strikeoffs

Printed fabric may be purchased from a number of companies, but sometimes a designer will want to include a print in the line that is exclusive to the company. This requires that the company buy a **croqui,** or a painting of the print; have the print put into repeat, or included in the line again; and decide on **colorways,** or the color composition. When these tasks are finalized, the painting is sent to a printing mill. The mill will print a few yards of fabric, called a **strikeoff,** and send them to the designer for approval.

Figure 10.7 The development team works together to edit and merchandise a collection.

10.32 List the steps in the color approval or strikeoff process at the company. Include whether the company uses original prints, where it buys most of its paintings, and if the paintings are put into repeat or recolored in-house or elsewhere.

_____

_____

_____

10.33 What is the minimum for executing an original print or a custom color? If available, attach a sample of a rejected labdip.

_____

_____

_____

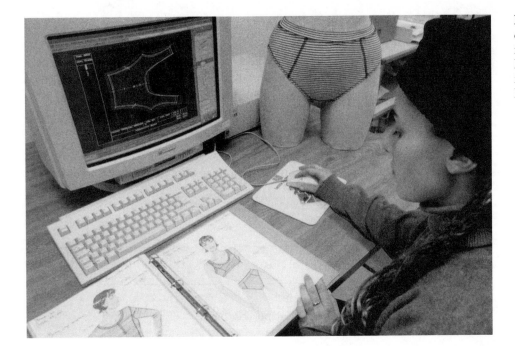

Figure 10.8 A technical designer makes a pattern from a sketch at Armor Lux manufacturing in Quimper, Brittany, France.

Technical Design and Follow-up

Specifications are a big part of designing and, correctly written, ensure that designers get what they want. At manufacturing companies, designers may give pattern makers sketches and a few measurements for guidance, or they may actually drape garments to perfect silhouettes. Each garment will eventually have its own specification sheet, or **spec sheet,** which includes detailed measurements and construction guidelines. Spec sheets may vary, depending on the company in which they are used, and may evolve as the preproduction process advances. Each item on the spec sheet can have critical impact on cost and on organization of time. Spec sheets may include the following:

- Style name

- Style number

- Technical sketch

- All measurements and tolerances

- All fabric and trim information

- Labor costs

- Size range

Retail product developers have a number of challenges. They often do not have in-house factories with pattern makers, and so do most of their manufacturing in distant factories whose pattern makers do the work. The developers often have to complete entire spec packages (also known as technical packages) to send overseas that tell factories every detail of what will be required when producing a style. Many times, specs can be used to give estimated costs so that items can be adjusted or canceled before a costly sample is made.

10.34 Who writes the specifications at the internship company?

_____

_____

_____

10.35 What qualifications does that person have?

_____

_____

_____

10.36 If available, attach or scan an example of a spec sheet or spec package.

_____

_____

_____

Editing and Adoption

After all prototypes have been received, fitted, and perfected, the development team will meet with key executives for this final step in the development process: editing and adoption. During this step, each style in the line will be scrutinized and its reason for inclusion in the line justified. Costs will be carefully reviewed. When the line has been finalized, responsibilities for its styles pass to the production team, and the developers proceed to work on other seasons. However, designers will usually still need to answer questions and help work out problems with styles that are in production.

Developing a product line is a creative, detailed, time-sensitive process; yet, it is one that can catapult a fashion business into the customer's closet and profitability.

Private Label and the Name Game

Sarah Riley is the buyer for the misses' sportswear department of a 15-unit specialty store chain. She is currently attending the Dallas Apparel and Accessories Market to purchase fall merchandise for her department. During this trip, Sarah has decided to investigate the possibility of ordering private label merchandise for her stores. She believes that there are a number of advantages to carrying private label goods, including the following:

- They can offer exclusivity to the merchandise assortment, as the label and selected styles are retained solely by the store.

- They can carry a higher markup on wholesale prices because the goods are not offered by competitors, thereby allowing for a better gross margin.

- They can be advertised with the confidence that competitive retailers will not be promoting identical merchandise.

- They can enhance the retailer's image by featuring the store name on the label.

As Sarah is reviewing the sportswear lines of her regular vendors at market, she realizes that many of these manufacturers offer the option of private label goods. The first requirement for purchasing private label merchandise from these vendors is not a problem: her store must provide the manufacturer with a graphic of the label logo and name or provide the actual labels. The second prerequisite, however, is causing Sarah much concern: a large minimum order is required for a private label purchase. All the manufacturers are consistent in stating that it is not cost-effective for them to produce and individually label small quantities of exclusive merchandise.

Sarah visits a number of vendors that she has not purchased from before and that specialize solely in producing private label merchandise. Although their minimum order quantities are smaller, they nonetheless require significant amounts. In addition, Sarah does not have a sales history with these manufacturers and wonders whether the quality and fit will be as reliable as with her regular vendors. Sarah also knows that late shipments, defective goods, and order substitutions on large amounts of merchandise could cripple her sales volume and even her entire fall season.

Sarah realizes that she will have to eliminate ordering from some of her regular merchandise suppliers to be able to allocate the open-to-buy money needed to accommodate the quantities required for private label purchases. She questions whether her clientele will find large amounts of the same styles unappealing, as her target market is a specialty store shopper. She also considers, however, that the private label merchandise is exclusive to her company and that it would provide the opportunity for competitive pricing. Price is becoming increasingly important to her target customer.

1. If you were in Sarah's position, what would you do? Why?

2. If you were one of the private label manufacturers Sarah had not purchased from previously, what would you do to solicit her business?

Licensing, Distribution, and Product Development— Developing the Footprint for a New Line

Known as a manufacturer of sock and hosiery products for women, men, and children, Hampton Hosiery is owned by a major international corporation that also operates several large divisions of product manufacturing and marketing for goods unrelated to socks and hosiery, such as handbags, active sportswear, gloves, and foods. The corporation as a whole has shown high profit margins for many years. As a result, the corporate executives have committed in the firm's long-range plan to expand one division annually. This year they have allocated funding for the expansion of Hampton Hosiery.

The Hampton Hosiery division has primarily sought out "middle America" as its target market, with moderately priced, traditionally styled sock and hosiery lines that cater to the entire family, from infants to adults. The corporation has recently raised the capital needed to increase Hampton Hosiery's production and distribution capabilities. The company's executives are currently evaluating various product development alternatives, marketing strategies, and retail opportunities that could potentially increase the company's market share through a successful move into a new product line for Hampton Hosiery.

The executives discuss the first alternative— establishing a licensing agreement with a popular designer. With this option the designer would agree to develop a line of women's or men's high-fashion socks or hosiery for Hampton Hosiery in exchange for royalties and a percentage of the line's sales volume. The designer and his or her staff would determine the color and style selection each season and coordinate these hosiery products with the designer's ready-to-wear lines. Hampton Hosiery would then produce the goods under the designer's label.

The executive team examines a second option—producing a budget line of socks and hosiery to sell to mass merchandisers and discount retailers. This product line would carry either a private label of the retailer's choice or a new label created by Hampton Hosiery. With this option, Hampton Hosiery would charge a lower markup on the line(s); however, large quantities would enable the company to make a hefty profit.

A third alternative is brought to the table: Hampton Hosiery could opt to manufacture a better line of hosiery or socks that would appeal to the higher-priced retail operations. Again, this potential line could either feature the prestigious retailers' names, possibly in conjunction with exclusive styles, or be labeled with a status brand invented by Hampton Hosiery.

The team of executives decides to brainstorm additional alternatives with a number of business consultants before determining a plan of action. Assume you are one of the business consultants hired by the corporation, and respond to the following questions:

1. What additional alternatives are available to Hampton Hosiery?

2. If you were an executive of the hosiery division, what would you recommend as the new product development strategy for the firm? How would you implement this strategy?

CHAPTER ELEVEN

Production

$\mathcal{O}$bjectives

- To examine preproduction planning needed to manufacture a product efficiently

- To evaluate domestic, foreign, in-house, and contractual production alternatives as they relate to manufacturing a product

- To explore the stages of the manufacturing process: production patternmaking, grading and marking, spreading and cutting, assembling, finishing and labeling, and distribution of the finished product

- To assess costing strategies as they relate to the wholesale price of a product

What Are the Stages and Strategies of Production?

Preproduction Planning

After styles for the line are selected and wholesale costs for these styles are calculated, preproduction planning begins. In planning for trade markets, fabric and trims are ordered for production samples and sales representatives' sample lines. Typical preproduction steps is presented in the following list:

- Order fabric and trims for sample lines.

- Begin making production samples and patterns.

- Cut and sew duplicates.

- Develop line sheets and swatch cards to be attached to sales representatives' lines.

- Send sample lines to sales representatives.

- Grade patterns.

- Construct specification sheets.

- Track sales made by representatives selling the line to build cutting tickets.

- Drop styles that did not sell well from the line.

- Inform sales representatives of deleted styles, and suggest replacements.

After the line is edited and the sales representatives have begun showing the line, a production pattern is drafted. The **production pattern** is a revised first pattern that is adjusted for fit, construction details, and placement on the fabric. The production pattern is then given to the **grader**, the person who adjusts it to various sizes, and to the **marker maker**, who creates a **marker**, or pattern layout, on the fabric that best suits the fabric and is most economical to produce. Pattern pieces are interlocked as closely as possible to ensure there is minimal wasted fabric. **Cutting tickets** are developed to indicate the minimum number of pieces that must be ordered to ensure profitability. They also instruct the cutter as to how many garments to make of each particular size. Today, much of grading, marker making, and cutting ticket formation is done by computer; often, the grading and marker making are done by one division or person in the company. The marker is then printed onto paper that is the same width as the fabric. The fabric is spread into layers, referred to as "laying up the cut." The marker is then laid over layers of the fabric onto large cutting tables to be separated into pieces by the **cutter** (Figure 11.1). Band knives that vibrate up and down are often used for cutting, as are lasers and old-fashioned shears, depending on the type of fabric and the technological resources of the company. Larger manufacturers use computers to grade the pattern, make the marker, and cut the pattern from the fabric. A more detailed discussion of the manufacturing process follows later in this chapter.

Figure 11.1 A cutter slices patterns through many layers of fabric.

11.1 Using the preproduction stages listed previously, describe where, when, how, and by whom the preproduction stages are accomplished by the internship organization if it is a manufacturer or design house.

_____

_____

Production Planning

Some companies cut to order, whereas others cut to stock. **Cut to order** refers to manufacturing goods after the buyers have submitted purchase orders. There is less risk involved in cutting garments to order; however, longer lead times are needed, and late orders often cannot be filled. **Cut to stock** refers to producing the amount of merchandise that corresponds to the amount of fabric purchased for a particular style. Larger companies cut to stock when they have a good track record with a specific style and are confident that it will sell well. These large companies often have fabric dyed to order or design an exclusive print. In both cases, they must purchase a significant quantity of yardage. A **purchasing plan** is then developed to calculate costs for and order fabrics and trims; this process is often referred to as **building orders**. Production flow charts are then drawn up to designate the dates when the fabric and trims will be received from suppliers, when cutting will be completed, when each stage of construction will occur, and when shipments will begin. There are two methods of production: sourcing to a contractor and manufacturing the products in-house.

11.2   Describe the production planning steps of the internship organization. Does the company cut to order or cut to stock? How is a purchasing plan used to facilitate building orders?

_____

_____

Offshore Production

When the costs of manufacturing spiraled upward because of domestic labor costs, as well as material and equipment expenses and availability, many American apparel and accessories manufacturers sought alternatives to U.S.-based production. Some searched for overseas operations in countries where the costs of production were far below those of the United States; others developed their own factories overseas in countries where hiring costly union labor was not a requirement. Countries such as Hong Kong, South Korea, and Taiwan became attractive centers for the production of American goods.

There are three basic ways in which a company may use offshore production for the manufacture of its products. First, the company may establish a **wholly owned factory** that the company totally finances and operates. It has the benefit of complete control in terms of personnel selection, manufacturing techniques, quality control, and timing of deliveries. Second, the company may choose a **joint-venture** alternative, which involves a partnership between the company and a contractor that performs all or part of the production process. The advantages of this option are that it affords the company some control, costs of the operation are often shared, and ownership of the production facility is not the responsibility of the company. Finally, the company can choose to use an **outside contractor**. An outside contractor is a production firm that requires payment from a manufacturer only for services provided.

11.3   Does the internship organization participate in offshore production? If so, specify whether the internship firm uses a wholly owned factory, a joint venture, or an outside contractor, and describe the process.

_____

_____

When a manufacturer in any country produces merchandise domestically, costs for labor, materials, promotion, and overhead are the primary calculations used to determine the wholesale price of goods. When a company based in one country decides to have its merchandise manufactured in another, a number of restrictions and expenses may be imposed that ultimately contribute to higher costs. **Duties,** or **tariffs**—fees levied on merchandise that comes from another country—are imposed by the government of the importing country. The main reason for duties or tariffs is to give domestically produced merchandise a more competitive edge through pricing. The government establishes a tariff schedule that specifically lists every conceivable type of product classification (e.g., men's sweaters, children's shorts, women's shoes) and the percentage of duty or tariff for each. The duty rate is based on a percentage of the product's appraised value and varies with each type of product. Sometimes the American government may wish to assist a foreign country with its economic problems by providing a **duty-free program**. In this scenario, goods may come into or exit the United States without any added tariff.

A **quota** refers to the amount of merchandise that a country's government will allow to be imported into its borders. Quota amounts are generally expressed in terms of units rather than dollars. In countries where production costs are comparable to those of the importer's country, no quotas are imposed. For example, the United States imposes quota restrictions on merchandise from the Far East where the labor costs are significantly lower; however, merchandise from France may be imported in any quantity.

11.4 Regarding the internship organization, how do duties/tariffs and quotas impact the firm's production and shipping decisions? Does the company export or import merchandise?

_____

_____

In-House Production

Company-owned production facilities are referred to as **in-house production,** or **inside shops**. The giants of the industry are among the very few manufacturers that produce the entire product. The major advantages of in-house production include: (1) better control over all operations (which often contributes to higher quality), (2) the ability to create exclusive merchandise, and (3) a shorter time frame for manufacturing. During in-house production, goods are not moved from one facility to another. The manufacturer's goods do not have to wait in line while another manufacturer's products are being constructed. The primary disadvantages of in-house production are the costs of operating a full production facility, the possible unavailability of skilled workers at an affordable wage, and the challenge of keeping the facility in operation during slow periods of production.

It is important to note that some large companies own or lease full production facilities overseas. This option combines the best of an inside shop with the advantages of offshore production. The manufacturer has complete control over the foreign factory yet receives the cost and labor benefits of foreign production. Mast Industries, Inc. (a major supplier of Limited Brands, Inc.) is an example of a corporation utilizing this option. Table 11.1 provides a comparison of contractors and in-house production alternatives.

11.5 If the internship organization is a manufacturer or design house, does it have in-house production? If so, are all or part of the processes needed to manufacture products completed in-house? If some of the steps are done outside of the company's factory, what are these, and where are they completed?

_____

_____

The Manufacturing Process

A flowchart of the production or manufacturing process as it relates to the various sectors of the fashion industry is shown as Figure 11.2. Next is an examination of the actual manufacturing steps, from development of the production pattern to distribution of the finished product. At the end of this chapter, costing activities for the various steps are presented.

The Production Pattern

As previously mentioned, the original pattern is created by the design division and is accomplished either through draping or flat patternmaking. The production pattern differs from the first pattern in a key way. The first pattern may be tailored to the figure of the fitting model or models working in the manufacturer's showroom. The production pattern strictly keeps to the company's size calculations. As fit is one of the most important selling points for fashion garments and some accessories, a perfected production pattern is critical to the success of a product.

Table 11.1
COMPARISON OF CONTRACTORS AND IN-HOUSE PRODUCTION

	Contractors	In-House Production
Labor	• They hire, lay off, do payroll, pay taxes and benefits. • They have access to additional trained workers as needed and can be responsive to seasonal demands. • They can be used to supplement in-house production time as needed; contractors will undoubtedly have the same seasons of business and slack as you do, so you need to have a well-established relationship, one that is profitable to them, if you want them to be available to you upon demand.	• You hire, lay off, do payroll, pay taxes and benefits. • You will need a backup source of skilled labor to meet seasonal demands; all your labor may be part-time/temporary, or you may have some full-time/permanent help that you supplement as necessary.
Overhead	• It is included in their price to you.	• You must include it as part of your costs, in addition to the wages and benefits you pay your employees.
Control of product	• You are paying them to produce according to your specifications and instructions. You are not present to oversee every step.	• You have total responsibility for, and control of, your production and the end product.
Cost	• Their piece price will be more than your in-house piece price because their price includes overhead and profit.	• Your piece price will be the direct costs of production—materials and labor only. In addition, you must include the overhead, labor benefits, and payroll taxes you will be paying.
Hassle	• You are not the only customer using the contractor's services: sometimes you cannot get your work done when you want it done. • It is necessary to constantly spot-check the production.	• You deal with all human resources issues. • You must purchase or lease equipment and maintain it. You, or someone, must oversee work you are paying for.
Ease	• The contractor deals with labor and overhead issues.	• In-house production involves no delivery and pickup of cut-and-sewn pieces. • Changes in production are easy to accommodate, as is fast turnaround on samples or other orders/items.

Source: Susan P. Gary and C. Ulasewicz, *Made in America: A Handbook for Design-Based Manufacturing of Apparel and Soft Products* (Sebastopol, CA: Garments Speak, 1998).

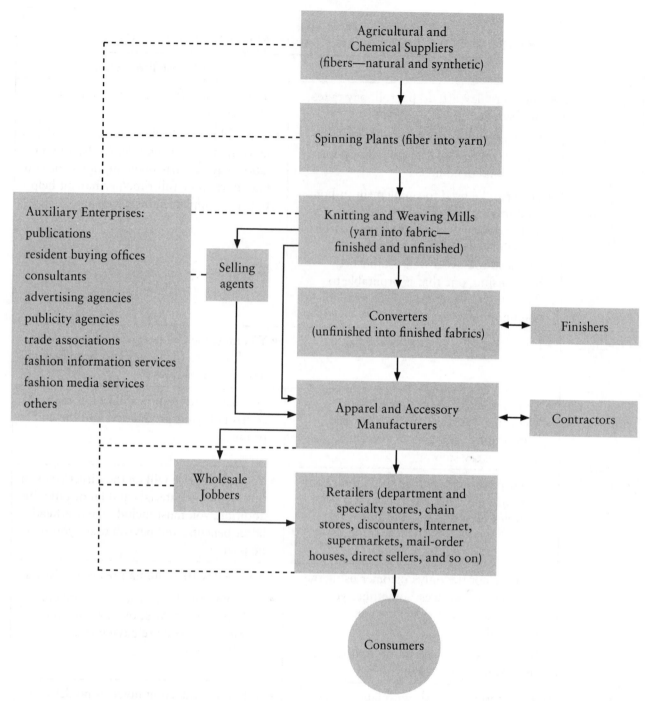

Figure 11.2 Flowchart of apparel, accessory, and soft goods products through levels of the fashion industry.

11.6 Who is responsible for developing the production pattern? What size specifications are used for a size 12 production pattern (or for a mid size carried by the company)?

_____

_____

Figure 11.3 illustrates the manufacturing stages and options for apparel, accessories, and soft goods products.

Grading and Marking

Grading is achieved manually or by computer. Using the manual means, the sample pattern is used as a guide to create other sizes by increasing or decreasing the pattern, using sizing guidelines that have been predetermined. More and more firms are using computerized systems for grading. The computer operator takes the initial pattern and marks key points with a digitizer that automatically adjusts the pattern to a range of sizes. Accuracy and time saving are major benefits of a computerized grading system. After grading is completed, a marker, or pattern layout, is constructed with the same width of the fabric to be used for that particular style.

11.7 If a manufacturer or design house, how does the internship organization conduct grading and marking—manually or by computer, or both? Describe the processes.

_____

_____

Spreading and Cutting

After the graded patterns and markers are constructed, the fabric is spread on a cutting table in layers over which the markers are placed. The number of layers can vary tremendously, depending on the density, nap, or print of the fabric as well as the cutting tools of the organization. As many as 500 layers of a very sheer fabric can be cut at one time, compared with as few as three layers of a bulky, patterned material. As mentioned previously, there are several cutting techniques: by hand, blade, or computerized laser. In cases in which a style is repeated from one seasonal line to another, **die cutting** may be used. Die cutting

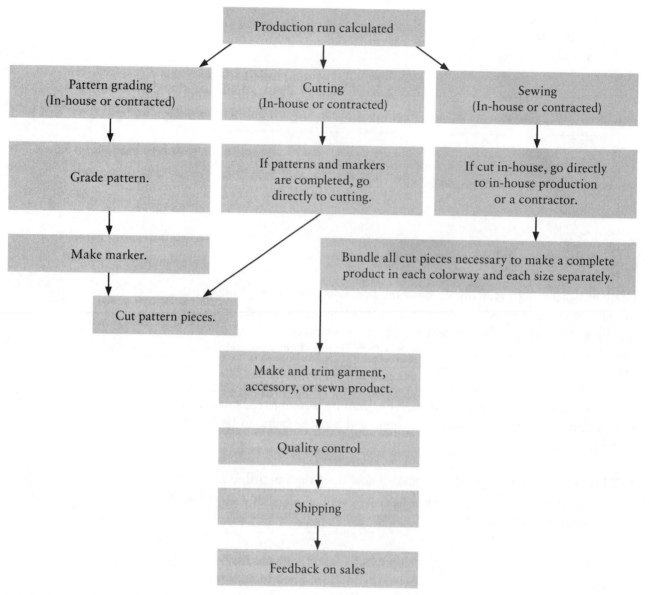

Figure 11.3 Production flowchart: options in manufacturing apparel, accessories, and soft goods.

is a process in which a die with sharp edges (resembling a cookie cutter) is developed to press through layers of fabric.

11.8 If applicable, describe the spreading and cutting stages of the internship organization's production process. Which tool is used for cutting? In what ways are computers utilized?

_____

_____

ssembling

The configuration of types and number of sewing operations needed to construct a garment are endless. It can take up to 200 sewing operations to assemble a man's tailored suit, for example. In a few situations, an individual worker may assemble an entire garment by machine and then later add handwork, as in the case of a finely tailored suit. For the most part, the fashion product is the result of a team effort called **assembly-line production**. Individual workers are trained to perform one or a few functions, passing the item or batch of items along to the following person in line, who completes the next sewing task, and so on down the line. These different steps culminate in the completion of a single product.

There are several types of equipment used in assembling fashion merchandise. Accessories, such as shoes and handbags, often require completely different machinery than do the soft goods of apparel or home accessories. For soft goods, there are the lock-stitch, chain-stitch, blind-stitch, and buttonhole machines. The **lock-stitch** machine sews a straight seam, whereas the **chain-stitch** machine generates an overlock that sews one edge over another. The **blind-stitcher** is used for hemming, and the **buttonhole** machine automatically creates buttonholes. More and more automated sewing is being introduced in factories as a means of reducing labor costs, saving production time, to ensure faster deliveries, and implementing consistent quality.

11.9 If applicable, describe the assembly processes used by the internship organization. Indicate the type of equipment that is used and the level of computerization.

_____

_____

Finishing and Labeling

After the product is assembled, it is moved on to finishers, who sew the buttons and sometimes add decorative embellishments as well, such as trims, beads, or appliqués (Figure 11.4). Additional functional finishes are also added at this stage. Pressing, for example, is a functional finish that can greatly impact the selling success of the final product. A number of labels are affixed to the product at this point. One identifies the designer or manufacturer; another provides information about the care of the item and fiber content. Finally, foreign-made merchandise, by law, must include a label indicating the country in which it was manufactured.

11.10 If applicable, discuss the finishing and labeling steps used for products manufactured by the internship organization.

_____

_____

Figure 11.4 Garment workers finish pants in the Sepal Group factory in Bangladesh for the clothing company of the American designer Tommy Hilfiger.

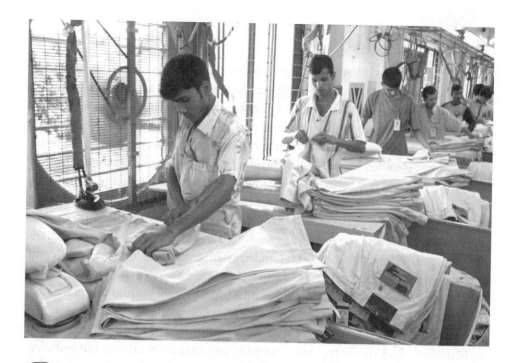

Distribution of the Finished Product

After the manufacturing steps are completed, the products are ready to be delivered to the clients' accounts. The merchandise is sorted according to style, color, and size and broken down into the orders that have been placed by the retail buyers. The merchandise is then packed and delivered according to the instructions the buyers have indicated on the purchase orders (Figure 11.5). Means of transportation, whether garments are packed flat or on hangers, and whether drop shipments to individual branch store locations are required are the types of specifications that buyers may place on shipments from manufacturers.

After the items have been selected in accordance with the purchase order, a packing slip is constructed. A **packing slip** is a form that indicates the style numbers and quantities contained in a specific container of merchandise. The receiving room personnel of the retail operation can quickly compare the packing slip with the purchase order to make certain that the delivery is accurate before completely unpacking the merchandise. The manufacturer also generates an invoice, a billing statement that reflects shipments made to the retail operation and denotes purchase order numbers.

11.11 Examine and describe the distribution steps used by the internship organization to deliver the finished products to its retail accounts or to direct customers, or both.

_____

_____

Costing the Product

Before the materials and trimmings are purchased and production quantities and schedules developed, the total cost of the finished product must be determined to make certain that it can be priced at a fair market value. To this end an approximate cost is established, based on the designer's original sample. After the designers or product developers have shown the line to merchandisers and the item has received enough support to produce it, these estimates are transformed into actual costs. The manufacturer calculates two types of costs:

1. First cost—The total amount of all direct costs of producing the item, including material and labor.

2. Wholesale cost—As a general rule, the first cost is increased to cover overhead expenses, selling expenses, and profit margin. The resulting amount is referred to as the wholesale cost.

Along with materials and trimmings, the expenses associated with manufacturing, promotion, sales and other personnel, overhead, and distribution must also be included. This complete calculation will allow the manufacturer to know exactly how much to charge the retail buyers in order to make a profit. A costing sheet is included in Figure 11.6.

Materials and Findings

Whether it is fabric for a dress, a lining for a coat, or leather for a belt, each component of a product must be calculated in terms of price and yardage for a

Romeo Blouse Company Costing Sheet

Date: _____

Style: _____

Pattern maker: _____

Designer: _____

    ❏ Miter

Label _____

    ❏ End Fold

Stock Pattern Reference: _____

Thread Color:

_____ Matching @ _____

_____

_____ Contrast @ _____

_____

Topstitching:

_____ Edge @ _____

_____

_____ 1/4 @ _____

_____

_____ Double Needle/Other @ _____

_____

Elastic:

_____ Width-Cut Length _____

_____ Width-Cut Length _____

_____

Button size and type: _____

Button Placement: _____

Curtain Color: _____

    ❏ Single   ❏ Double

Shoulder Pad Mill:_____ $ _____

Style # _____

Center Back Finished Length: _____

Special Notes: _____

_____

Yardages: _____

_____

Pattern Pieces-Fuse _____

_____

Comments: _____

_____

_____

Cutting Instructions: _____

_____

_____

Figure 11.6 A costing sheet lists the prices of the components of a product and often the costs of the labor to produce it.

single unit. For large manufacturers the price of piece goods and other product components may decrease with quantity purchases. As a result, costs are determined for single units and for purchases of varying sizes. For example, the price of a yard of fabric may be reduced by 20 percent if the company purchases more than 300 yards. It may drop another 5 percent with a 400-yard purchase. Findings, such as buttons, zippers, buckles, and decorative appliqués, must also be figured into the cost of the product.

11.12 How does the internship organization calculate materials and findings cost for a product it manufactures? Are quantity discounts an option for the company? If available, provide a costing sheet for materials and findings for a product manufactured by the company.

_____

_____

Production Labor

Production labor costs are varied, as they include the costs of making the patterns and grading, marking, cutting, and assembling goods. If personnel who perform these functions work on an hourly or weekly wage, or are paid a "piece rate," these expenses may be relatively simple to determine. Sometimes, outside contractors will provide a cost per unit for jobs such as cutting, sewing, and pressing. In a few situations, such as with a company producing hand-beaded sweaters, a worker may be paid on a "per-finished-piece" basis—a set amount for each completed item.

11.13 If applicable, what types of production labor costs are incurred by the internship organization? If available, provide a production labor costing sheet used by the internship organization.

_____

_____

Transportation

Shipping must also be considered when costing a product. Moving the garment from one production point to another is a time when freight costs will be incurred by the manufacturer. Although domestic shipping costs are significant, they do not compare with the costs related to overseas production; overseas shipments may include expenses for ground, sea, and air, depending on the country of origin and the speed of delivery required. If the product is manufactured abroad, the product components, labor, and shipping estimates are often totaled and referred to as a **landed cost**.

11.14 What transportation fees are incurred by the internship organization? Is merchandise produced domestically or overseas? If overseas, how are landed costs calculated?

_____

_____

Promotion

Advertising, fashion shows, and line catalogs illustrate a few of the many types of promotional activities conducted by manufacturers. With each promotional activity comes a unique set of expenses. Take, for example, the manufacturer developing a line catalog for retail buyers each season. Someone must oversee production of the catalog; models and a photographer must be hired, travel expenses may be incurred by the crew for the photo shoot, a graphic designer is needed to lay out the pages and insert the copy, a printer is needed to produce the finished piece—the list of related expenses for this single promotional tool goes on and on. Promotional expenses for staff, events, and selling tools must be prorated into the cost of goods each season. Promotion is examined in-depth in Chapter 12.

11.15 What promotional costs are underwritten by the internship organization? How are they calculated into the product cost?

_____

_____

Sales and Support Staff

In addition to the promotional staff, the costs associated with paying a sales force, a design or product development department, sample makers, fabric and trim buyers, merchandisers, and even the receptionists in the showroom and factory must be calculated as part of the cost of goods. Often, the manufacturer totals these salaries for one year and then divides the sum by the number of units produced and shipped in a year to determine a support staff fee that will be added to the cost of each item.

11.16 In terms of the internship organization, what sales and support staff salaries must be considered when costing products?

_____

_____

Overhead

Overhead refers to the expenses related to operating stores, offices, factories, and showrooms. Building costs (e.g., monthly rent or mortgage), utilities, insurance, taxes, maintenance of facilities, equipment, and supplies are examples of overhead costs. These expenses, too, are calculated into the price of a product, as they are an intangible cost of the product and necessary for manufacturing it.

11.17 Construct a list of overhead costs relating to the manufacturing of products by the internship organization. How are these expenses calculated into the cost of the company's products?

_____

_____

Distribution

Some manufacturers include the cost of the sales staff, such as manufacturer's representatives and showroom salespersons, as part of the distribution expense category. Others classify distribution expenses as costs associated with moving the product from the factory or warehouse to retail accounts that have ordered it. These costs can include packing materials and insurance in addition to labor and shipping costs. Regardless of the expense classification, the fees associated with shipping the goods to the consumer are part of a product's cost.

11.18 Describe the distribution expenses paid by the internship organization. How are these expenses calculated into the cost of the company's products?

_____

_____

Production Decisions—Domestic or Overseas?

Micky's is a contemporary misses' sportswear company based in New York City. The company produces fashion-forward casual apparel for contemporary women. The line is well known for its creative, relaxed designs with an athletic wear influence. Micky's has grown to be a key resource in the contemporary sportswear industry because of its innovative styling, excellent prices, superior quality, and consistent sizing and fit.

The owner of Micky's, Nancy, is actively involved in every facet of the business. She designs the line with the help of two design assistants and oversees the production aspects of the business with the support of an operations manager, a quality control director, and a production manager. Prior to major market weeks, Nancy introduces the new line to the sales representatives. During market weeks, she supervises the showroom and works directly with the retail buyers of Micky's key accounts by showing them the new collection and then later using their feedback to edit and improve the line. Nancy believes it is imperative that she has constant exposure to every aspect of the business in order to keep it thriving. Although she delegates job responsibilities, she believes it is her primary job—as the company owner—to oversee all operations of the firm.

Since the start-up of the company, Nancy has hired regional contractors to manufacture the company's line. She visits the contractors weekly, as they are located in New York and New Jersey. During her trips to the contractors' facilities, Nancy checks the production schedule, troubleshoots and solves problems, and inspects the quality of the finished garments in the shipping departments. She is able to monitor the delivery schedule of the merchandise by knowing the specific styles that will be produced in each location.

Recently, Nancy's production manager has been contacted by a number of overseas contractors interested in procuring Micky's manufacturing business. The production manager has done his homework, compiling a report for Nancy that summarizes the offers the foreign contractors have submitted. First, Nancy examines the quality and detailing of the finished garment samples the foreign contractors provided and determines that the quality is as good as—if not better—than that of her domestic sources. Next, she contacts the listing of clients the foreign contractors have provided as references. Finally, she takes a look at her production assistant's pricing summary. Nancy is amazed at the difference between the price quotes provided by the foreign contractors and what she is paying her U.S. contractors. The overseas manufacturers quote landed costs about 30 percent less than the prices she currently pays. She immediately realizes that this difference could afford her various opportunities, including passing the savings on to the customer, using the price reductions as additional profit for her company, hiring another person to help her with her work, and stepping up marketing activities. She feels like it's her birthday as she contemplates the potential new money stream.

On the other hand, Nancy is concerned that she will not have the production control she has enjoyed in the past if she utilizes foreign contractors. Currently, she knows firsthand how the finished garments look immediately after production. She can correct problems as they arise in the production process. She can view when and how garments are being shipped to retail accounts. She can answer questions about fabrics, construction, and fit in person and know that she has communicated clearly. If she uses foreign contractors, the opportunities for proactive problem solving in the line's production could be greatly minimized. In addition, she wants to support U.S. commerce by employing domestic manufacturers; she truly does not want to impact the jobs of the employees of her current contractors by sending her company's business overseas. However, Nancy knows that the hourly wages of the contractors' workers have risen steadily over the years and continue to increase. Additional employee benefits, such as health insurance, have also added to the costs of using domestic contractors. She anticipates that the wholesale costs of her line will have to increase as the labor costs of manufacturing rise. Nancy is concerned that the inevitable higher prices of domestic production will affect the retail sales of the line.

1. If you were in Nancy's position, which choice would you make—domestic or foreign production? Why?

2. Are there any alternatives that were not examined in the case study? What are they?

Production and Sales— Merchandise Coordinators on Board

Femme Flip, Inc., is a major player in the manufacturing sector of the misses' apparel industry. The company has been a key resource for almost a decade for large retail operations internally. The corporation operates several apparel divisions, including women's and men's sportswear, women's and misses' petite dresses, and licensed fashion accessories. Its retail clientele consists of major specialty and department store chains across the United States and Europe. The Femme Flip label is adored by the company's devoted target market—middle-aged, middle-income women with conservative fashion taste, an eye for quality, and the expectation of good fit and a positive price–value relationship. Femme Flip is a giant in the apparel industry, and the company continues to prosper with each season.

Recently, the president of the misses' sportswear division made an announcement to the division's personnel concerning distribution of the apparel line. She stated that the corporate executives jointly had made a major decision that would challenge traditional methods of product sales and distribution in the apparel industry: the misses' sportswear line would no longer be sold to the retail buyers through company sales representatives; those positions would be eliminated by the first of the year, and in their place the company was to hire a team of approximately 20 merchandise coordinators who would be trained and then assigned to specific geographical territories encompassing all of the company's major account areas. The merchandise coordinator's job responsibilities would include the following:

1. Working as a liaison between the company's major retail stores and Femme Flip through regular visits to the stores and consistent two-way communication

2. Collaborating with the store buyers, department managers, and sales associates to display and stock Femme Flip merchandise in the stores

3. Training the sales associates to sell the products to the customers more effectively

4. Presenting trunk shows and similar special events to the retail clientele

5. Writing reorders for fill-ins on available top-selling styles, as approved by the buyer

6. Communicating stock availability, selling trends, and fashion reports to the retail buyers and their staff

Many of the retail store buyers are very concerned about losing their sales representatives. Some have developed friendships with their reps after many years of working together to build their businesses. The buyers are upset with Femme Flip because they believe that the company made this decision to avoid paying the high salaries and commissions the sales representatives earned by employing industry "newbies" at a fraction of the cost. Retail buyers will now need to purchase the line each season in the New York showroom or at major apparel marts during market weeks, rather than through sales representatives who brought the new lines to the locations of their offices. This will add cost, time, and inconvenience to their jobs. The buyers worry that they will not have direct communication with the company regarding merchandise shipments, off-price goods, and top-selling styles. For the owners and buyers of smaller stores, Femme Flip may be the only reason they now need to travel to major apparel marts to view new lines. Because merchandise coordinators will work only with large retail accounts, the owners and buyers of smaller stores will be limited to communicating by telephone or Internet with a customer representative regarding issues of delivery, reorders, and returns.

The buyers are not the only people who are distraught over the elimination of the sales representatives' positions. Obviously, the sales reps are devastated. Financially, they will be without the substantial incomes they earned from Femme Flip. In addition, they fear that this move by such a major manufacturer could influence other companies to do the same, reducing the number of sales representative jobs available in the industry and perhaps ending the career track.

The corporate executives respond with several answers to the buyers' and sales representatives' objections. First, they indicate that the corporation is only able to maintain prices on the line and continue employing all others through this change. Second, they stress that replacing the sales representatives with merchandise coordinators is a move that aligns with the changing market. The merchandise coordinator position more directly benefits Femme Flip's primary target market, its first customer—the large retailer. Because the buyer is dealing with minimal staff and an overwhelming workload, the merchandise coordinator can ease the burden by assisting the buyer, department manager, sales associates, and, finally, the ultimate customer. Third, they emphasize their belief that the buyer of smaller stores with a successful track record of selling Femme Flip will continue to purchase the line. Although they admit they may lose some of these stores, the executives conclude that they are focusing the company's wholesale efforts on the clients that make the company profitable—the major department and specialty stores.

1. If you were a sales representative for Femme Flip, what would you do to maintain employment with the firm?

2. Do you agree or disagree with eliminating the sales representative position and adding the merchandise coordinator position? Why? Do you believe this is an industry trend?

CHAPTER TWELVE

Promotion and Publishing

Objectives

- To identify the buyer readiness state of the internship organization's target market

- To explore media and message selections for promotional activities

- To assess personal and nonpersonal communication channels

- To investigate methods of budgeting for promotions

- To identify the components of the promotional mix

- To examine sales promotion, publicity, and visual merchandising as they relate to the internship organization

- To recognize the importance of evaluating promotional efforts

What Is Promotion?

Promotion refers to the activities used to communicate the product attributes to the target consumer through four major tools: (1) advertising, (2) sales promotion, (3) publicity, and (4) personal selling.

Promotion involves the activities used to inform the potential consumer about the product. Some manufacturers and retailers use merchandising as promotional efforts to sell their products, such as window displays, product labeling and packaging, and signage. **Advertising** is paid, nonpersonal communication delivered through the mass media to communicate persuasive information about the product. **Sales promotions** provide short-term incentives to encourage sales of the product line. The cosmetic industry does an excellent job of using sales promotions to generate revenue through its use of gift with purchase (GWP) or purchase with purchase (PWP). **Publicity** refers to the nonpersonal creation of demand for a product by introducing commercially significant news about it through media efforts, at no cost to the sponsor.

Promotion can be transmitted to the consumer through many vehicles, including magazines and newspapers, television and radio, the Internet, outdoor displays, direct mail, novelties (e.g., calendars, pencils, memo tablets), catalogs, directories, and circulars. Through the messages the business sends in its promotional efforts, it emphasizes particular attributes or focuses on targeting how the customer wants to feel about him- or herself. Victoria's Secret, for example, sells self-image. Print and television advertisements using supermodels dressed in sexy lingerie imply that buying Victoria's Secret lingerie will make the consumer feel sensual and look attractive.

The executives working in public relations firms, advertising departments, or showrooms representing product lines make the following decisions with each product promotion:

- Identifying the buyer readiness state of the target market

- Choosing a message

- Choosing the media

- Setting the total promotional budget and mix

- Collecting feedback

Next, an examination of each of these decision levels will provide an overview of the responsibilities of key personnel working in the promotion sector of the apparel industry.

Buyer Readiness State of the Target Market

The preliminary stage of promotion decision making includes identifying the target market and determining its buyer readiness state to produce the desired

Figure 12.1 Adriana Lima and Doutzen Kroes promote the new Vintage Victoria collection at the Victoria's Secret Lexington Avenue store in New York City.

audience response. The **buyer readiness state** refers to the consumer's level of awareness and knowledge of a product.

For example, the customer will have a minimal buyer's readiness state when it comes to product introductions, such as a new fabric development or a new designer. The affective state is often utilized to promote existing products, as it focuses on the consumer's preference for, and level of conviction in, purchasing a specific product. The behavioral state focuses on motivating the consumer to purchase the product immediately, as illustrated by QVC's limited quantity offers.

12.1 Examine a product promoted by the internship organization, and identify the buyer readiness state of the target market.

_____

_____

Avenues of Promotion

The organization must decide on the message to be conveyed and to whom that message will be sent. The first question the organization should ask when developing an advertisement is "What do I (as a business) want or need to communicate?" The next questions are "What is the objective of the advertisement? What is it intended to accomplish, and when?" Is its objective to get the consumer to make a buying decision in the near future? to introduce a new product or service? The answers to these questions will help ensure that the advertising objectives are clear, specific, and targeted.

The primary goal of any promotional campaign is to increase sales. To determine the effectiveness of the campaign, the business needs not only to decide what should be accomplished through advertising but also to establish ways to measure the results. Retailers and manufacturers can measure the effectiveness of an advertising campaign by tracking increases in consumer traffic and sales volume, by noting increases in orders placed through the company Web site, or by tracking sales of the specific product promoted through the advertising campaign.

Choosing a Message

The second promotion decision for the public relations or advertising executive involves developing an effective message that accomplishes the following:

- Generates attention

- Stimulates interest

- Promotes desire

- Induces action

The message can be segmented into content, appeal, structure, and format. The message content reaches out to the target market through a rational, emotional, or moral appeal. The **rational appeal** is a promotion message that stresses common sense by showing that the product will produce claimed benefits. Skin care products with anti-aging ingredients are often advertised with a rational appeal: the promotions explain what the ingredients are, how they work, and why the customer needs them. **Emotional appeal** is a promotion message based on feelings, such as fear, love, humor, pride, romance, or joy. Think about fragrance and fine jewelry promotions. Often, companies producing or advertising these products choose an emotional appeal, such as romance, joy, or status, to market product lines to the consumer. **Moral appeal** reflects the audience's sense of what is right or wrong. There is an increase in the number of moral appeals used for promotion of fashion business and products. Some companies align with a cause; others identify a moral trend such as sustainability, recycling, or human rights in international labor.

The message structure may be open-ended or closed, one- or two-sided; it may present the strongest argument first or last. The message format varies with the type of media. Size, color, and illustration are all elements of print or display media messages. The speech pace and background music of a radio ad are part of its message format.

12.2 Select a promotional effort of the internship operation, and analyze its message purpose, appeal, content, structure, and format.

_____

_____

Personal and Nonpersonal Communication Channels

In the third stage of the promotion decision process, personal or nonpersonal communication channels are selected. **Personal communication channels** are those that direct a specific message to a specific customer group. They are classified as follows:

- **Advocate**—Uses a salesperson to contact potential buyers in the target market

- **Expert**—Uses a celebrity or well-known spokesperson to influence prospective consumers

- **Social**—Word of mouth from neighbors, family, friends, and associates

Personal communication channels can be stimulated in a number of ways. Identifying influential individuals and organizations is one method, as illustrated by the use of celebrities in promotional campaigns (Figure 12.2a). This can extend to one's local community as well. For example, the city council may implement a "Support Your Local Businesses" campaign that results in more customers' avoiding national chain stores and shopping at local, entrepreneurial businesses. Creating opinion leaders is yet another way to influence personal communication channels. Finally, developing advertising with high conversation value can impact communication channels: think about the cost, impact, and weeks of conversation initiated by the commercials aired during the Super Bowl.

12.3 Describe a personal communication channel selected by the internship organization. Is it an advocate, expert, or social channel?

_____

_____

_____

Nonpersonal communication channels are those promotional messages that utilize mass (undifferentiated) or selective (specialized) media through print, electronic, or display methods. Nonpersonal communication channels also include **atmospheres**, designed environments that create or reinforce the buyer's desire to buy a product. For example, Betsey Johnson's company decorates its showroom with bright pink silk flowers, bold patterns, and unique furniture—all with a "girly" look. The contemporary decor creates an exciting, youthful, colorful atmosphere that reflects Betsey Johnson's product line (Figure 12.2b).

Figure 12.2a Personal communication channel: Gwyneth Paltrow presents Estée Lauder's Pleasures by Gwyneth Paltrow.

(a)

Figure 12.2b Nonpersonal communication channel: Betsey Johnson's colorful showroom (see color insert) conveys the Betsey Johnson brand—even when she's not there.

(b)

12.4 Describe a nonpersonal communication channel selected by the internship organization.

_____

_____

Events, another nonpersonal communication channel, are designed occurrences that communicate particular messages to the target audience (Figure 12.3). For example, Cotton Incorporated, which represents cotton fiber and textile manufacturers, presents trend forecasts for each new season in order to familiarize designers and retail buyers with innovative fabrics made with cotton. Neiman Marcus's Fortnight presentations communicate messages to the target market, using, for example, a particular country as a theme.

12.5 How are atmospheres or events used as nonpersonal communication channels?

_____

_____

Figure 12.3 Event advertising: Agyness Deyn arrives at the *Elle* Style Awards.

Choosing the Media Type

When selecting a media type, the following factors are examined by public relations and advertising personnel:

- **The reach**, or number of persons in the target market

- **Frequency**, or number of times the message is presented

- Impact of the media source

- Target market media habits (the television channels they watch, the radio stations they listen to, and so on)

- The product itself

- The message

- The cost

- Source credibility

12.6 Select a promotion effort of the internship operation, and identify its media source and featured product. Describe the source credibility, media reach, frequency, and impact of the media source. Analyze the target market media habits, message, and cost as these variables relate to the product.

_____

_____

_____

 etting the Promotional Budget

Methods for establishing an organization's total promotional budget vary within different industries. A major cosmetics firm allocates 7 percent of sales for promotion expenditures, whereas a well-known discount operation appropriates 2.2 percent of sales volume for promotion costs. The following techniques are most commonly used to set the total promotional budget of an organization:

- Affordable method, the dollar amount the firm can afford at the moment

- Percentage of sales method, as based on sales volume

- Competitive-parity method, based on competitor's expenditures

- Analysis and costing of communication objectives and tasks

12.7 Which promotional budget method is used by the internship organization? Why is this method preferred?

_____

_____

Promotion budget assistance is often provided by external funding. Fiber, fabric, and garment producers frequently offer cooperative advertising monies. **Cooperative advertising** is when, in exchange for name or brand recognition, the producer will pay a specified percentage of promotional costs. The Wool Bureau and Cotton Incorporated provide cooperative advertising funds to garment manufacturers and retailers promoting their respective fibers and fabrics.

12.8 Does the internship organization utilize promotional assistance provided by suppliers? Special events, personnel training programs, trunk shows, giveaways, purchase-with-purchase items, catalogues, brochures, and direct mailers are some of the promotional alternatives offered by suppliers (e.g., fiber or apparel manufacturers). Describe the promotional assistance used by the internship organization.

_____

_____

etting the Promotional Mix

After the promotional budget is determined, it is divided between the following promotion tools:

- Advertising
- Sales promotions
- Publicity
- Personal selling

Advertising

Advertising can be designed to serve several purposes. **Institutional advertising** builds the organization's image and creates community goodwill. **Brand advertising** promotes a particular brand, whereas **sale advertising** announces specific value items. **Classified advertising** is a paid promotional message that provides information about a sale, service, or event. **Advocacy advertising** supports a particular cause. For example, a retailer recently ran a newspaper advertisement in which he announced that his entire inventory was composed of American-made products. In this advocacy advertisement, the retailer expressed his personal reasons for supporting domestic producers.

12.9 Examine the advertising efforts of the internship organization. Attach advertising samples, and describe the purpose and media type of each ad. List all forms of advertising media utilized by the organization.

_____

_____

12.10 Are the internship organization's advertising efforts externally or internally sponsored, or both? If the internship organization does minimal advertising, locate advertising examples from other sources to illustrate your understanding of advertising concepts.

_____

_____

Sales Promotions

Sales promotions are short-term incentives that encourage the sale of the product. Sales promotion techniques include samples, coupons, price packs, point-of-purchase displays, trade promotions, contests, sweepstakes, games, business conventions, and trade shows. For example, _Vogue_ magazine sponsored a give-away in which consumers who purchased a subscription to _Vogue_ received a tote bag at no cost upon submitting subscription payment (Figure 12.4).

12.11 Describe sales promotion efforts within the internship organization. If the organization offers no sales promotion activities, locate an example from another source.

_____

_____

Publicity

Press relations and product promotions can be examples of publicity efforts if they are unpaid and transmitted through the news media. For example, a branch store of Saks Fifth Avenue recruited the designer Diane von Furstenburg

Figure 12.4 Sales promotion: *Vogue* magazine subscription card, featuring a tote bag giveaway.

to promote her fashions and fragrances within the store. The local newspaper featured several articles on the designer's background, current lines, interests, and activities when mentioning her appearance. The retailer paid nothing for the newspaper publicity.

12.12 Analyze the publicity efforts of the internship organization. Locate examples of both positive and negative publicity. What techniques are used by the organization to gain positive publicity? If publicity solicitation is not used, what suggestions can you offer to gain favorable publicity for the internship organization?

_____

_____

Personal Selling

Personal selling, the fourth promotional tool, is examined in Chapter 7. A nonpersonal selling tool, visual merchandising, is presented next.

Visual Merchandising

Displays are often called "silent salespersons." They communicate information to the consumer, affecting purchasing behavior. Effective use of visual merchandising can modify consumer demand, buying habits, and patronage. The primary purpose of a display is to sell products while projecting a desired image. Displays can also speed up transactions, as in a self-service operation. They can encourage customers to add on purchases, such as displays of impulse items at the cash register. Window and interior displays are used throughout the industry to generate interest and sales (Figure 12.5).

12.13 Analyze the use of displays for creating sales within the internship organization, or locate an example elsewhere.

_____

_____

_____

Figure 12.5
BarberOsgerby window display for Tod's; Patrick Norguet's design.

Collecting Feedback

Evaluating the results of promotional efforts is a crucial, yet often overlooked, stage of promotion decision making. The most common form of promotion evaluation is an analysis of sales and profit impact before, during, and after the promotion effort occurs. Consumer surveys are sometimes used to evaluate consumer awareness, comprehension, and attitude changes resulting from promotion efforts. Advertising pretesting includes **direct ratings**, in which customers are asked which advertisement would influence them to buy the product. **Portfolio tests** are also used as advertising pretests. In portfolio tests, a group of consumers analyzes an assortment of ads and then is tested for recall and recognition.

12.14 Which evaluation methods are used by the internship organization to evaluate promotion results? Which methods would you recommend?

_____

_____

12.15 What are the disadvantages to the traditional technique of measuring sales and profit impact before, during, and after the occurrence of a promotion effort?

_____

_____

Some interns will work with an organization that provides promotional activities as its product. A magazine, a fashion event production company, and a public relations firm are examples of this type of organization. Although the product is the promotion, the organization must also price the product, define a target customer, determine how to reach this customer, and so forth. Many of the activities conducted by other kinds of fashion businesses, such as a retail store or an apparel manufacturer, are also implemented by a promotional company. As different as fashion businesses are, they share many of the same tasks, goals, and decisions.

12.16 If you are interning with an organization that offers promotion as its core product, describe the goals of the company and the responsibilities of its management and sales teams, and list a sample of its clients or customers.

_____

_____

Publishing

Many fashion companies publish information for employees or consumers, or both, through such vehicles as newsletters, brochures, mailers, catalogs, or Web sites. For other fashion firms, publications *are* the product. Promotion and publishing go hand in hand, as much of the publishing in the fashion industry relates to marketing a company, a product, an image, an idea, a person, or a sponsor. Internships, as well as career positions, in fashion publishing are usually available in three general areas: (1) advertising, (2) marketing, and (3) journalism.

Advertising is responsible for generating the income that comes from companies who pay to promote their products in the publication. This department is responsible for selling advertising to existing clients and in securing new ones. Advertising may also be responsible for producing marketing materials needed by clients. The **marketing division,** also referred to as consumer marketing and circulation, handles the direct sales of subscriptions and the sales of magazines at newsstands, bookstores, and other retail operations. This division also develops new offerings for the consumer via mail, television, the Internet, or other venues. In the area of journalism, a number of positions focus on research, writing, and editing. The **writer** conducts editorial reporting, most often related to fashion lifestyle trends in apparel, home decor, travel, celebrity, and so on. The **editor** determines noteworthy trends that set the scene in the fashion world and is ultimately responsible for content of the publication. An **editorial research assistant** checks article facts prior to publication through interviews and research, to verify accuracy. For some firms, a **catalog editor** oversees all content of the catalog, including proofing, visual layout, and editing. The photographer and **art director** orchestrate the visual images and the look of publications. Assistants to the photographer or art director are usually experienced in research and computer editing programs, such as Quark, Photoshop, and Illustrator.

Many corporate internship programs in the publishing industry place interns in the position of editorial assistant or under the supervision of one. The **editorial assistant** is responsible for supporting one or more editors with daily administrative work. The editorial assistant, or his or her intern, is primarily responsible for office work: maintaining updated contact lists, filing, sorting mail, faxing, scheduling meetings, drafting letters, preparing spreadsheets, and making appointments and copies. In some companies the editorial assistant has greater responsibilities, such as maintaining contacts with freelance editors, previewing manuscripts and story proposals, answering readers' mail, researching feature stories, writing headlines, and so on. Editorial assistants may support editors in the following departments: features, fashion market, fashion editorial, copy, art, production, research, or as the stylist's or photographer's assistant. Box 12.1 provides further information on securing and surviving the fashion publication internship.

The Fashion Magazine Internship

by Kimberly Lawson

It is the job a million fashion enthusiasts would kill for—the fashion magazine internship. If you are looking to get into fashion magazines as a career, an internship is one of the only ways to break into the business, especially if you want to work for a top-level fashion magazine like *Allure, Elle,* or the highly regarded *Vogue.* The biggest question of all for an internship seeker is how to find these highly sought after fashion magazine internships. Here are a few tips for getting your foot in the door:

- *Go straight to the source . . . in person.* One of the ways to find a fashion magazine internship is to go to the magazine itself. You can call the front desk and ask if there are any openings for interns. Better yet, send a résumé and cover letter to the magazine's editor, fashion assistants, or HR director on your own. They will be impressed by how driven and proactive you are.

- *Go straight to the source . . . online.* Many of the major fashion magazines are owned by the same company, such as Condé Nast, Hearst, or Time Warner. The official Web sites of these companies have job searches. Give the search a try, and a fashion magazine internship lead just may come up.

- *Start a blog.* How would you like to be handed a fashion magazine internship without even applying? It does not happen in all cases, but running your own fashion blog can get you great opportunities and

recognition. You can also use it to show potential employers your writing skills and how dedicated you are to fashion.

- *Go through your school.* If you go to a fashion school or a university with a well-respected fashion program, it should not be too hard to find an internship at a fashion magazine through your school's connections, such as alums or the campus career center. If you are not at a fashion school, it is still worth a try and, hopefully, one of your professors can track down leads to help you out.

Finding a lead for a fashion internship is not actually the hard part—it is landing the job that is hard! But you need to take these first steps, and it is important to search, search, search to find those leads.

The film *The Devil Wears Prada* left many aspiring fashion magazine interns wondering if its portrayal of a fashion magazine internship is realistic. This may come as a surprise to many, but much of what is seen in that movie is not an exaggeration; after all, it was written by someone who worked at *Vogue.* There are several things you will want to remember about fashion magazine internships:

- *It is a seasonal position.* Of course, every magazine has a different schedule. Top fashion magazines, such as *Allure* or *Marie Claire,* hire fashion interns for the season.

(continued on next page)

Usually, the fashion intern will start in late December or early January and work through May for the winter/spring season. If you impress the bosses during your fashion magazine internship, they will keep you on longer.

- *You will work your manicured fingers to the bone: long hours are required for fashion magazine interns.* One of the most accurate parts of *The Devil Wears Prada* was the extended hours that Anne Hathaway's character had to work. The amount of hours you are scheduled for means nothing. Expect to work 12-hour days, maybe shorter, maybe even longer. Most of the work will be running errands, going to showrooms to pick up items and collect samples, answering phones and e-mail, organizing the fashion closet, and anything else the fashion assistant may have you do. When your work is done, many times you will be asked to stay later, until the fashion assistants are finished with their work.

- *Do not practice running in heels (if you're a woman) with hot lattes; it is highly unlikely that you will have any interaction with the editor.* You will not have to worry about tiptoeing around Miranda Priestly; the fashion assistant will answer to the editor because he or she is the head boss. In turn, the fashion assistants will supervise the interns, but that does not mean they are not demanding.

- *You need to know how to write and sell.* Interns are expected to write, so be sure to have good clips on hand; include writing samples in your portfolio when you interview. Plan on writing while you are on the job. After all, it is a magazine. You may be asked to work with the advertising department. If so, you will sell, sell, sell. You had to sell yourself to get the position, so you know how to do this.

- *Enjoy the perks; they are rare, but they are there.* After you are established in your fashion magazine internship, you may get the one-in-a-thousand chance to fly across the country or perhaps out of the country, just like Lauren Conrad of *The Hills* did for her internship at *Teen Vogue*. Part of your work will probably include assisting on shoots and styling the models, which is a lot of fun. And even interns are gifted with high-fashion designer label items from the closet.

A fashion magazine internship certainly is not a walk in the park; in fact, it can be a run in high heels across hot pavement. It is, however, a good test to see who can and cannot make it in the industry. If you are specifically looking for a fashion magazine career, it is basically the only way to get your foot in the door. A few of the best places to begin your search for fashion magazine internships are Ed2010.com, DailyFashionJobs.com, and craigslist.com.

Kimberly Lawson is a FIDM graduate, professional blogger, and boutique owner and the mastermind behind DailyFashionJobs.com.

12.17 What are the personal qualities, skills, experiences, and education that the writer of a fashion publication must have?

_____

_____

_____

_____

_____

12.18 Through research or an interview, discover what a day in the life of a fashion writer is like. How much time does a writer typically spend on a one- to two-page story? What is the time period from assignment to submission of the article?

_____

_____

_____

_____

_____

12.19 What can the writer realistically anticipate in terms of actual outcomes (e.g., a story a day or an article a week)? How many articles are worked on simultaneously?

_____

_____

_____

_____

_____

12.20 Provide a summary that examines the writer's work in interviewing, researching, networking, writing, and reading.

_____

_____

_____

_____

12.21 What are the personal qualities, skills, experiences, and education that a successful candidate for the position of editor must have?

_____

_____

_____

_____

12.22 What are the personal qualities, skills, experiences, and education that the editorial assistant of a fashion publication should have?

_____

_____

_____

_____

12.23 What are the personal qualities, skills, experiences, and education that a successful intern must have to work successfully in all areas of a publishing house? Box 12.2 provides a starting point for examining the qualifications of a fashion magazine intern.

_____

_____

_____

_____

BOX 12.2

Sample Advertisement for an Internship with a Fashion Magazine

Magazine Intern Needed

The accessories/jewelry department at *Glossy Mag* seeks detail-oriented, highly motivated, organized, dependable interns for the spring semester. You must be able to commit to a minimum of three to five full days a week, to start as soon as possible. Positions are for college credit. Interns will be based in the fashion closet, working mostly with jewelry samples. Responsibilities include, but are not limited to: checking in and returning samples, creating trend boards, organizing the fashion closet, running errands (pick up and drop off at design houses or public relations showrooms), and assisting editors with special projects. Interns may also have the chance to assist at photo shoots or TV segments. Must have a strong interest in fashion. Please send a résumé and cover letter stating your availability and potential start date to Miranda Priestly at mpriestly@glossymag.com. Absolutely no phone calls, please.

The large publishing giants include Time Inc., the Hearst Corporation, and Condé Nast. Next, a list of affiliated magazines, by corporation, is presented, followed by Figure 12.6, which describes Condé Nast's summer intern program.

- Time Inc.—*InStyle, Entertainment Weekly, People*

- The Hearst Corporation—*Cosmopolitan, Esquire, Harper's Bazaar, Marie Claire, Town and Country*

- Condé Nast—*Vogue, Teen Vogue, Men's Vogue, W, Glamour, GQ, Allure, Lucky, Women's Wear Daily, Modern Bride, Bride, Vanity Fair, Self,* and more

Figure 12.6 Condé Nast careers and internship pages.

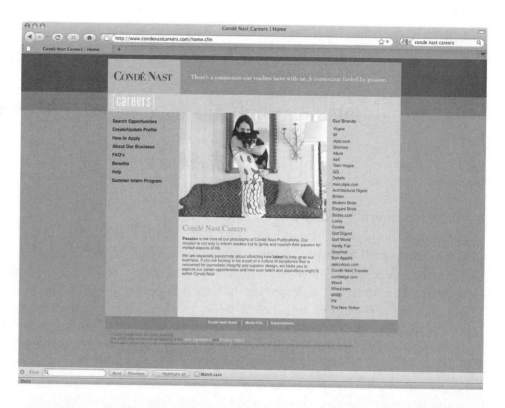

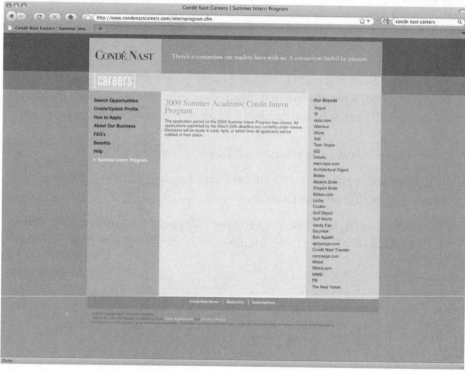

·❦[THE FASHION INTERN]❦·

12.24 Whether you are interning with a publisher or not, select one of these large publishing firms to research, and then write a corporate summary of about a page. Next, select one of the firm's publications and develop a profile for it. Include responses to the following queries: Who is the target market in terms of readers? What types of companies advertise in it? Examples? What is the publication's niche, or how does it differ from what is out there? Who are its competitors?

_____

_____

_____

_____

12.25 If you are an intern for a publication or a public relations firm, indicate the title of your supervisor and describe your job responsibilities. Draft a chart that illustrates the hierarchy in the organization—in other words, indicate who works for whom and what each person's title is.

_____

_____

_____

_____

Many public relations (PR) firms provide some of the services of a publisher. The big difference is that the public relations firm is paid by a person, a product, or a company—or by all three, under the same umbrella, such as the name of the designer, company, and brand—to promote it. The PR company will, for example, send articles and photographs to fashion editors of magazines, newspapers, and Web sites. PR representatives will seek out magazines and e-zine publishers to secure a feature article, an interview, or a photo feature on their clients. Box 12.3 provides an example of an article on a fashion designer, Catherine Malandrino, that was published in a French tourism magazine. Box 12.4 features a classified advertisement for interns to work in Malandrino's public relations department.

The Designer Catherine Malandrino

Malandrino's Inspiration

After Over 10 Years in New York, Catherine Malandrino Continues to Draw on French Roots for Her Designs

You live in New York City, but you've said that France continues to inspire you. Why?

I was born and raised in France. I gained experience in a Parisian atelier, where the tradition of craftsmanship and couture was born. Chanel, Paul Poiret, and Vionnet remain references in my work. I live in New York because I love to feel the vibrant energy of the city. It is a place where people come together to create a new world. Over the last 10 years, I have mixed both my New York and French identities by infusing the casual cool of the New York streets with the craftsmanship and refinement of French couture.

You worked in Paris for many years but were born in Grenoble. Where in France do you feel most at home?

I consider myself to be a citizen of the world and tend to draw inspiration from wherever I am, whether it is Tokyo, London, New York, or Paris. When I'm in France, I especially love to feel the romance of the streets of Paris, the warm sunlight of the south of France, and the fresh air of the Alps.

How often do you get to travel to France?

I visit France every two months. When I'm there for work, I visit my boutique in St. Germain, buy fabric, and visit exhibitions. During the summers, I enjoy the perfumes and colors of the south of France, while during the winters I spend my holidays around the fireplace in the Alps.

We've read that La Colombe d'Or in St.-Paul de Vence is one of your favorite hotels. Why is this?

When I was young I used to go to St.-Paul de Vence with my family. I love the people, the food is delicious, the crooked stone and the beautiful art pieces make me feel at home. La Colombe d'Or is one of my favorite places in the world and inspired me for my Malandrino Spring/Summer 2008 collection.

Any other favorite places in France?

Les Fermes de Marie in Megève, the market of St.-Tropez and Paris.

Do many tourists come by your boutique in St.-Germain?

My St. Germain boutique has a lot of worldwide customers because of my presence in New York, Japan, and Russia, so many women who are traveling will visit the boutique. At the same time, French people also discover my work through the St.-Germain boutique.

What advice do you have for Americans visiting France?

Get lost in Paris! Step away from the main avenues and stray down the side streets!

Any recommendations as to what to do—or where to shop?

Visitors should wander away from the main stores that you see all over the world and find small boutiques. They should also explore the Paris flea markets on weekends and walk along the Seine. Always visit the south of France, even in the winter, and travel from Monaco to St.-Tropez.

Any advice for tourists on what to wear in France?
"I Love NY" T-shirts with a miniskirt and high heels!

Source: Wigston, N. Maladrino's inspiration. *France Guide 2008*. New York: Maison de la France, retrieved from http://franceguide.v1.myvirtualpaper.com/franceguide/?page=6. Courtesy of franceguide.com.

❦[BOX 12.4]❦

*Catherine Malandrino Public Relations Internship**

Catherine Malandrino is seeking interns for the public relations department. With Fashion Week just around the corner, interns are needed immediately! Fashion Week responsibilities include:

- Assisting with production and coordination of the show
- Mailing invitations
- Coordinating celebrity samples

Other responsibilities include:

- Assisting with coordinating product placement in national and regional publications
- Tracking samples
- Tracking press coverage and assisting with credit requests
- Assisting with creation of weekly and monthly credit reports
- Maintaining publication library and press kit

Requirements:

- Applicant Personal Characteristics: organized, detail-oriented, determined, and motivated
- Applicant Qualifications: previous fashion experience and strong interpersonal skills

While we are seeking interns to start as soon as possible, summer inquiries are also welcome.
    Please send résumé and cover letter to: JRodas@catherinemalandrino.com

*Note: This is a sample internship advertisement that may not be available now.

Visual Merchandising—The Silent Selling Person

"You tell him," the store manager pleaded.

"Not me," the visual merchandising assistant replied. "You don't understand. I have to work with him every day."

Marie Millstein, the store manager, is concerned about the window display decisions made by the company's visual merchandising director, Travis van Gundy. The department store chain, which has 15 locations in New York State, carries a full range of budget to better apparel, accessories, and home furnishings. Travis and his team of assistants travel from branch store to branch store to install the primary window and interior displays. Travis is responsible for selecting the featured merchandise and designing the actual displays. Once again, Marie is dissatisfied with his choices of window merchandise.

Marie believes that the merchandise featured in the windows and displays should reflect the items that have been purchased in large quantities by the store's buyers; she believes that the window and interior displays are the most effective tools for promoting the merchandise purchased in quantity that she and her management and sales staffs must sell. Items carried in depth for newspaper and catalog advertising and those of large, private label purchases are the goods Marie would like to see promoted through these primary displays.

Travis, on the other hand, believes that the window and interior displays should be designed to catch the eyes of passersby, to stop them in their tracks and motivate them to enter the store and its departments and shop. He thinks that unique items from the store's merchandise assortment should be showcased in the windows and displays. He believes that alternate promotional efforts, such as newspaper advertisements and catalogs, will support the sales of merchandise that has been purchased in great depth. Travis does not want the store windows to look like those of the retailer's competitors, which feature basic merchandise in key displays. He believes that the store's displays should be dramatic and innovative; he sees his role as that of a stage director. Travis is not pleased that Marie does not appreciate his creative work.

Marie finally brings up her concerns about the selected display merchandise to Travis. She is determined to convince Travis that the merchandise featured in the store's advertising should also be displayed in the windows and interior displays. Travis, however, is adamant that his philosophy of display is correct. After all, Travis says, he is the one who has studied and trained in the field of visual merchandising. The discussion evolves to a heated debate that ends in an impasse. At Travis's suggestion, they decide to meet with the general merchandise manager, Carol Barnett, to discuss their conflicting views about the window and interior displays. Both parties agree that they will conform to Mrs. Barnett's decision.

1. Select the perspective of visual merchandising—Travis's or Marie's—that most closely resembles yours, and develop a list of talking points to present to the merchandise manager to persuade her to your point of view.

2. If you were in the position of Mrs. Barnett, the general merchandise manager, how would you resolve this conflict?

Consumer Buying Motives and Promotion

The promotional division of a major Internet company specializing in fashion apparel and accessories for the entire family is determining the focus of its winter holiday promotional campaign. The Internet firm carries trendy moderate to better merchandise that appeals to an international target market in a middle-class income level. The personnel attending the meeting include the Webmaster; the staff of the advertising department, including the advertising director, art director, copywriter, and photographer; the general merchandise manager; and the buyers for the women's, men's, and children's apparel departments. The primary objective of the meeting is to discuss and define the winter holiday promotional theme that will best appeal to the target market. As the image of the Web site is global, contemporary, and fashion forward, the theme must also reflect the company's personality. The group will begin by examining consumers' buying motives.

Meeting attendees discuss emotional versus rational buying motives; they debate appealing to the customer from the perspective of the joy of holiday giving as opposed to purchasing the best value and quality at the most reasonable price. They investigate the possibility of using psychogenic motives, focusing on ego by emphasizing the company's sophistication, forward fashion, and exclusive product offers. Finally, the team members examine the use of patronage as a foundation for the campaign. As they analyze the various buying motives, the advertising staff and buyers suggest techniques for implementing each approach through a variety of themes, such as World of Celebration, Fashion Frugalista, Making Memories, and so on. The general merchandise manager discusses how each of the projected major fashion trends would fit into the suggested themes.

At the conclusion of the meeting, each team member is assigned the task of formulating a proposal for the holiday promotional campaign by selecting a specific buying motive, creating a corresponding theme, and drafting implementation steps. The group will meet during the following week to select the most effective proposal.

1. If you were a member of the promotional division, would you choose an emotional, rational, psychogenic, or patronage motive? Why?

2. Using your selected approach, develop a new theme and implementation steps for this theme for the firm's holiday campaign.

APPENDIX A

Internship Learning Agreement

Print or type all responses except signatures. All three parties (the internship supervisor, the intern, and the academic sponsor) should retain a copy of this agreement.

Employer (Name of Organization): _____

Internship Supervisor (Name and Title): _____

Internship Academic Sponsor: _____

Job Description (List the duties, goals, and responsibilities that the intern will have. If possible, the duties and goals should be listed *by the intern* in an internship calendar format and attached to this form):

_____

_____

_____

_____

_____

Time Commitment (Number of weeks, days per week, hours per day):

_____

Amount of Academic Credit to Be Earned for Internship Course: _____

Level of Academic Credit to Be Earned for Internship Course: _____

Approvals

1. Approval of Internship Supervisor

I agree to supervise this student, to inform this student about information sources needed to complete *The Fashion Intern*, and to evaluate this student's work performance at the conclusion of the internship.

Name _____ Title _____

Signature _____ Telephone _____

Address _____ E-mail _____

_____

_____

2. Approval of Academic Internship Sponsor

I approve the placement as described above.

Name _____ Academic Institution _____

Signature _____ Telephone _____

Address _____ E-mail _____

_____

_____

3. Approval of Student

I agree to complete *The Fashion Intern*, to meet the academic requirements of the internship, and to provide my employer with high-quality work.

Name _____ Year in School _____

Signature _____ Student Number _____

Address during Internship: _____

_____

_____

Telephone Number _____

E-mail _____

Resources for Finding Internships and Researching Employers

*J*nternship Directories (online and at bookstores)

- *Vault Guide to Top Internships* (most recent edition)

- *National Directory of Arts Internships*

- *College Guide for Visual Arts 2009: Real-World Admission Guide for All Fine Arts, Design and New Media Majors* (Peterson's Guide for Visual Arts Majors)

- *Sheldon's Retail Trade of the United States*

*B*usiness Directories

- *Standard and Poor's* (www.standardandpoors.com)

- *Sheldon's Retail Guide*

- *National Retail Federation* (www.rtf.com)

- *NRF Stores* (www.stores.org)

- *Directory of Corporate Affiliations* (http://www.lexisnexis.com/dca)

- *Directory of Executive Recruiters* (www.kennedyinfo.com/js/der.html)

- *Harris Industrial Infosource Directory* (www.harrisinfo.com)

- *Hoover's* (www.hoovers.com)

Networking

- Alumni
- Professional associations
- Faculty
- Past and present employers
- Family and friends
- Fellow students
- The Fashion Group International career seminars, located throughout the United States (e.g., Chicago, Kansas City, Dallas, Denver)
- Guest speakers on campus
- Career fairs

Fashion and Trade Associations

American Advertising Federation (www.aaf.org)

Advertising Council (www.adcouncil.org)

American Association of Advertising Agencies (www.aaaa.org)

American Association of Exporters and Importers (www.aaei.org)

Apparel Manufacturers' Association (www.apparelandfootwear.org)

American Society of Media Photographers (www.asmp.com)

Personal Care Products Council (www.personalcarecouncil.org)

Council of Fashion Designers of America (www.cfda.org)

Direct Marketing Association (www.the-dma.org)

Institute of Store Planners (www.ispo.org)

International Apparel Federation (www.iafnet.com)

American Jewelry Design Council (www.ajdc.org)

Costume Designers Guild (www.costumedesignersguild.com)

National Retail Federation (www.nrf.com)

Retail Advertising and Marketing Association (www.rama-nrf.org)

National Textile Association (www.nationaltextile.org)

The Fashion Association (fashion.infomat.com)

The Fashion Group International, Inc. (www.fgi.org)

The Woolmark Company (www.wool.com)

Cotton Incorporated (www.cottoninc.com)

Mohair Council of America (www.mohairusa.com)

Newspapers

The *Wall Street Journal*

The *New York Times*

National Business Employment Weekly

Crain's New York Business

The *National Ad Search*

Women's Wear Daily (WWD)

Magazines

Business Week

Forbes

Fortune

Entrepreneur

Stores

Industry-Specific Reference Materials

Women's Wear Daily (WWD)

Fur Council of Canada (www.furcouncil.com)

O'Dwyer's Public Relations News

The Standard Directory of Advertising Agencies—The Salesman's Guide

Thomas Register of American Manufacturers

Top Private Companies (by state)

Trade Periodicals and E-zines

(See http://www.magazinecity.com for additional selections)

Advertising and Beauty Industry

Adweek

Advertising Age

California Apparel News

DMNews

Multichannel Merchant

DIRECT

American Salon

Beauty Fashion

Cosmetic News

Cosmetic World

Beauty Industry Report

Nailpro

SpaFinder

Spa

Spa Life Magazine

WWD BeautyBiz

Children's Wear

Earnshaw's

General Fashion, Apparel, and Textiles

AAMA Newsletter

Apparel Magazine

California Apparel News

Surface

Textile World

WWD Collections

WWD Fast

Menswear

Sportswear International

WWD Men's

Visual Display and Packaging

VMSD

Signs of the Times

Packaging Digest

Packaging World

Shopper Marketing

Intimate Apparel News

Apparel News

Textiles

Bobbin

Davidson's Textile Bluebook

Fiberarts

The International Textiles Magazine

Textiles Panamericanos

Textile World

Accessories

Accessories Magazine

Manufacturing Jewelers & Suppliers of America (MJSA Journal)

Footwear News

Accessory Merchandising

The Goldsmith—hr: Watches

WWD Accessories

Fashion and Color Trend Forecasting Services

The Color Association of the United States (CAUS)
409 West 44th Street
New York, NY
Tel: (212) 582-6884
Fax: (212) 757-4557
www.colorassociation.com

The Doneger Group
463 Seventh Avenue
New York, NY 10018
Tel: (212) 564-1255
Fax: (212) 564-3971
www.doneger.com
www.tobereport.com (Tobé Report)
www.mpnews.com (Margit Publications)

Design Options
110 East 9th Street, Suite B769
Los Angeles, CA 90079
Tel: (213) 622-9094
DONow@design-options.com
www.designoptions.com

Pantone Color Institute
590 Commerce Boulevard
Carlstadt, NJ 07072
Tel: (201) 935-5500
Fax: (201) 896-0242
www.pantone.com

Promostyl (subsidiary office; headquartered in Paris)
853 Broadway, Suite 803
New York, NY 10003
Tel: (212) 921-7930
www.promostyl.com

Trend Union
30 Boulevard Saint Jacques
75014 Paris
France
Tel: 01 44 08 68 80
www.trendunion.com

Worth Global Style Network (West Coast)
(London-based Internet trend service)
9300 Wilshire Blvd., Suite 405
Beverly Hills, CA 90212
Tel: (310) 385-5999
www.wgsn.com

Online and Internet Research—
A Few of the Many Databases

American Business Disk
library.dialog.com/bluesheets/html/bl0531.html

Business Dateline
library.dialog.com/bluesheets/html/bl0635.html

Canadian Employment
www.canadajobs.com

Canadian Universities
www.canadian-universities.net

Career Dreams Incorporated
www.careerdreams.org

Career Mosaic
careermosaic.com

Career Path
www.careerpath.com

Colorado Online Jobs Connection
http://www.coloradojobs.com

Cool Works
www.coolworks.com/showme/

Corporate Development Network
www.metropark.com/cdn

Creative Jobs
www.creativejobscentral.com/fashion-internships/employment

Dun's International Business Locator
www.dnbibl.com/mddi/ibl

Dun's Million Dollar Plus
www.dnbmdd.com/mddi

Ed2010
www.ed2010.com

Encyclopedia of Associations
library.dialog.com/bluesheets/html/bl0114.html

Fashion Positions
www.dailyfashionjobs.com

Fashion Jobs
www.thefashiontool.com

Find a Job
www.monster.com

Find an Internship
www.freefashioninternships.com

Help Wanted
www.helpwanted.com

Hispanic and Latino Businesses
www.hispanicstar.com

Locate a Job
www.hotjobs.com

HR Unlimited
www.sonnet.com

Infomat
www.infomat.com

Infoseek: Find a Job
www.infoseek.com/Getting_It_Done/Finda_job?sv=N3

Intern Zoo
www.internzoo.com

International Fashion Jobs
www.fibre2fashion.com

Job Bank USA
www.jobbankusa.com

Job Search
www.careerbuilder.com
www.jobsearch.com

Job Web
www.jobweb.org

Los Angeles Times
www.latimes.com

Lycos Career Guide
www.lycos.com

Monstertrak
www.monstertrak.com/career-guide/college-internships

NationJob Network
www.nationjob.com

New York Times
www.nytimes.com

LexisNexis
w3.nexis.com/new

Online Career Counseling
www.careerplannet.com

Rising Star Internships
www.rsinternships.com

Simply Hired
www.simplyhired.com

Snag a Job
www.snagajob.com

Snelling Staffing Services
www.snelling.com

U.S. Exports of Merchandise
www.census.gov

U.S. Federal Government
www.fedworld.gov

U.S. News Online
www.usnews.com

Vault Internships
www.vault.com/jobs/jobboard/industry

The Woodmoor Group, Inc.
www.careerbuilder.com

Yahoo! Classifieds
classifieds.yahoo.com

*I*nternational and U.S. Apparel Markets and Marts

Atlanta
AmericasMart Atlanta
240 Peachtree Street
Atlanta, GA 30303
(404) 220-3000
www.americasmart.com

Boston

Boston Collective and Connecticut Menswear Market
Crown Plaza – Cromwell Court
Boston, MA 02125
(508) 655-7158
www.bostoncollective.com

California

California Market Center
110 East 9th St.
Los Angeles, CA 90079
(213) 630-3600
www.californiamarketcenter.com

Canada

Alberta Fashion Market
P.O. Box 66037
Edmonton, Canada ab t5s 1k9
(780) 455-1881
www.trendsapparel.com

Toronto Fashion Incubator
www.fashionincubator.com/resources/selling_your_line/canadian-fashion-trade-sh.shtml

Ontario Fashion Exhibitors
160 Tycos Drive, Suite 2219, Box 218
Toronto, Canada M6B 1W8
(416) 596-2401
www.ofeshows.ca/welcome.php

Charlotte

Charlotte International Trade Center
200 North College Street
Charlotte, NC 28202
(704) 335-9100
www.internationaltradecenter.info

Chicago

Chicago Apparel Center
350 North Orleans Street
Chicago, IL 60654
(312) 527-4141
www.merchandisemart.com

Dallas

Dallas Market Center
2300 Stemmons Freeway
Dallas, TX 75207
(214) 655-6100
www.dallasmarketcenter.com

Denver

Denver Merchandise Mart
451 East 58th Avenue, #4270
Denver, CO 80216
(303) 292-6278
www.denvermart.com

Kansas City

Kansas City Apparel and Accessories Sales Association
P.O. Box 28381
Kansas City, MO 64188
(816) 231-6446

Los Angeles

The New Mart
127 East Ninth
Los Angeles, CA 90015
(213) 627-0671
www.newmart.net

Miami

Miami International Merchandise Mart
711 N.W. 72nd Avenue
Miami, FL 33126
(305) 261-2900
www.miamimart.net

Minneapolis

Minneapolis Apparel Mart
Hyatt Merchandise Mart
3001 Nicolette Mall
Minneapolis, MN 55403
(612) 333-5226
(800) 272-6972
www.northstarfashion.com

New York

Fashion Center Headquarters
249 West 39th Street
New York, NY 10018
(212) 764-9600
www.fashioncenter.com

Pittsburgh

Pittsburgh Expo Center
322 Mall Boulevard
Monroeville, PA 15146
(888) 366-4660
www.pittsburghfashionmart.com

Portland

Portland Apparel Mart
Montgomery Park
2701 N.W. Vaughn Street
Portland, OR 97210
(503) 228-7275

San Francisco

Market Northern California
3701 Sacramento Street, Suite 204
San Francisco, CA 94118
(415) 328-1221
info@fashionmarketnorcal.com

Seattle

Seattle International Trade Center
2601 Elliott Avenue, Suite 1333
Seattle, WA 98121
(206) 441-3000

Singapore

Textile and Fashion Federation
190 Middle Road
Singapore, 239055
Malaysia
65-6735-8390
www.taff.org.sg

Internship Programs and Program Placement

Careers in Fashion
http://jobsinfashion.com
This Web site is a great way to find out about internships and other career opportunities. Many topics are discussed, including education and training, recruiting, résumés, and salary. The site is geared toward current fashion students and people curious about starting a career in fashion.

The first topic discussed is the various design institutes the site recommends. There is also a list of reviewed books that would be good supplemental reading. These books touch on virtually every area of the fashion industry. The site also provides a great overview of each area. The Recruiter Rolodex is a personalized job search this site can do for an applicant. There is a fee for this, but the Rolodex has many contacts, including international companies.

A favorite aspect of this Web site is its interview checklist. It divides the information given into three categories: before the interview, during the interview, and after the interview. Before the interview, it is suggested you familiarize yourself with the company through its Web site and current publications. You should also make a list of questions you want to ask during the interview and be prepared to answer questions about your abilities, strengths, and weaknesses. During the interview it is suggested you sell yourself through both your words and your actions. You should also evaluate the company and end on a positive note. After the interview you should make note of any important information. There should then be a follow-up on your part, by mail and phone.

Rising Star Internships
www.rsinternships.com
Experience America is a company that helps place international students and foreign professionals in internship positions. The internships are unpaid and located in the San Francisco Bay area. Depending on the country, there may be related fees, terms, and conditions; these are provided for the applicant upon request. Experience America will try to match your internship to your educational background. One area mentioned on the site is fashion design. The firm is able to locate internships with both small and large companies. Placement usually takes 6 to 8 weeks. To apply, one must contact Experience America by e-mail to request an information packet.

Internships at Abercrombie and Fitch
www.abercrombieandfitch.com/anf/careers
The internship program at Abercrombie and Fitch works a little differently from those at most retail stores. The company actually trains the intern as a manager in training (MIT). These positions are especially designed for college seniors and those recently graduated as a way to integrate them into higher positions within the company. The MIT program lasts approximately 90 days, and the trainee goes through a formal training schedule. Once this program is completed, the trainee will qualify for the next position up the ladder: assistant manager. From there, it is possible to continue to aim higher on up the employment ladder, armed with the internship experience with Abercrombie and Fitch.

Liz Claiborne, Inc., Internship Program
http://www.lizclaiborne.com/careers/external/internship.asp
This summer internship program is scheduled for June through August, for 8 to 10 weeks. Internships are offered in the following areas: design, merchandising,

planning, buying, sales, finance, information technology, human resources, and marketing/public relations. An intern is placed in an area that matches his or her interests and is involved in the daily workings of that area.

Each intern is given a summer project that takes 5 to 6 weeks to complete. The summer project creates a hands-on experience that allows interns to gain more exposure to their field while providing a portfolio addition. The program exposes interns to other areas of the company through field trips and other activities in which the interns can interact with each other. There are also weekly brown bag lunch talks by guest speakers on topics such as licensing, design, and e-commerce.

Internship opportunities are available in a number of the corporation's brands, including Juicy Couture, Kate Spade, Liz Claiborne, DKNY Jeans, and Lucky Brand. The program is designed for flexibility, as interns can work part-time, 20 hours per week, or full-time, 40 hours per week. Qualifications include sophomore through senior college enrollment, a minimum GPA of 2.8, and eligibility to receive college credit. Some internships require certain majors; others are open to any major. Placement is based on need in each area and interests of the candidate. These are unpaid internships. Prior retail experience is a plus.

London College of Fashion (LCF) Internship Program
http://www.fashion.arts.ac.uk
The internship is an optional part of the LCF program and is subject to application approval for all students. Students on the semester program may apply to work in an unpaid internship for a minimum of 120 hours. A minimum GPA of 3.5 or equivalent is required, as is fashion experience in a work setting. The internship experience is equivalent to six course credits. Assessment is based on a written journal and formal presentation at the end of the program. In the past, students have been placed in public relations, design, buying, merchandising, marketing, retailing, and trend forecasting with the following companies:

Buying offices and retailers, including

- Arcadia Group

- Earl Jean

- Harvey Nichols

- Liberty

- Joseph

- Burberry

Public relations departments and companies representing

- Ketchams

- Agnès b.

- Nicole Fahri

- Sophia Swire

- Beverly Cable

- Browns

- Vivienne Westwood

- Whistles

Designers, including

- Ben de Lisi

- Boyd

- Vivienne Westwood

- Ozwald Boateng

- Fake London

- Sweaty Betty

- Shelley Fox

- English Eccentrics

Costume designers, including

- The Globe Theater

- The English National Opera

- Angels and Bermans

- The National Archive Library

Daily Activity Journal

*J*ntroduction

The Daily Activity Journal is both a personal diary and a work log. It is suggested that, during the internship, you maintain a small notebook in which you can jot down information you will need to remember, things to do, and brief summaries of your daily activities. The CD-ROM that accompanies this text allows you to record your internship experiences electronically and to construct an effective daily activity journal. Before starting your journal, please see the following guidelines.

An effective daily activity journal:

- contains entries that indicate dates, hours worked, a description of job responsibilities for each day, and reflections of your workday;

- may include some brief entries and some that are several pages in length;

- indicates what was learned from each workday—sometimes what not to do, what you should have done, or how to handle problems;

- is written in daily (If you attempt to reconstruct a week's worth of work, it will be obvious); and

- concludes with a final entry that summarizes your views of the internship experience.

An ineffective daily activity journal:

- is sloppy, too brief, vague, or boring to review; it is more like a log of your work hours than a reflection on, and evaluation of, your work experiences;

- contains vague entries that were not recorded daily, with little attention to detail; and

- often says, "same as yesterday." Most employees learn something new each day (let's hope!), although on some days the learning is more subtle. An ineffective journal skims the surface, rather than looking inward.

Daily Activity Journal

Date _____

Hours Worked _____

Department _____

Today

Work Responsibilities:

_____

_____

_____

New Learning Experiences:

_____

_____

_____

Summary of Workday:

_____

_____

_____

Things to Remember:

_____

_____

_____

Tomorrow

Questions to Ask:

_____

_____

_____

Things to Do:

_____

_____

_____

Weekly Activity Report

Student Intern's Name _____ Week Number _____

Company Name _____ Date _____

Work Schedule					
Date	Day of Week	From	To	# of Hours Worked	Primary Duties
	M				
	Tu				
	W				
	Th				
	F				
	Sa				
	Su				
Total Hours Worked This Week:					

Descriptive summary of this week's activities (including duties performed, training, exposure to new areas of the internship organization, and so on):

_____

_____

_____

_____

_____

_____

Successes:

_____

_____

_____

_____

_____

Challenges:

_____

_____

_____

_____

_____

Self-Evaluation of This Week's Performance:

_____

_____

_____

_____

_____

_____

Student's Internship Summary

List the routine duties of the _____

(internship employer's job title)

_____

_____

_____

_____

_____

_____

List your routine duties as the student intern.

_____

_____

_____

_____

_____

_____

As in most industries, various segments of the fashion industry have unique buzzwords—words or phrases used by industry personnel. List these terms and their definitions.

_____

_____

_____

_____

_____

_____

Indicate your income (internship salary), if the internship was paid.

_____

_____

_____

_____

_____

_____

List any expenses incurred during the internship experience, or attach a spreadsheet of these.

_____

_____

_____

_____

_____

_____

Indicate the anticipated salary range for a career in _____.
                                                      (employer's position)

_____

_____

_____

_____

_____

_____

From your internship experience, examine the qualifications and attributes of a successful _____.

(employer's position)

_____

_____

_____

_____

_____

_____

Based on your internship experience, discuss the qualifications and attributes of a successful student intern in this position.

_____

_____

_____

_____

_____

_____

Which areas of work and study, as well as cocurricular experiences, would assist a student preparing for a career in this employment area?

_____

_____

_____

_____

_____

_____

Internship Supervisor's Intern Evaluation: Rating Chart and Short Answer Questions

Intern _____

Organization _____

Instructions: Please indicate your evaluation of the intern during the work experience period. Rate each characteristic by placing an X in the appropriate column and write comments related to ratings as desired.

Rating: 1. Exceptional   2. Above Average   3. Average   4. Below Average   5. Not Observed

Characteristics	Rating	Comments
Work Habits		
Is reliable under pressure		
Practices punctuality and good attendance		
Accepts criticism constructively		
Shows consistent quality of work		
Demonstrates logical thinking ability		
Exhibits decision-making ability, self-direction		
Is organized		
Knowledge of Work		
Understands systems and procedures		
Performs job efficiently		
Understands and follows instructions		
Shows knowledge of department		

Characteristics	Rating	Comments

Human Relations

    Exhibits cooperation with coworkers

    Demonstrates leadership qualities

    Is receptive to supervision

    Handles customers tactfully

Personal Attributes

    Dresses in an appropriate manner

    Is emotionally mature

    Shows enthusiasm for job

    Exhibits initiative and creativity

Areas of Strength:

_____

_____

_____

_____

Areas Needing Improvement:

_____

_____

_____

_____

Prediction: What is your estimation of the probable success of this intern in this field?

_____

_____

_____

_____

Comments/Suggestions: Please add any suggestions you may have that might be helpful in the preparation of students for their careers.

_____

_____

_____

_____

Is it acceptable to forward a copy of this evaluation to the intern?

____ Yes   ____ No

Signed _____ Date _____

Title _____

Address _____

Telephone _____

E-mail _____

Internship Supervisor's Intern Evaluation: Checklist/Rating Scale

Organization's Name and Address _____

Supervisor _____

Intern _____

Total Number of Hours Worked _____

Please answer the questions below by placing a check mark next to the appropriate answer.

1. Compared with other student interns I have supervised, this intern's performance was

    ❏ excellent

    ❏ above average

    ❏ average

    ❏ below average

    ❏ unsatisfactory

    ❏ I have not supervised an intern before.

2. When evaluating an intern, which of the following qualities are most important? Please rank from 1 to 5, with 1 being most important and 5 being least important.

    _____ promptness

    _____ motivation

    _____ personal initiative

    _____ professionalism

    _____ quality of work

3. On a scale of 1 to 5, with 1 being excellent and 5 being unsatisfactory, please rate the intern's performance in the following areas:

_____ dependability   _____ quality of work

_____ motivation   _____ ability to learn

_____ personal initiative   _____ attitude

_____ professionalism   _____ other (please specify) _____

4. When assigned a task, the intern

❏ needed little guidance/worked independently

❏ needed some guidance/worked independently at times

❏ needed regular supervision/rarely worked independently

5. The student intern arrived to work on time

❏ always   ❏ usually   ❏ rarely   ❏ never

6. The quality of the intern's work was

❏ excellent

❏ above average

❏ average

❏ below average

❏ unsatisfactory

7. The intern completed most tasks

❏ with enthusiasm

❏ with average diligence

❏ without enthusiasm

8. The intern worked well with other employees.

❏ Yes   ❏ No

9. The intern respected company policies.

❏ Yes   ❏ No

10. The intern was (check all that apply)

❑ diligent   ❑ mature   ❑ immature   ❑ unreliable

❑ careless   ❑ responsible   ❑ dependable   ❑ indifferent

❑ other (please specify) _____

11. The intern met the objectives/goals specified at the beginning of the internship.

❑ Yes   ❑ No   ❑ Goals were not specified

12. The intern learned (check all that apply)

❑ quickly ❑ with some difficulty

❑ easily ❑ with great difficulty

13. The intern's overall performance was

❑ excellent (A)

❑ above average (B)

❑ average (C)

❑ unsatisfactory

14. Do you wish for this evaluation to remain confidential—for us to not share it with the intern you supervised?

❑ Yes   ❑ No

Comments (use an additional page if necessary):

_____

_____

_____

_____

Signature _____ Date _____

Title _____

Address _____

Telephone _____

E-mail _____

Thank you for supervising the student intern. Your time and expertise are greatly appreciated.

Intern's Internship Supervisor Evaluation

Date _____

Name _____

Title/Dept. _____

Semester/Term of Internship _____

Organization's Name and Address _____

_____

_____

_____

Supervisor's Name and Title _____

_____

Telephone Number _____

E-mail Address _____

Please give a brief description of your internship job responsibilities:

_____

_____

_____

_____

_____

_____

Rate the following characteristics of your employer:

	Highest Performance			Lowest Performance		Comments
Training	1	2	3	4	5	
Attitude	1	2	3	4	5	
Assistance and Support	1	2	3	4	5	
Direction/goal setting	1	2	3	4	5	
Communication	1	2	3	4	5	
Overall supervision	1	2	3	4	5	
Valuable work assignments	1	2	3	4	5	
Availability	1	2	3	4	5	

Additional Comments/Suggestions:

_____

_____

_____

_____

_____

_____

_____

_____

_____

_____

Would you recommend this organization to future internship candidates?
_____ Yes   _____ No

If so, please list contact person, location, and telephone number.

_____

_____

_____

Signature _____

Intern's Self-Evaluation

Date _____

Name _____

Title/Dept. _____

Semester/Term of Internship _____

Organization's Name and Address _____

_____

_____

_____

Supervisor's Name and Title _____

_____

Telephone Number _____

E-mail Address _____

Please give a brief description of your internship job responsibilities:

_____

_____

_____

_____

_____

_____

_____

Rank yourself on the following characteristics as they reflect your performance during the internship experience:

	Highest Performance			Lowest Performance		Comments
Motivation	5	4	3	2	1	
Attitude	5	4	3	2	1	
Ability	5	4	3	2	1	
Availability	5	4	3	2	1	
Organization	5	4	3	2	1	
Self-direction	5	4	3	2	1	
Attendance/punctuality	5	4	3	2	1	
Interpersonal skills	5	4	3	2	1	
Leadership ability	5	4	3	2	1	
Knowledge of organization	5	4	3	2	1	

Did you complete the training program for the internship effectively and within the allocated time? _____ Yes _____ No

As part of your evaluation, provide a discussion of the following:

Did you accomplish your predetermined goals?

_____

_____

_____

How did your supervisor help you the most?

_____

_____

_____

Would you recommend this firm again for internship students?

_____

_____

_____

What do you feel the benefits of the internship experience are to you, an upper-level student?

_____

_____

_____

Are there ways we could better prepare students for an internship experience?

_____

_____

_____

Additional Comments/Suggestions:

_____

_____

_____

On a grading scale of A through F, what grade would you assign yourself as a student intern? _____

Signature _____

Glossary

Administered vertical marketing system   Coordinates successive stages of production and distribution through the size and power of one of the parties, not through common ownership.

Advertising   Paid, nonpersonal communication delivered through mass media. Advertising is used to communicate persuasive information about the product in a nonpersonal presentation financed by the seller.

Advocacy advertising   Promotional messages that support a particular cause.

Advocate channel   Uses a salesperson to contact potential buyers in the target market.

Art director   Coordinates visual images used in promotions.

Assembly-line production   Manufacturing process that is segmented into steps that culminate in a single product.

Assortment   The total number of items in the product mix.

Atmospheres   Designed environments that create or reinforce the buyer's desire to buy a product.

Augmented level   Product level that incorporates such extras as installation, delivery, credit, after-sale services, warranty, advertising, and promotion.

Basic items   *See* **Staple items.**

Blind-stitcher   A machine used for hemming.

Boutique   A very specialized retailing operation ("little shops," as translated from French).

Boutique layout   Divides the business into individual shopping areas, each with its own theme.

Branch division area   Responsible for the organization's outlets that are not within the company's headquarters.

Brand   A name, term, sign, symbol, or design, or a combination of these, that is intended to identify the goods or services of one seller or group of sellers and to differentiate them from those of competitors.

Brand advertising   Promotes a particular brand, as opposed to sale advertising, which announces the specific value of item(s).

Branding   A label, image, or word(s) for which developers create an image or personality.

Brand mark   The part of a brand that can be recognized but that cannot be spoken.

Brand name   The part of a brand that can be vocalized.

Breadth   The number of different product lines the organization carries.

Break-even point   The level of operations at which revenue from sales and total costs (expenses) are equal.

Building orders   Production flow charts that are drawn up to designate the dates when the fabric and trims will be received from suppliers, when cutting will be received from suppliers, when cutting will be completed, when each stage of construction will occur, and when shipments will begin.

Business location   Refers to the physical site of the company, destinations to which catalogs are mailed, or the company's Web site and Internet links, whether it is a manufacturing service or retail operation.

Buttonholer   A machine that automatically creates buttonholes.

Buyer readiness state   The consumer's level of awareness and knowledge; commonly used for new product introduction, such as a recent fabrication or development.

Buyers   The individuals who determine the merchandise needs of departments or entire companies and ultimately make the inventory purchases.

Buying motives   The reasons the customer will react to, or buy, a particular product.

Capital items   Goods that are part of the finished product, such as specialized equipment.

Catalog editor   A person who oversees the contents of a publication's catalog, including proofing, visual layout, and editing.

Central business district   The historical center of a town; the area where downtown businesses were established in the development of the city.

Chain operations   Multiple outlets operating under common ownership.

Chain-stitch   A machine that generates an overlock that sews one edge over another.

Channel of distribution   The avenue selected for moving goods from producer to consumer.

Chronological résumé A résumé that lists a person's education and experiences sequentially with the most recent dates indicated first.

Classified advertising A paid promotional message that provides information about a service, sale, or specific value item(s).

Click and brick Store that has both a traditional brick-and-mortar facility and an online presence.

Closed competitive environment A market that is saturated with a high level of competition.

Collection A group of styles with a common theme that is presented for a specific season to buyers.

Colorways The color composition of a product; the color choices available for a specific item.

Company image The combination of thoughts, feelings, beliefs, opinions, and visions people have about the company and its products.

Consistency How closely related the various product lines are in end use, production requirements, and distribution channels.

Consumer cooperative association A group of actual consumers who own all the shares in a retail operation.

Consumer research Involves finding everything out about the customer's characteristics and behavior by analyzing demographics and psychographics.

Contractors Factories that are hired to make and finish goods. Contractors may be domestic or offshore.

Contractual vertical system Consists of independent firms at different levels of production and distribution that integrates their programs through retailer cooperatives and franchise organizations.

Control The division responsible for monitoring the firm's financial status through accounting, management information systems, credit and collections, budgeting, and inventory control. Control also refers to the point in the strategic planning process at which results are compared with goals and objectives.

Convenience goods Products the consumer purchases frequently, quickly, and with minimal effort spent in comparison shopping.

Conventional marketing channel Consists of an independent producer and one or more wholesalers and retailers.

Cooperative advertising When, in exchange for name or brand recognition, the producer pays a specified percentage of promotional costs.

Coordinated group lines Found primarily in the sportswear and home accessories markets, each group is built around coordinating fabrics and includes items that may be mixed and matched to form a variety of ensembles.

Copyright The exclusive right to reproduce, publish, and sell material in the form of a literary, musical, or artistic work.

Core basics Basic styles that are carried every season in colors that may change slightly. Fabrics can also change with each season (e.g., corduroy in fall, linen in spring).

Core level Represents the main benefit or service provided by the product.

Corporate culture The way things are professionally done in a company; accepted or preferred business conduct.

Corporate vertical system Combines successive stages of production and distribution under single ownership.

Corporation Stockholders invest in a business but do not necessarily share in management decisions.

Cover letter A letter of application used to introduce the writer and seek out job opportunities.

Croqui A print, painting, or similar image of a textile pattern, or form used to draw garments.

Cross shopping The consumer's selection of both high and low priced merchandise from better to budget retail providers via online, catalog, and brick-and-mortar store.

Culture The behavior and beliefs typical of a group or class.

Customary pricing Assumes that customers expect a certain product to be available at a certain price and that significant deviation in either direction from that customary price will result in decreased demand.

Customer research Involves finding out everything about the customer's characteristics and behavior by analyzing demographics and psychographics.

Cut to order Manufacturing goods after the buyers have submitted purchase orders to reduce the risk involved in making products before orders; however, longer lead times are needed, and late orders often cannot be filled.

Cut to stock Refers to producing the amount of merchandise that corresponds to the amount of fabric purchased for a particular style.

Cutter Separates into pieces the marker that is laid over layers of the fabric on large cutting tables.

Cutting tickets Lists that indicate the minimum number of pieces that must be ordered to ensure profitability; also can indicate number of units to be produced.

Decline stage The final phase of the product life cycle, once consumers have lost interest and sales have dropped off.

Demographics The breakdown of the population into statistical categories, such as age, gender, education, occupation, income, household size, and marital status. Demographics are also quantitative factors that can help predict available income.

Department store Features hard lines, such as home furnishings and electronics, and soft lines, such as apparel and accessories.

Depth   The number of variants offered in each product of the line, such as sizes and colors.

Design-driven brand   A brand that is led by a designer expressing his or her own artistic vision and personal sense of style.

Die cutting   A process that resembles cookie cutting, in which a die with sharp edges is pressed through layers of fabric.

Digital portfolio   *See* **e-portfolio**

Dimensions   The assortment, in detail, of the items in a product mix.

Direct competitors   Those firms carrying similar products at comparable prices and catering to similar target markets.

Direct market brand   A brand that is both the name of the store (usually a specialty store) and the name on the label. Examples include Ann Taylor, Express, IKEA, and Banana Republic.

Direct merchant   Someone who works directly with fabric mills and manufacturers, eliminating the markups of middlemen.

Direct ratings   Advertising pretesting that includes feedback from customers who were asked which advertisement would influence them to buy the product.

Discount and off-price stores   Firms that sell merchandise at below-market prices.

Distributed storefront (also called mall storefront model)   Model of online retailing that simulates the brick-and-mortar shopping mall.

Downward vertical   Commonly used channel of communication, often from management to staff.

Dual distribution   *See* **Multichannel marketing systems.**

Durable goods   Tangible goods that normally survive many uses. Apparel, home accessories, footwear, and fabrics are examples of durable goods.

Duties (also called tariffs)   Fees levied on merchandise that comes from another country, imposed by the government of the importing country.

Duty-free program   Involves government assistance to a foreign country with economic problems that is provided by waiving charges on imports or exports.

Editing and merchandising   Styles are changed, eliminated, and added during the fitting process. Frequent line review meetings are held to put styles into cohesive collections, then to finalize the line.

Editor   In fashion publishing, the person who determines noteworthy trends and who is ultimately responsible for the content of his or her publication.

Editorial assistant   The career position in publication in which help with promotions and articles is provided.

Editorial research assistant   A person who checks the facts of a publication's articles, through interviews and research, to verify accuracy.

Elastic Demand is referred to as elastic when changes in price affect customer purchases. For example, when prices go up, demand often decreases.

Emotional appeal Promotion message based on feelings, such as fear, love, humor, pride, romance, or joy.

Entertailing Combining an interesting retail environment with appealing activities and desirable merchandise.

E-portfolio (also called digital portfolio) Web-based resource that allows a person to document academic, work, and extracurricular achievements, reflect on past experiences, and display the work on the Web.

E-portfolio abstract A summary of the portfolio's contents intended to guide the reader through the portfolio.

Events Activities such as fashion shows, wardrobing seminars, and wedding expos that are developed and implemented by an event planner or public relations directors.

Exclusive distribution strategy Selecting preferred better stores because of the company's high-end price points and limited production capacity.

Exclusives Items that only a certain retailer or manufacturer carries, often within a specific geographic area.

External environment The outside influences on a business, including social/demographic, natural, political/legal, technological, and economic factors.

Fabric and color stories Groups of fabrics and colors that will ultimately compose collections.

Factory outlets Retail stores owned and operated by manufacturers, usually selling only goods produced by the manufacturers at discount prices (e.g., Hanes, Coach, and Ralph Lauren).

Fashion items Products subject to seasonal and trend changes, frequently available in a wide range of styles with a life expectancy that is relatively brief.

Finance and accounting Company division responsible for the procedures put into place to run the finances of the firm.

First cost The total of all direct costs of producing the item, including material and labor.

Fittings When designers and production staff meet and fit the garments on fitting models after prototypes are received.

Flame bait The e-mail that starts a flame war.

Flame wars A series of angry letters, most of them from two or three people, directed toward each other, that can dominate the tone of an exchange and destroy the camaraderie of the recipients.

Flaming When a person expresses a strongly held opinion online without holding back any emotion.

Flea markets Open-air shopping areas in which multiple vendors sell their wares.

Flexible markup policy A plan that allows the company to apply different levels of markup to varying merchandise classifications.

Forecasting The process of identifying fashion trends, interpreting them for a particular customer or market, and communicating them to designers.
A forecaster is a type of market researcher who knows the fashion market and anticipates its influences.

Formal communication Involves the use of employee handbooks, suggestion systems, newsletters, bulletins, meetings, and education.

Formal internship program Usually offered by a large company. A group of student interns will go through preplanned classes and activities in a structured internship program.

Formal level The product and its accompanying attributes, such as packaging, brand name, quality, styling, and features.

Franchise Manufacturer, wholesale, or service company that sells a smaller firm or individual the right to conduct a business in a specified manner within a certain period of time.

Free-form layout An interior floorplan in which displays of varying shapes and sizes are arranged in a random fashion. The resulting image is relaxed and friendly and has been shown to increase the number of impulse purchases customers make.

Frequency The number of times a promotional message is presented about a product.

Functional résumé One in which a person's education and experiences are grouped by skills and functions, rather than by dates of employment.

General line Refers to a wide variety of merchandise or to an inventory of great breadth.

General product classification Groupings based on similar product characteristics that enable companies to develop marketing strategies for specific products.

Grader The person who adjusts the production pattern to various sizes; grading may also be done by computer.

Grapevine Verbal messages that frequently travel faster than messages sent through official channels.

Grid layout An interior layout in which displays are arranged in a rectangular fashion so that the aisles are parallel. It is a formal and organized environment, especially appropriate for self-service operations.

Growth stage A product enters this stage of the product life cycle when a larger number of consumers begins to accept and purchase it.

Hard goods Products such as appliances, electronics, and home furnishings.

High-end goods Fashion businesses may define merchandise in terms of pricing, with high-end goods being at the top.

Horizontal Communication of messages between those in similar personnel positions, such as manager to manager or employee to employee.

Horizontal marketing channel The joining of two or more companies to distribute merchandise by contracting on a permanent or temporary basis or by creating a separate company.

Human resources Division of the company responsible for overseeing employees; recruiting, hiring, training, promoting, terminating, etc., employees within legal guidelines and company culture.

Image How the brand or company is intended to be perceived and how it is developed best to attract the target customer.

Independent representative *See* **Multiple line rep.**

Indirect competitors Companies providing different products at varying prices that may be purchased by the target market.

Industrial products Products that are necessary to the manufacturing process.

Informal communication The casual use of vertical and horizontal lines for verbal communication, often employee to employee.

Informal internship The supervisor of the internship organization and the student develop an individual program that will meet the employer's needs and the student's internship requirements.

Information flow Pertains to directed promotional efforts used to influence product sales from one party to other parties in the channel.

In-house production (also called inside shop) Company-owned production facility.

Inside shop *See* **In-house production.**

Inspiration Influences that direct the general trend direction a fashion company will take for an upcoming season.

Institutional advertising Advertising that builds the organization's image and creates community goodwill.

In-stock basics Items that are always carried and that change minimally. These items have a long selling life and are in demand season after season. Examples are white cotton T-shirts and five-pocket denim jeans.

Intangible products Goods that cannot be touched or held, such as a service or an idea.

Intensive distribution strategy Selling products to a specific type of retailer throughout the country.

Introductory stage The first stage of the product life cycle. This is the time when innovative goods that appeal to fashion leaders, or trendsetters, are first offered.

Inventory Selection of products available for sale by a fashion operation.

Invoice   A billing statement that reflects shipments made to the retail operation and denotes purchase order numbers.

Item line   A selection of only one type of product (e.g., a T-shirt or a pair of jeans), organized around groups of fabrics and showing a range of colors.

Joint-venture   A production alternative involving a partnership between the company and a contractor that performs all or part of the production process.

Key items   Not-too-trendy, but not-too-basic, fashion items that are the must-haves for the season, offered in many colors or a variety of fabrics. These are usually advertised and carried in-depth.

Keystoning   Retail price developed by doubling the wholesale price.

Key vendors   Lines from manufacturers that feature the greatest proportion of inventory.

Knockoff   A copy of another style, either line for line or with a few small changes.

Labdips   Swatches of dyed fabric shown to the product development team for color approval prior to dyeing large yardages of fabric.

Labeling   Part of the packaging, referring to the printed information that describes the product and appearing on or with the package.

Landed cost   For a product manufactured abroad, the total estimates for product components, labor, and shipping.

Layout   The arrangement of the physical facilities in a business. The ideal layout contributes to efficient operations, increased productivity, and higher sales.

Lead time   The period between receipt of the order by the producer and receipt of goods by the consumer.

Leased departments   Arrangements in which a retailer rents space within the store to another company (e.g., Estée Lauder, BCBG, and DSW Shoes).

Letter of application   A brief letter including an explanation about the job you are interested in, how you heard about it, and why your qualifications fit the job.

Licensees   Manufacturers that pay for the right to use a designer's, sports team's, celebrity's, or character's name and develop lines under those names.

Limited line   Operations feature a particular product category with depth of selection.

Line   A seasonal collection of groups of styles.

Line appeal   The attraction of a group of products to a customer.

Line balance   The cohesiveness and variety make it hard for buyers or customers to choose just one thing from a line—they should want to buy everything.

Line plan   The line plan shows the number of styles in the line, number and types of fabrics to be used, colors and sizes per style, anticipated stock-keeping units, and approximate preferred costs.

Line sheet   Provides information about the products being sold. Often, it includes style sketches and an order form for the retail buyers to use.

Line structure   The number and types of styles in a product's line.

Lock-stitch   A machine that sews a straight seam.

Long-range forecasting   Forecasting that refers to researching economic trends related to consumer spending patterns and the business climate by looking into the future.

Loss leader   A product offered at an extremely low price, thereby generating little or no profit and perhaps even a loss. Loss leaders are used to attract customers or get their attention.

Low-end goods   Representing budget price points. These goods are the lowest-priced in the merchandise assortment.

Mall storefront model   *See* **Distributed storefront.**

Management   Leading, planning, organizing, directing, delegating, motivating, and communicating in a supervisory capacity, with the goal of making the business and its employees successful.

Manufacturer   A company that creates, produces, markets, and distributes lines on a continual basis.

Manufacturer's representatives   *See* **Sales representatives.**

Markdown   A decrease in the selling price of an item.

Marker   The layout of pattern pieces for a particular style and size of a product.

Marker maker   One who creates a pattern layout on the fabric that best suits the fabric and is most economical to produce. Pattern pieces are interlocked as closely together as possible to ensure there is little fabric waste.

Market analysis   The study of general market trends. Market analysis can be split into long-range and short-range forecasting.

Market positioning   Arranging for a product or product lines to occupy a distinctive and desirable place for a specific market in the minds of target customers.

Market repositioning   New activities a company implements to accomplish more effectively its objectives and goals.

Market segmentation   The process of dividing the total market into smaller population sections that share similar characteristics.

Marketing calendar   A calendar that indicates line preview dates and release dates by season, start and end shipping dates, weekly or monthly sales, and weekly or monthly shipping plans.

Marketing channel   The function of moving goods from producer to consumer.

Marketing communications   An umbrella term referring to all the activities a business undertakes to "talk" to its target market, including printed marketing brochures and other marketing messages, advertising, sales promotions, publicity, and public relations.

Markup   The amount of money added to the cost of the product to establish the selling price.

Materials and parts   Goods that enter the manufacturer's product completely, such as raw materials and manufactured materials and parts.

Maturity stage   The point in the product life cycle when the product is at either a peak or plateau in sales.

Merchandise assortment   The selection of products available for sale in a fashion operation.

Merchandise coordinator   Personnel who work for a salary, and possibly a commission, and who assist with the maufacturer's product line in the actual retail store.

Merchandiser   The person who works with the product development team to decide what to make and who then organizes and controls the entire product development process.

Merchandising   Includes responsibility for all the activities involved in buying and selling merchandise.

Merchandising-driven brand (also called void-filling brand)   A market-based brand that supplies a void in the market, or an underserved customer, and that creates a product to appeal specifically to that customer.

Merchandising calendar   The product development team's schedule. Its goal is to deliver the right product (in terms of style, quality, and price) at the right time.

Merchandising/operating results (MOR)   Statistical information on national retail sales that is compiled by the National Retail Federation.

Mission statement   A statement that articulates and guides the firm's vision.

Moral appeal   Promotional message that reflects the audience's sense of what is right or wrong.

Multichannel marketing systems (also called dual distribution)   Systems that operate on two different customer levels.

Multiple line representatives (also called independent rep)   Salesperson who represents several lines that work well together, are noncompetitive, and can be sold to the same buyers.

Neighborhoods   Locations in which residential areas are heavily concentrated.

Netiquette   The use of good manners to communicate online.

Nondurable goods   Tangible goods that are normally consumed in one or a few uses.

Nonpersonal communication channels   Promotional messages distributed through mass media (undifferentiated) or selective media (specialized), using print, electronic, or display methods.

Nonstore selling   Those retailing activities that do not require a physical facility to which consumers come to shop.

Office etiquette   The protocol of office conduct in most business settings.

Open competitive environment   A market in which there is a low level of competition.

Operations   The division of a company that is responsible for the maintenance of the business facilities, purchasing of supplies and equipment to operate the business, customer services, and security. Operations are also the procedures put in place to run the business.

Opinion leader   The person in a reference group who exerts the most influence on the purchase decisions of group members.

Organizational structure   Defines the chain of command, communication, and authority within the business.

Outside contractor   A production firm that requires payment from a manufacturer only for services provided.

Overhead   Expenses related to operating stores, offices, factories, or showrooms, such as rent and utilities.

Ownership group   A parent corporation that owns divisions of a business.

Packaging   The container or wrapper for a product.

Packing slip   A form that indicates the style numbers and quantities contained in a specific container of merchandise.

Partnership   Two or more people who invest their time and money in a business and maintain liability for its debts.

Payment flow   Describes how and when channel members pay their bills and to whom the payments are made.

Penetration pricing   A strategy designed to capture a large share of the mass market by offering the product at a low price.

Personal communication channels   Those promotional channels that direct a specific message to a specific customer group. They are classified as advocate, expert, and social.

Personal selling   A form of direct sales that consists of oral presentations to one or more prospective buyers.

Personnel   The division of a company responsible for overseeing human resources; the employees of the organization.

Physical distribution   The tasks of planning, implementing, and controlling the physical flow of materials and final goods from point of origin to point of use to meet the needs of customers at a profit.

Physical flow   Refers to the movement of the actual product from raw materials to end users.

Population density   The number of people per square mile in a given area. This is an important characteristic for businesses that rely on high-traffic volume.

Portfolio   A compilation of products or samples that illustrate a person's work skills and values.

Portfolio test   A measure in which a group of consumers analyzes an assortment of ads and is then tested for recall and recognition.

Power center   An area that combines the drawing potential of a large regional mall with the convenience of a neighborhood shopping center.

Premiums   Items intended to promote a specific brand; usually sold in return for proofs-of-purchase, they may be manufactured by an apparel or accessory producer for a nonapparel company.

Prestige pricing   Assumes that customers infer a relationship between price and quality and will not buy a product if the price is too low.

Price ceiling   The maximum price a consumer is willing to pay, determined by fashion retailers and manufacturers.

Price floor   The minimum price that can be charged based on cost.

Price lining   A marketing strategy based on retail goods at a preferred customer price point.

Price setting   A technique for establishing price that is often used by retailers or manufacturers in selling a product that is new to the market or in selling to an elite group of buyers not sensitive to price.

Price zones   Refers to the range of prices that a customer will pay for an item.

Private brand   A name owned exclusively by a particular retailer.

Private label   A name owned exclusively by a particular fashion operation that is extensively marketed with a definite image.

Product   Anything offered to a market for attention, acquisition, use, or consumption.

Product assortment   *See* **Product mix**.

Product development   Creating and manufacturing a product from start to finish.

Product level   The layers of a product, tangible and intangible: the three levels are core, formal, and augmented.

Product life cycle (also called the fashion diffusion process)   A model designed to identify the selling stage of a particular product by estimating its level of customer acceptance.

Product line   A group of products that are closely related, because they function in a similar manner.

Product mix (also called product assortment)   The set of all product lines and items that a particular seller offers for sale to buyers.

Product research   Involves anticipating the sales potential of new products, recognizing how lines are structured, identifying preferred product design and characteristics, and determining which items must be in the line.

Product specifications   The measurements, construction, and components of a product. Designers, or technical designers, may provide manufacturers with specific production guidelines, called specs.

Production pattern   A revised first pattern that is adjusted for fit, construction details, and placement on the fabric.

Promotion   The activities used to communicate the product's attributes to target consumers through four major tools: advertising, sales promotion, publicity, and personal selling.

Promotional pricing   A strategy that keeps prices at a minimum, despite the possibility that a company's services and physical space may suffer, in the belief that there are always some customers who care more about low prices.

Prospecting letter   A brief letter constructed to show interest in the firm and to request information about any internship opportunities.

Prototypes   First samples that are ordered for in-house designers, manufacturer's representatives, or showroom salespersons.

Psychographics   Qualitative factors that help predict a consumer's willingness to spend income. These include interests, personality, and lifestyle.

Psychological pricing   Refers to using odd versus even numbers as endings on retail prices in order to create the illusion of bargain pricing.

Public relations   Division of a company concerned with all nonpersonal selling activities, including sales promotions, advertising, and publicity.

Publicity   The nonpersonal creation of demand for a product by introducing commercially significant news about it through media efforts, at no cost to the sponsor.

Purchasing plan   A plan developed by the manufacturer for calculating costs for, and ordering, fabrics and trims. Also, a plan developed by the buyer to calculate sales, inventory, and amount of money available to purchase new goods by month.

Quota   The amount of merchandise that a country's government will allow to be imported into its borders.

Rational appeal   Promotional message that stresses common sense by showing that the product will produce claimed benefits.

Reach   The number of persons in a product's target market.

Reference groups   Groups who are influential in shaping people's attitudes and opinions.

Research and development   Company division responsible for the organization's work in developing new products or updating and improving existing ones.

Résumé   A one- or two-page summary of one's goals, education, experience, and skills.

Retailers   Entities that sell products to the ultimate consumer, including the vast range of bricks-and-mortar stores (e.g., department stores, mass merchants, specialty stores, boutiques, discount stores, off-price stores, outlet stores) as well as catalogs and online stores.

Retail label   A tag attached to the product with a retailer's name on it.

Retail layout   The arrangement and method of the physical facilities in a business. The ideal layout contributes to efficient operations, increased productivity, and higher sales.

Road sales   A term used to describe selling the product to the retail store buyer through sales representatives.

Sales forecast   A forecast that includes projections of sales by category, style, color, and size, based on historical data and statistical analysis. This information may be used to place preliminary fabric orders and to block out production time in factories. For retailers, the forecast is used to project the amount of money to be spent on new merchandise.

Sales promotions   Short-term incentives that encourage product sales.

Sales representatives (also called manufacturer's reps)   Salespersons who are salaried or commissioned, or both, and who sell the line to retail buyers in a specified territory, either at the buyer's location or during trade shows.

Scannable résumé   An electronic résumé that is formatted to be transmitted by e-mail.

Seasonal patterns   Distinct changes in activity within a calendar year that are related to changing seasons and holidays.

Secondary vendors   Lines carried in smaller quantities.

Selective distribution strategy   Choosing to sell lines to specific, targeted operations.

Services   Activities, ideas, benefits, or indulgences that are offered for sale.

Shopping-cart technology   Internet model that accepts credit card charges via a secure server.

Shopping centers   Centers and malls that provide the customer with one-stop shopping. They include neighborhood shopping centers, community shopping centers, regional shopping malls, and power centers.

Shopping goods   When in the process of selection and purchase, the customer compares similar products, or shopping goods, on the basis of quality, price, and style.

Short-range forecasting   The type of planning a company does to advance its goals in the near future.

Single unit   Business that has one outlet, often owner managed.

Social channel   Word-of-mouth from neighbors, family, friends, and associates comprises the social channel.

Social classes   Homogeneous divisions of families and individuals within a society.

Soft goods   Textile and apparel products, including accessories.

Sole proprietorship   One person owns a business and assumes personal responsibility for its debts.

Sourcing   Locating the suppliers or manufacturers, or both, for a product.

Space value   The value of each square foot of space in a retail store in terms of its generating sales revenue.

Specialty   Stores or manufacturers that sell or produce a specific classification of merchandise.

Specialty goods   Products with unique characteristics or brand identification, or both.

Spec sheet   Specification list providing detailed measurements and construction guidelines.

Staple items (also called basic items)   Merchandise that is in demand for extended periods of time and not subject to rapid style changes.

Storefront model   A basic model for retailing online; conceived to simulate a bricks-and-mortar store.

Store label   A label with the retailer's name on it, such as Neiman Marcus or Saks Fifth Avenue.

Strikeoff   A few yards of fabric printed by a mill and sent to the designer for approval.

Style development   When, upon establishing fabric, trend, and color directions, the designer can begin sketching individual styles.

Styling direction   Product line concepts that synthesize theme, silhouette, color, and fabric.

Supplies and services   Items that do not enter the finished product in any form. They include operating supplies, maintenance and repair items, maintenance and repair services, and business advisory services.

Tangible products   Goods that can be physically held.

Target demographics   Specific characteristics, such as age, income, and education, that are shared by a given population that a business aims to attract.

Target market   A homogenous group of customers with similar characteristics, needs, and desires.

Tariffs   *See* **Duties.**

Title flow   The passage of ownership of goods from one marketing organization to another.

Tracking plan   A plotted pattern that is created from observing the movements of random samples of shoppers in the business. The flow of customer traffic, as well as the places where customers tend to touch merchandise, pick it up, and buy it, are indicated on a floor plan of the store.

Trademark   A brand or part of a brand that has legal protection because a company has exclusive rights to use the brand name or brand mark, or both.

Trendy items   Products that are very exciting but carried minimally; items that pull the customer into the store. Often these are impulse items showcasing a wild fashion color, a unique fabric, or a very forward style.

Uncontrollable variables   Influences and events that cannot be controlled by the management of the organization.

Unsought goods   Goods the customer does not know about or knows about but does not normally think of buying. Customers may be introduced to these products through advertising. Promotion is the key to selling unsought goods.

Upward vertical   Communication from an employee to a manager.

Variety stores   Stores that carry a wide range of merchandise and that are often referred to as general merchandise stores.

Vertical integration   *See* **Vertical marketing channel.**

Vertical marketing channel (also called vertical integration)   Consists of producers, wholesalers, and retailers, cooperating as a unified group or operating under the same ownership.

Void-filling brand   *See* **Merchandising-driven brand.**

Wholesale cost   The first cost, which is increased to cover overhead expenses, selling expenses, and a profit margin.

Wholesaler   Someone who buys merchandise from a manufacturer and then sells the goods to a retailer for subsequent resale to the consumer.

Wholly owned factory   A factory that the company totally finances and operates. These factories have the benefit of complete control in terms of personnel selection, manufacturing techniques, quality control, and timing of delivery.

Writer   Author of advertising copy, publicity articles, or magazine editorials.

Credits

Chapter 1

1.2   © Johannes Mann/Corbis
Box 1.3 figure   Courtesy of AIU
Box 1.4 all figures   Courtesy of Global Experiences
Box 1.5 figure   © Colleen Greene Photography

Chapter 2

2.1   © Fancy/Veer/Corbis

Chapter 3

3.3   © Image Source/Corbis
3.4   © Fancy/Veer/Corbis
3.5   © Adrianna Williams/zefa/Corbis
3.6   © Harry Vorsteher/zefa/Corbis
3.7   www.landsend.com
3.9   Courtesy of 963Collective www.963collective.com
      & Miacro

Chapter 4

4.1   © Radius Images/Corbis
4.2   © Virgo Productions/zefa/Corbis
4.3   © PictureNet/Blend Images/Corbis

Chapter 5

5.1   © Mark Peterson/CORBIS
Box 5.1 figure   © WWD/Condé Nast
5.2   © Condé Nast Publications
5.3   © Rose Hartman/CORBIS
5.4   © James Leynse/Corbis
5.5   © Joey Nigh/Corbis
5.6   Courtesy of Smart Fixtures, www.smartfixtures.com
5.7 (top)   © WWD/Condé Nast
5.7 (bottom)   © Michael Reynolds/epa/Corbis
5.9   © WWD/Condé Nast
5.12   © Andrew Kent/Corbis

Chapter 6

6.1   © WWD/Condé Nast
6.3   © Patterson Graham/Corbis
6.4   © SHANNON STAPLETON/Reuters/Corbis
6.5   © Radius Images/Corbis

Chapter 7

7.1   Courtesy of Condé Nast Publications
7.2   © WWD/Condé Nast
Box 7.1 figure   © 2009 Lands' End
7.3   © Gillian Laub/Corbis

Chapter 8

8.2   © Corbis
8.3   © Robert Sorbo/Sygma/Corbis
8.4   © 2009 Rogers Publishing Limited.
8.5   © 2008–2009 Standard Style
Box 8.1 figure   © 2009 Lands' End
8.6   © 2007–2009 GILT GROUPE, INC

Chapter 9

9.1   © 2009 Make-Up Art Cosmetics Inc. All worldwide
      rights reserved.
9.2   © 2009 Make-Up Art Cosmetics Inc. All worldwide
      rights reserved.
9.5   © 2009 Kenneth Cole Productions, Inc.
9.6   © John Aquino/ W Magazine/Condé Nast
9.7   © WWD/Condé Nast Publications

Chapter 10

10.2   Courtesy of miacro, www.miacrodesign.com
10.3   Courtesy of miacro, www.miacrodesign.com
Box 10.1 figure   The Doneger Group
10.3   © WWD/Condé Nast Publications
10.4   © Anna Clopet/CORBIS
10.5   © Seth Wenig/Reuters/Corbis
10.6   © Image Source/Corbis
10.7   © ANNEBICQUE BERNARD/CORBIS SYGMA

Chapter 11

11.1   © Bettmann/CORBIS
11.4   © Andrew Holbrooke/Corbis
11.5   © Patrice Latron/Corbis

Chapter 12

12.1   © Andrew Marks/Corbis
12.2a   © Mario Anzuoni/Reuters/Corbis
12.2b   © WWD/Condé Nast Publications
12.3   © Rune Hellestad/Corbis
12.4   © Vogue/Condé Nast Publications
12.5   © Robert Mitra/W Magazine/Condé Nast Publications
12.6   Courtesy of Condé Nast Publications

Index

426688